Anonymous

The Fortnightly review

Anonymous

The Fortnightly review

ISBN/EAN: 9783337775476

Printed in Europe, USA, Canada, Australia, Japan

Cover: Foto ©ninafisch / pixelio.de

More available books at **www.hansebooks.com**

FORTNIGHTLY REVIEW.

EDITED BY

GEORGE HENRY LEWES.

CONTENTS.

		PAGE
I. The Englifh Conftitution: No. I. The Cabinet. By WALTER BAGEHOT		1
II. The Belton Eftate. Chapters I. and II. By ANTHONY TROLLOPE	.	24
III. The Influence of Rationalifm. By GEORGE ELIOT		43
IV. Perfonal Recollections of Prefident Lincoln. By M. D. CONWAY .	.	56
V. The Heart and the Brain. By the EDITOR		66
VI. Atalanta in Calydon. By the HON. LEICESTER WARREN . .	.	75
VII. On Atoms. By SIR JOHN HERSCHEL	.	81
VIII. Principles of Succefs in Literature. By the EDITOR . .	.	85
IX. The Iron-Mafters' Trade-Union. By F. HARRISON . . .	.	96
X. Public Affairs	.	117
XI. Notices of New Books. By GEORGE ELIOT, F. T. PALGRAVE, JOHN DENNIS, and the EDITOR	.	124

LONDON:

CHAPMAN AND HALL, 193, PICCADILLY;

AND ALL BOOKSELLERS.

LEIPZIG: BROCKHAUS.   ROTTERDAM: KRAMERS.

1865.

[*The Right of Tranflation is referved.*]

THE FORTNIGHTLY REVIEW.

EDITED BY GEORGE HENRY LEWES.

It has often been regretted that England has no journal similar to the *Revue des Deux Mondes*, treating of subjects which interest cultivated and thoughtful readers, and published at intervals which are neither too distant for influence on the passing questions, nor too brief for deliberation.

The FORTNIGHTLY REVIEW will be established to meet this demand. It will address the cultivated readers of all classes by its treatment of topics specially interesting to each; and it is hoped that the latitude which will be given to the expression of individual opinion may render it acceptable to a very various public. As one means of securing the best aid of the best writers on questions of LITERATURE, ART, SCIENCE, PHILOSOPHY, FINANCE, and POLITICS generally, we propose to remove all those restrictions of party and of editorial "consistency" which in other journals hamper the full and free expression of opinion; and we shall ask each writer to express his own views and sentiments with all the force of sincerity. He will never be required to express the views of an Editor or of a Party. He will not be asked to repress opinions or sentiments because they are distasteful to an Editor, or inconsistent with what may have formerly appeared in the REVIEW. He will be asked to say what he really thinks and really feels; to say it on his own responsibility, and to leave its appreciation to the public.

In discussing questions that have an agitating influence, and admit diversity of aspects—questions upon which men feel deeply and think variously—two courses are open to an effective journal: either to become the organ of a Party, and to maintain a vigilant consistency which will secure the intensive force gained by limitation; or to withdraw itself from all such limitations, and rely on the extensive force to be gained from a wide and liberal range. The latter course will be ours. Every Party has its organ. The FORTNIGHTLY REVIEW will seek its public amid all parties.

It must not be understood from this that the REVIEW is without its purpose, or without a consistency of its own; but the consistency will be of one tendency, not of doctrine; and the purpose will be that of aiding Progress in all directions. The REVIEW will be liberal, and its liberalism so thorough as to include great diversity of individual opinion within its catholic unity of purpose. This is avowedly an experiment. National culture and public improvement really take place through very various means, and under very different guidance. Men never altogether think alike, even when they act in unison. In the FORTNIGHLY REVIEW we shall endeavour to further the cause of Progress by illumination from many minds. We shall encourage, rather than repress, diversity of opinion, satisfied if we can secure the higher uniformity which results from the constant presence of sincerity and talent.

We do not disguise from ourselves the difficulties of our task. Even with the best aid from contributors, we shall at first have to contend against the impatience of readers at the advocacy of opinions which they disapprove. Some will complain that our liberalism is too lax; others that it is too stringent. And, indeed, to adjust the limits beyond which even our desire for the free expression of opinion will not permit our contributors to pass, will be a serious difficulty. We must rely on the tact and sympathy of our contributors, and on the candid construction of our readers. The *Revue des Deux Mondes* has proved with what admirable success a Journal may admit the utmost diversity of opinion. Nor can we doubt that an English public would be tolerant of equal diversity, justified by equal talent.

The FORTNIGHTLY REVIEW will be published on the 1st and 15th of every month. Price Two Shillings.

CHAPMAN & HALL, 193, PICCADILLY.

FORTNIGHTLY REVIEW ADVERTISER.
No. 1.—May 15, 1865.

Just published, crown 8vo., price 9s. cloth,

EVENINGS IN ARCADIA.
Edited by JOHN DENNIS.

Athenæum.—"The notion of the book is a happy one. Pictures of rural life taken from our best poets, social criticism, and apropos anecdote, should form a tempting entertainment.... The friends talk like men of taste and culture upon a subject which they thoroughly enjoy. Their tone is kindly, their remarks are sensible, and for the most part just, while the gravity of criticism is a good deal relieved by pleasant gossip. A book with these qualities, and rich moreover in poetical selections, can hardly be uninteresting."

The Reader.—"This volume would form an attractive means of introduction to a knowledge of the best English poetry."

St. James's Chronicle.—"Mr. Dennis has conferred a great boon upon the lovers of English poetry.... We shall be greatly surprised if the work does not at once take standard rank among the highest class of critical literature."

Morning Post.—"In his criticisms the author is frequently very happy, and has brought to his task a close acquaintance with the works, not only of England's most famous poets, but of many who are comparatively obscure. No lover of verse can fail to draw pleasure from the work."

Daily News.—"A good and clever book. The style is highly classical and chaste."

Pall Mall Gazette.—"Sensible and unaffected. We have no hesitation in recommending the book to all our readers."

Press.—"We leave Mr. Dennis with a recommendation to all who love rural poetry and thoughtful criticism to read his charming volume."

Weekly Review.—"We find these criticisms to be sound, sagacious, genial, competent in appreciation, tender, glowing, and graceful in expression."

Nonconformist.—"We cordially commend the book to lovers of poetry. The author displays throughout a vigorous and an independent judgment."

Illustrated London News.—"A more delightful companion during a solitary hour, either in summer beneath the spreading oak, or in winter by the fireside, it would not be easy to command."

Just published, fcap. 4to. cloth, 8s.

ATALANTA IN CALYDON.
A TRAGEDY.
By ALGERNON CHARLES SWINBURNE.

London Review.—"Would be considered a work of unusual beauty even if it came forth under the signature of the most established reputation: as the work of a new poet it is surprising."

Notes and Queries.—"Moulded on the form of the ancient tragedy, and introduced by a long tribute, in Greek verse, to the memory of Walter Savage Landor, this very ably and powerfully written drama does not present temptations to general readers. But the time will come when its merits will be widely recognised."

Athenæum.—"A grand word-picture, in which the influence of no contemporary can be traced."

MR. PENNELL'S NEW VOLUME.
In fcap. 8vo. cloth, 5s.

CRESCENT?
And other Lyrics.
By H. CHOLMONDELEY PENNELL, Author of "Puck on Pegasus," &c.

Athenæum.—"Language alike strong and musical.... The first of Mr. Pennell's eight poems is a passionate protest against the sickly plaint, ever on the lips of idlers, but scouted by all honest workers, that the age of poetry is past; and if there were not other and stronger voices raised against this cry of fretful weakness, the nervous and deep-rolling lines of 'Crescent?' would of themselves be a sufficient answer to the ignoble wail. Others may sneer at the marvels that surround them, and prate about the day of little men, finding in the imputed decay of human intellect a proof that Nature herself has entered on a cold decrepitude; but Mr. Pennell has learnt a different lesson.... Other men have heard music in the factory's roar, and caught melody from the crash of iron hammers; but few have translated it into better words than the following.... The writer has proved himself a man of cultivated taste."

John Bull.—"Mr. Pennell is a stalwart champion of his age, and in reading his ringing lines we feel that most assuredly there is a charm for the poet even in the most material of modern life. The following stanzas come from a master hand."....

Scotsman.—"Real and undoubted poetic talent.... Mr. Pennell always shows himself a master of the art of versification."

Spectator.—"Like all the author's writing, 'Crescent?' has thought in it and considerable power."

Reader.—"Hitherto we have known Mr. Pennell principally by his 'Puck on Pegasus,' and other like frolicsome effusions. His present volume shows us that he is undoubtedly capable of writing serious verse of much more than average merit. His stanzas on 'Fire!' are especially vigorous, and in the 'Two Champions' he essays, with a boldness which success justifies, poetry of a highly imaginative description."

London Review.—"Mr. Pennell writes with nerve and force. ... The best poem in the book is 'The Fiend in the Family;' a ghastly story, not of these days, but of the old feudal times. The whole legend is charged with a dusky and mysterious horror, and is told with great intensity and power."

Public Opinion.—"Several years ago Mr. Pennell gave amusement and delight to many readers by the publication of a volume of poems of a facetious kind, entitled 'Puck on Pegasus.' One or two of the poems in the volume, called 'The Night Mail North,' and 'The Derby Day,' displayed unusual vigour and vivid descriptive power. While reading 'The Night Mail North,' the reader seemed hurried along and amazed by the swiftness and skilfulness of the verses; and it was felt that so much dash and skilfulness in rhyme clearly heralded a new poet, who would be likely to become the Laureate of the active wonders of the present age. It was thought, however, by many of Mr. Pennell's friends that he could not write serious poetry; and we suppose he has issued the present volume to undeceive them.... The passage we quote below could only emanate from a real poet. ... Scattered here and there are lines of exquisite beauty, musical as rills and eminent with cluster thoughts.... We have sincere pleasure in acknowledging that Mr. Pennell is a true poet, who may, by determining to be simple, one day become the undisputed guest of fame. 'The Picture Gallery' has some capital lines, and a depth of thought that remind us of the subtleties of Browning.

"Instances are rare of a poet being able to evoke from his lyre strains grave and gay with satisfactory success—but Mr. Pennell has already done these things, and is beginning to make a reputation of which he may be justly proud."

By the same Author, 7s. 6d.,

PUCK ON PEGASUS.
Fourth Edition, enlarged and revised, with upwards of 50 original Illustrations by Leech, Tenniel, Phiz, George Cruikshank, and Portch.

LONDON: EDWARD MOXON & CO., DOVER STREET, W.

Lately published, in small 8vo. cloth, 6s.

ELSIE; FLIGHTS TO FAIRYLAND, &c.
By J. CRAWFORD WILSON,
Author of "Jonathan Oldaker," "Gitanilla," &c.

Literary Gazette.—"A poem which entitles the author to very high praise."

Illustrated London News.—"Written with some spirit, much grace, and no little pathos."

Illustrated Times.—"'Flights to Fairy Land' are stories on the Ingoldsby model, *but* poetic and refined."

News of the World.—"A succession of beautiful images."

Sunday Times.—"True in that best and highest of truths—true to nature."

Brighton Herald.—"The strong points in his verse are its pathos and its humour."

Observer.—"A very pleasing collection of poems."

Christian Times.—"None who regard Cowper as a true poet will dispute Mr. Wilson's right to the same designation."

Athenæum.—"We have seldom read verses which breathe more earnestly 'the hate of hate, the scorn of scorn, the love of love.'"

Pall Mall Gazette.—"Mr. Wilson is inferior to few who have chosen to tell in rhymed lines a sad tale of real life."

The Reader.—"Mr. Crawford Wilson has no lack of power, and is wonderfully sustained and fluent; his efforts will win the applause of many, and the respect of all."

Public Opinion.—"As a pleasing and elegant poet, Mr. Wilson deserves hearty praise; his muse is delicate, and loves to worship beauty in all its attributes. He is a poet for whom the ladies ought to feel some respect, for he dwells on their constancy and goodness in eloquent strains."

Lately published, crown 8vo. cloth, 9s.

ST. THOMAS À BECKET.
And other Poems.
By JOHN POYER.

Cambridge Chronicle.—"The work of a new and genuine poet."
Morning Advertiser.—"Mr. Poyer discourses on poetry so well."
News of the World.—"Exceedingly good and elevated in character."

Fcap. 4to., beautifully printed, 10s. 6d.

A NEW VOLUME OF POEMS.
By MAJOR W. B. LUMLEY.
Author of "The Ironsides; a Tale of the English Commonwealth."

CONTENTS:

1. A LAMENT FOR THE LATE PRINCE CONSORT.
2. THE VICTIM OF FASHION.
3. THE MOTHER'S PRAYER.
4. THE MARATHON OF THE EAST.
5. VIVE ET SEMPER SPERO.
6. THE LAST REQUEST.
7. RELIGION À LA MODE.
8. STANZAS TO SAINT ANNE.
9. ITALY.
10. MIDSUMMER'S NIGHT.
11. THE LAND'S END, CORNWALL.
12. ELLENBEL.
13. THE ADIEU.
14. VOLUNTEERING.
15. PALMAM QUI MERUIT FERAT.
16. A TRIBUTE TO THE LOVED AND HONOURED MEMORY OF RICHARD COBDEN.

The little Sonata styled "The Adieu" has been set to an Air composed by the Author, the Music of which is appended to this work.

MOXON'S MINIATURE POETS.

Messrs. MOXON have the pleasure to announce (by kind permission of Messrs. Chapman and Hall) that Vol. II. of this favourite Series will consist of a POPULAR SELECTION from the WORKS of ROBERT BROWNING. Part II., price Sixpence, was issued with the Magazines for May; Part III. June 1.

MOXON'S MINIATURE POETS, Vol. III., will be issued this Month, and will be LOCKER'S POEMS, Illustrated by DOYLE and MILLAIS.

Just published, in fcap. 8vo. cloth, 7s.

THE ROMANCE OF THE SCARLET LEAF;
Poems and Ballads.
WITH ADAPTATIONS FROM THE PROVENÇAL TROUBADOURS.
By HAMILTON AÏDÉ,
Author of "Rita," "Mr. and Mrs. Faulconbridge," &c.

LONDON: EDWARD MOXON & CO., DOVER STREET, W.

NEW AND STANDARD WORKS.

I.
HISTORY OF ENGLAND, from the Fall of Wolsey to the Death of Elizabeth.
By JAMES ANTHONY FROUDE, M.A., late Fellow of Exeter College, Oxford. Revised Editions of the First Eight Volumes.
    Vols. I. to IV.—REIGN OF HENRY VIII. 54s.
    Vols. V. and VI.—REIGNS OF EDWARD VI. AND MARY, 22s.
    Vols. VII. and VIII.—REIGN OF ELIZABETH, Vols. I. and II. 28s.

II.
THE HISTORY OF ENGLAND from the Accession of James II. By LORD MACAULAY. Three Editions, as follows:—
    LIBRARY EDITION, 8 vols. 8vo. £4.
    CABINET EDITION, 8 vols. post 8vo. 48s.
    PEOPLE'S EDITION, 4 vols. crown 8vo. 16s.

III.
AN ESSAY ON THE HISTORY OF THE ENGLISH GOVERNMENT AND CONSTITUTION, from the Reign of Henry VII. to the Present Time. By JOHN, EARL RUSSELL. New Edition, with a new Introduction. 8vo. 12s.

IV.
SIR JOHN ELIOT, a Biography: 1590—1632. By JOHN FORSTER. With Two Portraits on Steel, from the originals at Port Eliot. 2 vols. crown 8vo. 30s.

V.
THE CONSTITUTIONAL HISTORY OF ENGLAND, since the Accession of George III.: 1760—1860. By THOMAS ERSKINE MAY, C.B. 2 vols. 8vo. 33s.

VI.
HISTORY OF CIVILIZATION. By HENRY THOMAS BUCKLE. 2 vols. £1 17s.
    Vol. I.—ENGLAND AND FRANCE. Fourth Edition, 21s.
    Vol. II.—SPAIN AND SCOTLAND. Second Edition, 16s.

VII.
HISTORY OF THE RISE AND INFLUENCE OF THE SPIRIT OF RATIONALISM IN EUROPE. By W. E. H. LECKY, M.A. 2 vols. 8vo. 25s.

VIII.
AN EXAMINATION OF SIR W. HAMILTON'S PHILOSOPHY, and of the Principal Philosophical Questions Discussed in his Writings. By JOHN STUART MILL. 8vo. 14s.

IX.
HISTORY OF THE ROMANS UNDER THE EMPIRE. By CHARLES MERIVALE, B.D., Chaplain [to the Speaker. CABINET EDITION in course of publication, in Eight Monthly Volumes, 6s. each.

X.
THE CONVERSION OF THE ROMAN EMPIRE: the Boyle Lectures for the year 1864, delivered at the Chapel Royal, Whitehall. By the same Author. 8vo. 8s. 6d.

XI.
ESSAYS IN ECCLESIASTICAL BIOGRAPHY. By the Right Hon. Sir J. STEPHEN, LL.D. Fourth Edition. 8vo. 14s.

XII.
CRITICAL AND HISTORICAL ESSAYS contributed to the *Edinburgh Review*. By the Right Hon. Lord MACAULAY.
    LIBRARY EDITION, 3 vols. 8vo. 36s. | In POCKET VOLUMES, 3 vols. fcap. 21s.
    TRAVELLER'S EDITION, in 1 vol. 21s. | PEOPLE'S EDITION, 2 vols. crown 8vo. 8s.

XIII.
MISCELLANEOUS WRITINGS OF LORD MACAULAY. LIBRARY EDITION, in 2 vols. 8vo., with Portrait, 21s. Also the PEOPLE'S EDITION, complete in 1 vol. crown 8vo. 4s. 6d.

XIV.
HISTORICAL STUDIES. By HERMAN MERIVALE. 8vo. 12s. 6d.
    I.—ON SOME OF THE PRECURSORS OF THE FRENCH REVOLUTION.
    II.—STUDIES FROM THE HISTORY OF THE SEVENTEENTH CENTURY.
    III.—LEISURE HOURS OF A TOURIST.

XV.
HISTORICAL LECTURES ON THE LIFE OF OUR LORD JESUS CHRIST. By C. J. ELLICOTT, D.D., Lord Bishop of Gloucester and Bristol. Fourth Edition. 8vo. 10s. 6d.

XVI.
CONYBEARE AND HOWSON'S LIFE AND EPISTLES OF ST. PAUL. With numerous Illustrations. Three Editions, as follows:—
    LIBRARY EDITION, 2 vols. 4to. 48s.
    INTERMEDIATE EDITION, 2 vols. square crown 8vo. 31s. 6d.
    PEOPLE'S EDITION, slightly condensed, 2 vols. crown 8vo. 12s.

LONDON: LONGMAN, GREEN, & CO., PATERNOSTER ROW.

CHAPMAN AND HALL'S NEW PUBLICATIONS.

MR. THOMAS ADOLPHUS TROLLOPE'S NEW WORK.
A HISTORY OF THE COMMONWEALTH OF FLORENCE,
From the Earliest Independence of the Commune to the Fall of the Republic in 1531.
By THOMAS ADOLPHUS TROLLOPE. Vols. I. and II., demy 8vo. 30s.

MR. HEPWORTH DIXON'S NEW WORK.
THE HOLY LAND.
By W. HEPWORTH DIXON. With Steel Engravings and Woodcuts. 2 Vols. demy 8vo. 24s.

MR. CARLYLE'S NEW WORK.
THE HISTORY OF FREDERICK THE GREAT.
By THOMAS CARLYLE. Vols. V. and VI., 40s., completing the work.

NEW WORK BY MR. CHARLES DICKENS.
In Monthly Parts, uniform with the Original Editions of "Pickwick," "David Copperfield," &c.
Parts I. to XIV. now ready, 1s. each of
OUR MUTUAL FRIEND.
By CHARLES DICKENS. To be completed in Twenty Monthly Parts. With Illustrations by Marcus Stone.
Vol. I. handsomely bound, 11s.

NEW SERIAL BY ANTHONY TROLLOPE.
To be completed in Twenty Monthly Parts, uniform with "Orley Farm."
Now ready, Parts I. to XVII., 1s. each.
CAN YOU FORGIVE HER?
By ANTHONY TROLLOPE, author of "Dr. Thorne," "Rachel Ray," &c. With Illustrations.
Vol. I., handsomely bound, is now ready, 11s.

MR. WALTER WHITE'S NEW BOOK OF TRAVEL.
EASTERN ENGLAND.
FROM THE THAMES TO THE HUMBER.
By WALTER WHITE. 2 Vols., post 8vo. [*In May.*

M. ESQUIROS'S NEW WORK.
CORNWALL AND ITS COASTS.
By ALPHONSE ESQUIROS, Author of "The English at Home." Post 8vo. [*In May.*

A WORK ON PANAMA.
By CHARLES J. BIDWELL. Demy 8vo. [*In May.*

HERR FREYTAG'S NEW WORK.
THE LOST MANUSCRIPT.
By HERR FREYTAG. Translated by Mrs. Malcolm. 2 Vols., post 8vo. [*In May.*

MR. EDMUND YATES'S NEW WORK.
THE BUSINESS OF PLEASURE.
By EDMUND YATES. 2 Vols., post 8vo. [*In May.*

CARL MARIA VON WEBER;
THE LIFE OF AN ARTIST.
From the German of his son, Baron Max Maria Von Weber.
By J. PALGRAVE SIMPSON, M.A. 2 Vols., post 8vo. 22s.

NEW WORK BY CHARLES LEVER.
LUTTRELL OF ARRAN.
By CHARLES LEVER, Author of "Harry Lorrequer," "Charles O'Malley," &c.
With 32 Illustrations by Phiz. Demy 8vo. 17s.

193, PICCADILLY.

NEW WORKS & NEW EDITIONS PUBLISHED BY MACMILLAN & CO.

NEW WORK BY THE AUTHOR OF "THE HEIR OF REDCLYFFE."

THE CLEVER WOMAN OF THE FAMILY. By the Author of "The Heir of Redclyffe." 2 Vols. crown 8vo. cl., 12s.

"There is a good deal of carefully written dialogue, and the story flows on easily and agreeably."—*Saturday Review.*
"This bright and very agreeable book."—*Daily News.*

CAWNPORE. By G. O. Trevelyan, Author of "The Competition Wallah." Illustrated with a Plan of Cawnpore, and two Engravings from Photographs of the Burial-ground and the Well. The History is drawn from authentic and in many cases from new sources. Crown 8vo. cloth, 10s. 6d.

THE COMPETITION WALLAH. By G. O. Trevelyan. Crown 8vo. cloth, 9s.

"The earlier letters are especially interesting for their racy description of European life in India, as seen by the quick eye and measured by the sharp satire of an intelligent new comer. Those that follow are of more serious import, seeking to elicit the truth about the Hindoo character, and English influences, good and bad, upon it, as well as to suggest some better course of treatment than that hitherto adopted."—*Examiner.*

In Type and Text, Paper and Binding, *the best*, and in price *the cheapest.* The Globe Edition of

SHAKESPEARE'S PLAYS AND POEMS. Complete in One compact Volume, from the best Cambridge Text. 3s. 6d.

THE CAMBRIDGE SHAKESPEARE.

THE WORKS OF WILLIAM SHAKESPEARE. Edited by W. G. CLARK and W. ALDIS WRIGHT. To be completed in Eight Volumes, demy 8vo., each 10s. 6d. Shortly will be published Volume VI., containing:—Henry VIII. Troilus and Cressida, Coriolanus, Titus Andronicus, Romeo and Juliet, and a Reprint of the Quarto of 1597. The Editors hope that Volumes VII. and VIII. completing the work, will be ready for publication before the close of the present year.

BALLADS AND SONGS OF BRITTANY. By Tom TAYLOR. Translated from the "Barsaz-Breiz" of Vicomte Hersart de la Villemarqué. With some of the Original Melodies harmonised by Mrs. TOM TAYLOR. With Illustrations by J. Tissot, J. E. Millais, R.A., J. Tenniel, C. Keene, F. Corbould, and H. K. Browne. Small 4to. cloth, 12s.

"The book has every external attraction; it is beautifully got up and illustrated; the pieces are real translations from genuine ancient Breton poems, and the translations are executed with great spirit and power. The poems are really vigorous and beautiful."—*Saturday Review.*

GOBLIN MARKET, AND OTHER POEMS. By CHRISTINA G. ROSSETTI. With Two Illustrations from Designs by D. G. ROSSETTI. Second Edition, fcap. 8vo. cl., 5s.

"The poetical art of Miss Rossetti is simple, firm, and deep.... She can point to finished work—to work which it would be difficult to mend."—*Times.*

By the same Author,

THE PRINCE'S PROGRESS, AND OTHER POEMS. By CHRISTINA G. ROSSETTI. [*In the Press.*

GOLDEN TREASURY SERIES.

THE POETICAL WORKS OF ROBERT BURNS. Edited, from the best printed and manuscript Authorities, with copious Glossarial Index, and a Biographical Memoir, by ALEXANDER SMITH. Two vols., handsomely bound in cloth, with Vignette and Design by J. B.; engraved by SHAW. 9s.

"Beyond all question this is the most beautiful edition of Burns yet out."—*Daily Review.*

THE POETICAL WORKS of JOHN MILTON. Edited, with Text collated from the best Authorities, and with Critical and Explanatory Notes, by DAVID MASSON. (This will form part of the GOLDEN TREASURY SERIES.) [*In the Press.*

In a few days will be published, crown 8vo. cloth,

LETTERS FROM EGYPT. By Lady Duff-Gordon.

THE COAL QUESTION; An Inquiry concerning the Progress of the Nation and the Probable Exhaustion of our Coal Mines. By W. STANLEY JEVONS, M.A., Fellow of University College, London. 8vo. cloth, 10s. 6d.

WORDS AND PLACES; or, Etymological Illustrations of History, Ethnology, and Geography. With a Map showing the settlements of the Celts, Saxons, Danes, and Norwegians in the British Isles and Northern France. By the Rev. ISAAC TAYLOR, M.A. A New Edition, crown 8vo. cloth, 12s. 6d.

Shortly will be published,

CENTRAL AND EASTERN ARABIA. By William GIFFORD PALGRAVE.

In 1864 Mr. Palgrave read before the Royal Geographical Society, "Notes of a Journey from Gaza through the interior of Arabia to El Khatif on the Persian Gulf, and thence to Oman." The *Quarterly Review* (April, 1865), speaking of this paper, says:—

"An Oxford first-class man told a stirring tale of adventure in an absolutely new and virgin country, hitherto unvisited except under conditions which reduced the traveller to the category of a mere senseless corpse in a coffin. He told his tale, too, more as Herodotus would have recited at Olympia, than like a commonplace voyager of the nineteenth century. He spoke with all the spirit and picturesqueness of the old Greek, combined with the careful eloquence of a trained orator, and his crowded audience admired and applauded the accomplishments of the speaker, no less than they appreciated the interest of the primeval Eastern country thus brought before their eyes."

This day is published,

ST. PAUL'S EPISTLE TO THE GALATIANS. A Revised Text, with Notes and Dissertations. By J. D. LIGHTFOOT, D.D., Hulsean Professor of Divinity in the University of Cambridge. 8vo. cloth, 10s. 6d.

THE SYNONYMS OF THE NEW TESTAMENT. By RICHARD CHENEVIX TRENCH, D.D., Archbishop of Dublin. New and Revised Edition, in 1 vol. 8vo., 10s. 6d. [*This day.*

DISCUSSIONS ON THE GOSPELS. In Two Parts. Part I. On the Language employed by Our Lord and His disciples. Part II. On the Original Language of St. Matthew's Gospel, the Origin and Authenticity of the Gospels. By the Rev. ALEXANDER ROBERTS, D.D. Second Edition, revised and enlarged. 8vo. cloth, 18s.

"A most valuable contribution to our biblical literature."—*Saturday Review.*

THE HISTORY OF CHRISTIAN NAMES. By the Author of "The Heir of Redclyffe." 2 vols. crown 8vo. cloth, £1 1s.

ESSAYS IN CRITICISM. By Matthew Arnold, Professor of Poetry in the University of Oxford. Fcap. 8vo. cl., 6s.

ESSAYS, BIOGRAPHICAL AND CRITICAL; chiefly on the English Poets. By DAVID MASSON, M.A., Professor of English Literature in University College, London. 8vo. cloth, 12s. 6d.

BRITISH NOVELISTS AND THEIR STYLES; being a critical Sketch of the History of British Prose Fiction. By DAVID MASSON, M.A. Crown 8vo. cloth, 7s. 6d.

Also by the same Author,

RECENT BRITISH PHILOSOPHY; a Review with Criticisms. By DAVID MASSON. [*In the Press.*

Second Annual Publication.

THE STATESMAN'S YEAR-BOOK; A Statistical, Genealogical, and Historical Account of the States and Sovereigns of the Civilised World for the Year 1865. By FREDERICK MARTIN. Crown 8vo. strongly bound in cloth, 10s. 6d.
"As indispensable as Bradshaw."—*Times.*

MANUAL OF POLITICAL ECONOMY. By Henry FAWCETT, M.A., Professor of Political Economy in the University of Cambridge. Second Edition. Crown 8vo. cloth, 12s.

STEPHEN.—GENERAL VIEW of the CRIMINAL LAW OF ENGLAND. By J. FITZJAMES STEPHEN, Barrister-at-Law, Recorder of Newark-on-Trent. 8vo. cloth, 18s.

"Readers feel in this book the confidence which attaches to the writing of a man who has great practical acquaintance with the matter of which he writes, and lawyers will agree that it fully satisfies the standard of professional accuracy."—*Saturday Review.*

THE ROMAN AND THE TEUTON. A Series of Lectures delivered before the University of Cambridge. By CHARLES KINGSLEY, M.A., Professor of Modern History. 8vo. cloth, 12s.

STIMULANTS AND NARCOTICS; Their Mutual Relations. With Original Researches on the Action of Alcohol, Æther, and Chloroform, on the Vital Organism. By FRANCIS E. ANSTIE, M.D., M.R.C.P., Assistant Physician in Westminster Hospital, Lecturer on Materia Medica and Therapeutics to the School, and formerly Lecturer on Toxicology. 8vo. cloth, 14s.

"In this very able and very interesting book we have a full exposition of researches and reflections on an important and highly comprehensive part of medical science, on which Dr. Anstie has been employed during many years."—*Examiner.*

MACMILLAN & CO., LONDON AND CAMBRIDGE.

CHAPMAN AND HALL'S NEW PUBLICATIONS.

Sixth Edition, in Four Volumes, fcap. 8vo., with Portrait, 24s.
ELIZABETH BARRETT BROWNING'S POETICAL WORKS.
Including 'AURORA LEIGH.'

A New Edition, in Three Volumes, fcap. 8vo., 22s. 6d.
ROBERT BROWNING'S POETICAL WORKS.
With a Photographic Portrait of the Author.

Second Edition, crown 8vo. 8s. 6d.
A NEW VOLUME OF POEMS.—'DRAMATIS PERSONÆ.'
By ROBERT BROWNING.

In Two Volumes, fcap. 8vo.,
OWEN MEREDITH'S POEMS.
COLLECTED EDITION. [*In the Press.*

Collected Edition, in Three Volumes, fcap. 8vo. 16s.
HENRY TAYLOR'S PLAYS AND POEMS.
PHILIP VAN ARTEVELDE, &c.

DYCE'S SHAKESPEARE.
"The best text of Shakespeare which has yet appeared. . . . Mr. Dyce's edition is a great work, worthy of his reputation, and for the present it contains the standard text."—*Times*, Jan. 20, 1864.

A New Edition, to be completed in Eight Volumes, demy 8vo. 10s. each,
THE WORKS OF SHAKESPEARE.
Edited by the Rev. ALEXANDER DYCE.

This Edition is not a mere reprint of that which appeared in 1857; on the contrary, it will present a text very materially altered and amended from beginning to end, with a large body of Critical Notes, almost entirely new, and with a Glossary, in which the language of the poet, his allusions to customs, &c., will be fully explained.

To be published every alternate Month. Vols. I. to V. are now ready.

In Two Volumes, post 8vo., with Illustrations, 24s.,
THE LIFE OF LAURENCE STERNE.
By PERCY FITZGERALD, M.A., M.R.I.A.

THE LIFE OF THORWALDSEN.
FROM THE DANISH.
By the Rev. M. R. BARNARD. 1 vol. post 8vo. 9s.

In demy 8vo., with Portrait, 16s.
THE LIFE OF GENERAL WOLFE.
By R. WRIGHT.

A FAMOUS FORGERY;
BEING THE STORY OF THE UNFORTUNATE DOCTOR DODD.
By PERCY FITZGERALD. 1 vol. post 8vo. 8s.

In demy 8vo. 22s.
ENGLISH WRITERS.
THE WRITERS BEFORE CHAUCER.
With an Introductory Sketch of the Four Periods of English Literature. By HENRY MORLEY.

LUTHER'S LETTERS TO WOMEN.
Collected by Dr. ZIMMERMANN. Translated by Mrs. MALCOLM. 1 vol. post 8vo. 5s.

Demy 8vo. 20s.
THROUGH MACEDONIA TO THE ALBANIAN LAKES.
By MARY ADELAIDE WALKER. With 12 beautiful Illustrations.

SCENES OF WONDER AND CURIOSITY IN CALIFORNIA.
By JAMES M. HUTCHINS. With above 100 Illustrations. Demy 8vo. 12s.

193, PICCADILLY.

WORKS PUBLISHED BY SMITH, ELDER & CO.

New Work by Mr. Ruskin.

Kings' Treasures and Queens' Gardens. By JOHN RUSKIN, M.A. Fcap. 8vo. [*Nearly Ready.*]

Commemoration of Dante.

The Inferno of Dante. Translated in the Metre of the Original, by the Rev. JAMES FORD, M.A., Prebendary of Exeter. With a Portrait. Crown 8vo., 10s. 6d.
*** The Italian text is printed on the opposite pages of the Translation, for the use of Students.

The Early Italian Poets, from Ciullo D'Alcamo to Dante Alighieri (1100, 1200, 1300). In the Original Metres. Together with Dante's "Vita Nuova." Translated by D. G. ROSSETTI. Crown 8vo., 12s.

The Lake Country. By E. LYNN LINTON. Illustrated by W. J. Linton. With a Map. A handsome 4to. volume, printed by Messrs. Clay and Co., on tinted paper, and richly bound in cloth gilt, One Guinea.

The Cornhill Gallery. Containing One Hundred Engravings from Drawings on Wood (being Designs for the Illustration of "The Cornhill Magazine") by

FREDERICK LEIGHTON, A.R.A.	J. NOEL PATON, R.A.S.	W. M. THACKERAY.
JOHN EVERETT MILLAIS, R.A.	FREDERICK SANDYS.	FREDERICK WALKER.
GEORGE DU MAURIER.	GEORGE A. SALA.	

Engraved by the Brothers Dalziel, W. J. Linton, and Joseph Swain, and printed in tint on Cardboard, size 13½ in. by 10¼ in., by the Brothers Dalziel, with Index to the Pictures. In one handsome volume, richly bound, One Guinea. As separate Pictures in elegant Portfolio, One Guinea.

Grimm's Life of Michael Angelo. Translated by F. E. BUNNETT, translator of Gervinus's "Shakespeare Commentaries." With a Photographic Portrait. Copyright Edition. 2 vols., crown 8vo., 24s.

Recollections and Anecdotes of the Camp, the Court, and the Clubs, at the close of the last War with France. By Captain R. H. GRONOW. With Illustrations New Edition, comprising the First and Second Series in One Volume. Crown 8vo., 6s.

Celebrities of London and Paris; being a Third Series of Reminiscences and Anecdotes of the Court, the Camp, and the Clubs. Containing a Correct Account of the Coup D'Etat. By Captain GRONOW. With a Coloured Frontispiece. Crown 8vo., 9s.

On Capital Punishment. Based on Professor Millermaier's "Die Todesstrafe." Edited by JOHN MACRAE MAIR, M.A., of the Middle Temple, Esq., Barrister-at-Law. Crown 8vo., 6s.

Waterloo; the Downfall of the First Napoleon. A History of the Campaign of 1815. With Maps and Plans. Demy 8vo., 15s.

Romola. By GEORGE ELIOT, Author of "Adam Bede," "Scenes of Clerical Life," and "Silas Marner," &c. New Edition, with Five Illustrations. Crown 8vo. [*Nearly Ready.*]

Aristotle. A Chapter from the History of Science, including Analyses of Aristotle's Scientific Writings. By GEORGE HENRY LEWES. Demy 8vo., 15s.

The Life of Goethe. By GEORGE HENRY LEWES. New Edition. Partly re-written. With a Portrait. One Volume. Demy 8vo., 16s.

Studies in Animal Life. By GEORGE HENRY LEWES. With Coloured Frontispiece, and other Illustrations. Crown 8vo., 5s.

Life in Nature. By JAMES HINTON. Crown 8vo., 6s.

Man and His Dwelling Place. An Essay towards the Interpretation of Nature. By JAMES HINTON. Second Edition. Crown 8vo., 6s.

Shakespeare Commentaries. By Dr. G. G. GERVINUS, Professor at Heidelberg. Translated under the Author's Superintendence by F. E. BUNNETT. Two vols. Demy 8vo., 24s.

LONDON: SMITH, ELDER & CO., 65, CORNHILL.

NOW READY AT ALL THE LIBRARIES.

DEDICATED, BY EXPRESS PERMISSION, TO THE RT. HON. W. E. GLADSTONE, M.P., H.M. Chancellor of the Exchequer.

THE WEDGWOODS; being a Life of JOSIAH WEDGWOOD, with Notices of his Works and their Productions, Memoirs of the Wedgwood and other Families, and a History of the Early Potteries of Staffordshire. By LLEWELLYNN JEWITT, F.S.A. Illustrated. With Portrait, after Sir Joshua Reynolds, engraved by John Taylor Wedgwood, and with upwards of 150 exquisite Engravings, comprising Portraits, Views, Examples of Pottery of every period, specimens of Plymouth, Bristol, New Hall, and other China, and of every variety of Wedgwood Ware. In 1 vol. 8vo., 18s.

A HISTORY OF CARICATURE AND GROTESQUE IN LITERATURE AND ART. By THOMAS WRIGHT, Esq., M.A., F.S.A., &c. With Illustrations from various Sources, drawn and engraved by F. W. Fairholt, Esq., F.S.A. Small 4to. cloth, red edges, 21s.

Saturday Review.—"The present volume has been expected for some time with much interest, and will be welcomed as a very satisfactory attempt to illustrate a novel and a very curious subject. It may safely be said that the volume is of the highest value. It is a work which few living scholars could have produced, and it reflects great honour on the diligent antiquary to whom we owe this important addition to our literature."

Athenæum.—"Mr. Wright has chosen a subject of the most fascinating and wealthy order. . . . . The illustrations, of which there are several hundreds, are drawn with characteristic fidelity and spirit."

Notes and Queries.—"A compendious history of literary and pictorial satire, which is at once learned and useful."

Pall Mall Gazette.—"An interesting, curious, compendious, and a more than commonly amusing book."

Art-Journal.—"A learned, entertaining, and instructive book."

By the same Author.

DOMESTIC MANNERS and SENTIMENTS in ENGLAND during the MIDDLE AGES. With numerous Illustrations by F. W. Fairholt, Esq. Fcap. 4to., 21s.

The CELT, the ROMAN, and the SAXON. Illustrated. New Edition. Post 8vo., 12s.

GATHERED LEAVES: a Collection of the Poetical Works of the late FRANK E. SMEDLEY. With a Memorial Preface by EDMUND YATES, a Portrait, and numerous Illustrations. Imitation half morocco, 8s. 6d.

By the same Author.

FRANK FAIRLEGH; or, Scenes from the Life of a Private Pupil. 2s. 6d.; or 3s. 6d. in cloth.

LEWIS ARUNDEL; or, the Railroad of Life. 3s.; or 4s. in cloth.

HARRY COVERDALE'S COURTSHIP, and All that Came of It. 2s. 6d.; or 3s. 6d. in cloth.

THE OLD FOREST RANGER; or, Wild Sports of India on the Neilgherry Hills, in the Jungles, and on the Plains. By COLONEL WALTER CAMPBELL, of Skipness, late of the 7th Royal Fusiliers. Third Edition. Small 8vo., superbly illustrated, 8s.

THE TIGER PRINCE: or, Adventures in the Wilds of Abyssinia. By W. DALTON. With Eight Illustrations. Crown 8vo., 5s.

SCENES FROM THE DRAMA OF EUROPEAN HISTORY. By W. H. DAVENPORT ADAMS. Crown 8vo., 5s.

THE PRINCE OF THE HOUSE OF DAVID; or, Three Years in the Holy City. With Eight Illustrations. New Edition, fcap., 3s. 6d.

NAOMI; or, The Last Days of Jerusalem. By Mrs. J. B. WEBB. New Edition, with Designs by Gilbert and Bartlett. Fcap., 7s. 6d.

THE LIFE OF DR. ARNOLD. By E. J. WORBOISE. Second Edition, fcap., 3s. 6d.

ORIGINAL POEMS FOR INFANT MINDS. Illustrated Edition, cloth gilt, 5s. Cheap Edition, in 2 vols., price 1s. 6d. each.

WEALE'S SERIES.

A TREATISE ON LOGIC, pure and applied. By S. H. EMMENS. 1s. 6d.
PRACTICAL HINTS FOR INVESTING MONEY. By F. PLAYFORD. 1s.
THE LAW of FRIENDLY, BUILDING, LOAN, and OTHER SOCIETIES. By N. WHITE. 1s.
OUTLINES of MODERN FARMING. By R. SCOTT BURN. 2 vols., illustrated, strongly bound, 14s.
ENGLISH DICTIONARY. By HYDE CLARKE. 3s. 6d.; or strongly bound, 4s. 6d.

LONDON: VIRTUE BROTHERS & CO., 1, AMEN CORNER.

TRÜBNER & CO.'S PUBLICATIONS.

BY MISS FRANCES POWER COBBE.
STUDIES NEW AND OLD ON ETHICAL AND SOCIAL SUBJECTS. Crown 8vo. cloth. [*In the press.*

ITALICS: Brief Notes on Politics, People, and Places in Italy in 1864. Post 8vo. cloth, 12s. 6d.

AN ESSAY ON INTUITIVE MORALS. THE THEORY OF MORALS. Post 8vo. cloth, 5s.

RELIGIOUS DUTY. Post 8vo. cloth, 7s. 6d.

BROKEN LIGHTS: an Inquiry into the present Condition and Future Prospects of Religious Faith. *Second Edition.* Crown 8vo. cloth, 5s.

THE CITIES OF THE PAST. Foolscap 8vo. cloth, 3s. 6d.

THANKSGIVING: a Chapter of Religious Duty. 24mo., 1s.

BY THEODORE PARKER.
THE COLLECTED WORKS OF THEODORE PARKER. Edited by FRANCES POWER COBBE. 12 Vols. 8vo. cloth, price 6s. each volume.

CONTENTS.

Vol. I., Discourse of Matters pertaining to Religion; with Preface by the Editor.
Vol. II., Ten Sermons, and Prayers.
Vol. III., Discourses of Theology.
Vol. IV., Discourses of Politics.
Vols. V. and VI., Discourses of Slavery, 2 vols.
Vol. VII., Discourses of Social Science.
Vol. VIII., Miscellaneous Discourses.
Vols. IX. and X., Critical Writings, 2 vols.
Vol. XI., Theism, Atheism, and the Popular Theology.
Vol. XII., Autobiographical and Miscellaneous Pieces.

LESSONS FROM THE WORLD OF MATTER AND THE WORLD OF MAN. Selected from Notes of his unpublished Sermons, by RUFUS LEIGHTON, and edited by FRANCES POWER COBBE. In 1 vol. Crown 8vo., 350 pp., cloth. Portrait, 7s. 6d.

BY AUGUSTE COMTE.
A GENERAL VIEW OF POSITIVISM. Translated by Dr. J. H. BRIDGES. Crown 8vo. cloth, 8s. 6d.

POSITIVE PHILOSOPHY. Translated and condensed by HARRIET MARTINEAU. 2 vols., post 8vo. cloth, 16s.

THE CATECHISM OF POSITIVE RELIGION. Translated by R. CONGREVE. 12mo. cloth, 6s. 6d.

BY PROFESSOR FRANCIS W. NEWMAN.
THEISM, DOCTRINAL AND PRACTICAL; or Didactic Religious Utterances. 4to. cloth, 8s. 6d.

LECTURES ON POLITICAL ECONOMY. Crown 8vo. cloth, 5s.

PHASES OF FAITH; or Passages from the History of my Creed. New Edition; with Reply to Professor HENRY ROGERS, author of the "Eclipse of Faith." Crown 8vo. cloth, 3s. 6d.

THE SOUL, ITS SORROWS AND ITS ASPIRATIONS; an Essay towards the Natural History of the Soul, as the True Basis of Theology. Seventh Edition. Crown 8vo. cloth, 3s. 6d.

CATHOLIC UNION: Essays towards a Church of the Future, as the Organisation of Philanthropy. Crown 8vo. cloth, 3s. 6d.

A HISTORY of the HEBREW MONARCHY from the Administration of Samuel to the Babylonish Captivity. Second Edition. Large post 8vo. cloth, 8s. 6d.

BY WILLIAM RATHBONE GREG.
THE CREED OF CHRISTENDOM: its Foundations and Superstructure. Crown 8vo. cloth, 6s.

BY PROFESSOR RENAN.
THE LIFE OF JESUS. The Authorised Translation. Revised by the Author. Demy 8vo. cloth, 10s. 6d. Cheap Edition, crown 8vo., 1s. 6d.

AN ESSAY ON THE AGE AND ANTIQUITY OF THE BOOK OF NABATHÆAN AGRICULTURE. To which is added an Inaugural Lecture on the Position of the Shemitic Nations in the History of Civilisation. Crown 8vo., 164 pp., cloth, 3s. 6d.

BY BENEDICT DE SPINOZA.
TRACTATUS THEOLOGICO-POLITICUS: A Critical Inquiry into the History, Purpose, and Authenticity of the Hebrew Scriptures; with the Right to Free Thought and Free Discussion asserted, and shown to be not only consistent but necessarily bound up with True Piety and Good Government. Translated from the Latin. With an Introduction and Notes by the Editor. 8vo. cloth, 10s. 6d.

BY JEAN PAUL FREDERIC RICHTER.
LEVANA: or the Doctrine of Education. Translated. 12mo. cloth, 7s. 6d.

FLOWER, FRUIT, AND THORN PIECES. Translated. 2 vols. 12mo. cloth.

TITAN: a Romance. Translated by CHARLES T. BROOKS. 2 vols., 12mo. cloth, 18s.

HESPERUS. Translated by CHARLES T. BROOKS. [*In the Press.*

THE LIFE OF JEAN PAUL FREDERIC RICHTER. Compiled from various sources. Preceded by his Autobiography. By ELIZA BUCKMINSTER LEE. Third Edition, 12mo. cloth, 7s. 6d.

PUBLICATIONS OF THE ANTHROPOLOGICAL SOCIETY.
THE ANTHROPOLOGICAL REVIEW; and Journal of the Anthropological Society of London. Vol. I. 8vo. cloth, 16s. Vol. II., 8vo. cloth, 18s.

ON THE NEGRO'S PLACE IN NATURE. By JAMES HUNT, Ph.D., F.S.A., F.R.S.L. 8vo., 1s.

INTRODUCTORY ADDRESS on the STUDY OF ANTHROPOLOGY. By Dr. JAMES HUNT. 8vo., 1s.

ANNUAL ADDRESS TO THE ANTHROPOLOGICAL SOCIETY, January 5, 1864. By Dr. JAMES HUNT. 8vo., 1s.

MEMOIRS READ BEFORE THE ANTHROPOLOGICAL SOCIETY OF LONDON. 8vo. cloth, 21s.

JOURNAL OF THE ROYAL ASIATIC SOCIETY OF GREAT BRITAIN AND IRELAND. New Series. Vol. I., 8vo. cloth. [*Shortly.*

HISTORY OF THE SECT OF MAHARAJAS OR VALLABHACHARYAS IN WESTERN INDIA. With a Plate. 8vo. cloth, 12s.

BY MAJOR EVANS BELL.
THE MYSORE REVERSION "AN EXCEPTIONAL CASE." 8vo. cloth, 6s. 6d.

THE EMPIRE IN INDIA. Letters from Madras, and other places. Post 8vo., 420 pp., cloth, 8s. 6d.

THE ENGLISH IN INDIA. Letters from Nagpore, written in 1857-8. Post 8vo., 206 pp., cloth, 5s.

BY HORACE HAYMAN WILSON.
ESSAYS AND LECTURES CHIEFLY ON THE RELIGION OF THE HINDUS. Collected and edited by Dr. REINHOLD ROST. 2 vols., 8vo. cloth, 21s.

ESSAYS, ANALYTICAL, CRITICAL, AND PHILOLOGICAL, ON SUBJECTS CONNECTED WITH SANSKRIT LITERATURE. Collected and edited by Dr. REINHOLD ROST. 3 vols., 8vo. cloth, 36s.

THE VISHNU PURANA: a System of Hindu Mythology and Tradition. Translated from the original Sanskrit, and illustrated by Notes derived chiefly from other Puranas, by H. H. WILSON. Edited by Dr. FITZ EDWARD HALL. Vol. I., 8vo. cloth, 10s. 6d. [*Vols. II. to IV. in the Press.*

BY STEFANOS XENOS.
EAST AND WEST: a Diplomatic History of the Annexation of the Ionian Islands to the Kingdom of Greece. Accompanied by a Translation of the Despatches exchanged between the Greek Government and its Plenipotentiary at London, and a Collection of the Principal Treaties, Conventions, and Protocols, concerning the Ionian Islands and Greece, concluded between 1797 and 1864. Royal 8vo. cloth, 12s.

BY PROFESSOR BERNHARD VON COTTA.
GEOLOGY AND HISTORY. A Popular Exposition of all that is known of the Earth and its Inhabitants in Pre-historic Times. Post 8vo. cloth, 2s.

MARTIN'S HISTORY OF FRANCE.
THE AGE OF LOUIS XIV. By HENRI MARTIN. Translated from the Fourth Paris Edition with the Author's sanction and co-operation. By MARY L. BOOTH. 2 vols., 8vo. cloth, 36s.

LONDON: TRÜBNER & CO., 60, PATERNOSTER ROW.

THE SHILLING MAGAZINE.
A MONTHLY MISCELLANY. ILLUSTRATED. Edited by SAMUEL LUCAS, M.A.
No. I. Now Ready.
CONTENTS.

PHEMIE KELLER. Chapters I., II., III., IV., V. By the Author of "George Geith," &c. (With an Illustration.)
GOLD. By Bonamy Price, M.A.
DRAMATIC LITERATURE. By Robert Bell, F.S.A.
THE PICTURES OF 1865. By Tom Taylor.
BENJAMIN DISRAELI.
WIT AND WISDOM FROM WEST AFRICA. By W. Stirling (of Keir), M.P.

THE GOLDEN ROSE. By W. J. Thomas, F.S.A. (With an Illustration.)
THE WILD FLOWER OF RAVENSWORTH. Chapters I., II., III. (With an Illustration.)
FROM PETRARCA. By Edwin Arnold, M.A.
WHAT'S O'CLOCK. By J. Carpenter (Greenwich Observatory).
IRON SHIPS AND TURRETS. By C. D. Yonge, M.A.

NEW NOVEL BY THE AUTHOR OF "EAST LYNNE," NEVER BEFORE PUBLISHED.
On June 5th, will be published, in 3 vols.,
MILDRED ARKELL. By the Author of "East Lynne."

This day is published, in 1 vol.,
WIT AND WISDOM FROM WEST AFRICA; or, a Book of Proverbial Philosophy, Idioms, Enigmas, and Laconisms. Compiled by RICHARD F. BURTON, late H.M.'s Consul for the Bight of Biafra and Fernando Po, Author of "A Pilgrimage to El Medinah and Meccah," "A Mission to Dahomey," &c. [Ready.

NEW NOVEL BY THE AUTHOR OF "THE FIELD OF LIFE."
This day is published, in 3 vols.,
A WOMAN'S WAY; a Novel. By the Author of "The Field of Life." [Ready this day.

NEW STORY OF LANCASHIRE LIFE, BY BENJAMIN BRIERLY.
This day is published, in 2 vols.,
IRKDALE; a Lancashire Story. By Benjamin Brierly. [Ready.

NEW WORK BY M. LAMARTINE.
Shortly will be published, in 2 vols.,
BIOGRAPHIES OF EMINENT MEN AND WOMEN. By Alphonse De Lamartine.

NEW WORKS IN CIRCULATION AT ALL THE LIBRARIES.
MY DIARY IN AMERICA IN THE MIDST OF WAR. By George Augustus Sala. The Second Edition Revised, in 2 vols., is ready.
THEO LEIGH; a Novel. By Annie Thomas, Author of "Dennis Donne." In 3 vols.
BITTER SWEETS; a Love Story. By Joseph Hatton. In 3 Vols.
GEORGE GEITH OF FEN COURT, the Novel by F. G. Trafford, author of "City and Suburb," &c. In 3 vols. Third Edition.
MASANIELLO OF NAPLES. By Mrs. Horace St. John.
SHOOTING AND FISHING IN THE RIVERS, PRAIRIES, AND BACKWOODS OF NORTH AMERICA. By B. H. Revoil.
FACES FOR FORTUNES. By Augustus Mayhew, Author of "How to Marry and Whom to Marry," "The Greatest Plague in Life."
"There is no sound in this world so beautiful as the laughter of woman. In the hope of hearing it, this book was written."—*Preface.*

NEW EDITION OF "DENIS DONNE."
Shortly will be published, in 1 vol., 6s.
DENIS DONNE; a Novel. By Annie Thomas, Author of "Theo Leigh."

This day is published, in 1 vol., 6s.
THE WORLD IN THE CHURCH. By the Author of "George Geith of Fen Court," "Too Much Alone," &c.

Also, uniform with the above, New Editions of

CITY AND SUBURB. 6s.	MAURICE DERING. 6s.	SWORD AND GOWN. 4s. 6d.
JOHN MARCHMONT'S LEGACY. 6s.	TREVLYN HOLD. 6s.	TOO MUCH ALONE. 6s.
SEVEN SONS OF MAMMON. 6s.	GUY LIVINGSTONE. 5s.	DUTCH PICTURES. By Sala. 5s.
RECOMMENDED TO MERCY. 6s.	BARREN HONOUR. 6s.	TWO PRIMA DONNAS. 5s.
ELEANOR'S VICTORY. 6s.	BORDER AND BASTILE. 6s.	BUNDLE OF BALLADS. 6s.
BUCKLAND'S FISH HATCHING. 5s.		

TINSLEY BROTHERS, 18, CATHERINE STREET, STRAND.

DEDICATED, BY SPECIAL PERMISSION, TO H.R.H. THE PRINCE OF WALES.

THE ART-JOURNAL:
A MONTHLY JOURNAL OF

The Fine Arts, the Arts of Manufacture, Industry, &c.

EDITED BY S. C. HALL, ESQ., F.S.A.

PRICE 2s. 6D. MONTHLY.

The ART-JOURNAL is, by the elegance and value of its engraved Illustrations, a work especially calculated for the Drawing-room of all persons of taste and refinement.

It is addressed to the Artist, the Amateur, the Manufacturer, and the Artisan, representing the Fine Arts and the Arts of Industry.

The most eminent and experienced writers on Art, in all its varied ramifications, communicate with the public through its pages.

The Principal Writers for the Year 1865 *are—*

JOHN RUSKIN, M.A.	REV. E. L. CUTTS, M.A.
DR. CRACE CALVERT, F.R.S.	HENRY MURRAY, F.S.A.;
F. W. FAIRHOLT, F.S.A.	PROFESSOR T. C. ARCHER.
J. B. ATKINSON.	J. T. WALLER, LL.D.'
LLEWELLYNN JEWITT, F.S.A.	MADAME BODICHON.
J. B. PYNE.	HENRY OTTLEY.
REV. C. BOUTELL, M.A.	JAMES DAFFORNE.
PETER CUNNINGHAM, F.S.A.	MRS. S. C. HALL.
W. CHAFFERS, F.S.A.	S. C. HALL, F.S.A. ETC. ETC.

The JUNE Number will contain a full descriptive and critical account of the Pictures and Sculpture now exhibiting at the Royal Academy, by an eminent writer on Art.

THE ENGRAVINGS,

Of which each Monthly Part contains *three* on steel and about *fifty* on wood, are from pictures by renowned artists; landscapes, portraits, historical and archæological relics, objects of recent or remote Art-manufacture, &c., being suggestive examples for the Amateur, the Student, and the Manufacturer. The engravings are in all cases from *original pictures*, principally of the British school.

The general intelligence treats of all matters connected with Art; all recent discoveries; biographies; provincial movements; reviews of Art-works, &c.

The ART-JOURNAL is designed to aid and promote that love and appreciation of Art which has, of late years, influenced, more or less, every class of the community.

This high object is sought to be effected by liberal and judicious expenditure of capital, and by unremitting industry, rendering Art-literature popular by avoiding, as far as possible, dry technical details, while conveying the utmost attainable amount of useful information.

The ART-JOURNAL will be supplied by any Bookseller in Town or Country.

LONDON: JAMES S. VIRTUE, 26, IVY LANE.

NEW NOVELS
PUBLISHED BY CHAPMAN AND HALL.

NEVER FORGOTTEN.
By PERCIVAL FITZGERALD. 3 vols.

"The character of Captain Fermor is an original creation, and deserves to be studied. . . . The minor characters are thoroughly life-like. . . . Indeed, the story is full of humour, and there is really pathos in it also. The descriptive passages are very cleverly written, and the dialogue is crisp and sparkling. From the author of a book which possesses so many merits, we may fairly expect much."—*Saturday Review.*

CYRIL BLOUNT; or, Trust Money.
By the Author of "Recommended to Mercy." 3 vols. [*May* 1.

STRATHMORE.
By OUIDA. 3 vols. [*In May.*

ON GUARD.
By MISS THOMAS, Author of "Denis Donne." 3 vols.

THE WOMAN I LOVED, AND THE WOMAN WHO LOVED ME.
By the Author of "Agnes Tremorne." 1 vol. [*In May.*

MILES BULLER; or, The Little World of Onniegate.
3 vols.

CRUMBS FROM A SPORTSMAN'S TABLE.
By CHARLES CLARKE, Author of "Charlie Thornhill," &c. 2 vols.

SIGNE'S HISTORY. A Norwegian Tale.
By MAGDALENE THORESEN. Translated by the Rev. M. R. BARNARD. 1 vol. post 8vo.

LANGLEYHAUGH; a Tale of an Anglo-Saxon Family.
By G. W. FEATHERSTONHAUGH, Author of "The Canoe Voyage," &c. 2 vols. post 8vo. [*In May.*

THE BROOKES OF BRIDLEMERE.
By WHYTE MELVILLE. Third Edition. 3 vols.

QUITE ALONE.
By GEORGE AUGUSTUS SALA. 3 vols.

WHICH IS THE WINNER?
By CHARLES CLARKE. 3 vols.

CAPTAIN HERBERT. A Sea Story.
3 vols.

193, PICCADILLY.

MESSRS. BELL AND DALDY'S PUBLICATIONS.

DR. RICHARDSON'S NEW DICTIONARY OF THE ENGLISH LANGUAGE. Combining Explanation with Etymology, and copiously Illustrated by Quotations from the best authorities. New Edition, with a Supplement containing additional Words and further Illustrations. In Two Vols. 4to. £4 14s. 6d. Half bound in russia, £5 15s. 6d. Russia, £6 12s.

⁎ The Supplement separately, 4to. 12s.

An 8vo. EDITION, without the Quotations, 15s. Half-russia, 20s. Russia, 24s.

"It is an admirable addition to our Lexicography, supplying a great desideratum, as exhibiting the biography of each word—its birth, parentage, and education, the changes that have befallen it, the company it has kept, and the connections it has formed—by rich series of quotations, all in chronological order. This is such a Dictionary as perhaps no other language could ever boast."—*Quarterly Review.*

Immediately, in crown 8vo.,

Sydonie's Dowry. By the Author of "Denise," "Mademoiselle Mori," &c.

Shortly, in crown 8vo.,

Henri de Rohan. By the Author of "Arnold Delahaize."

In the press, medium 8vo., with Illustrations,

The History and Natural History of Precious Stones, Precious Metals, and Gems. By C. W. KING, M.A., Fellow of Trinity College, Cambridge, and Author of "Antique Gems," and "The Gnostics and their Remains."

Royal 8vo. 15s.,

The Gnostics and their Remains, Ancient and Mediæval. By C. W. KING, M.A., Author of "Antique Gems."

Lays of the Western Gael, and other Poems. By SAMUEL FERGUSON, Author of "The Forging of the Anchor." Fcap. 8vo. 5s.

Jerusalem Explored: being a Description of the Ancient and Modern City, with upwards of One Hundred Illustrations, consisting of Views, Ground-plans, and Sections. By Dr. ERMETE PIEROTTI, Doctor of Mathematics, Architect-Engineer to his Excellency Soorraya Pasha of Jerusalem, and Architect of the Holy Land. (Translated by the Rev. T. G. Bonney, M.A., Fellow of St. John's College, Cambridge.) 2 vols. Imp. 4to. £5 5s.

The Customs and Traditions of Palestine. By E. PIEROTTI, Author of "Jerusalem Explored." 9s.

The Book of Psalms: a New Translation, with Introductions and Notes, Critical and Explanatory. By the Rev. J. J. STEWART PEROWNE, B.D., Vice-Principal of Lampeter College, and Examining Chaplain to the Lord Bishop of Norwich. 8vo. Vol. I. 14s.

Two Vols. 8vo. 21s.,

A History of the Intellectual Development of Europe. By JOHN WILLIAM DRAPER, M.D., LL.D.

"His narrative is accurate and graphic, and his grasp of historical truth powerful and tenacious."—*Saturday Review.*

"It is one of the best attempts to treat the entire history of man on a scientific theory."—*Athenæum.*

Host and Guest: a Book about Dinners, Wines, and Desserts. By A. V. KIRWAN, of the Middle Temple, Esq. Crown 8vo. 9s.

Seventh Edition, in Two Vols. 8vo. 21s.

A Practical Treatise on Banking. By the late JAMES WILLIAM GILBART, F.R.S., one of the Directors of the London and Westminster Bank, and formerly General Manager.

Shortly, in square 16mo., with Illustrations,

Aunt Sally's Life. By Mrs. Alfred Gatty.

In crown 8vo. 6s. 6d.,

Lacon in Council. By the Author of "Illustrations of Æschylus," &c.

Dedicated by permission to Her Majesty the Queen.

In Six Vols., 30s.,

A Popular Edition of Miss Agnes Strickland's Lives of the Queens of England, carefully revised.

In small 8vo. 5s.,

Fifty Modern Poems. By William Allingham, Author of "Laurence Bloomfield," "Day and Night Songs," &c.

Fcap. 8vo. 6s. 6d.,

Anthologia Latina. A Selection of Choice Latin Poetry, with Notes. By the Rev. F. ST. JOHN THACKERAY, Assistant Master, Eton College.

Crown 8vo. 6s. 6d.,

Sermons. By George Jehoshaphat Mountain, D.D., D.C.L., late Bishop of Quebec. Published at the request of the Synod of the Diocese.

Just completed, in Four Vols., half-bound, £2 2s.; or, in Eleven Parts, £2,

Lowndes's Bibliographer's Manual of English Literature; containing an Account of Rare, Curious, and Useful Books, published in or relating to Great Britain and Ireland, from the Invention of Printing; with Bibliographical and Critical Notices, Collations of the Rarer Articles, and the prices at which they have been sold. New Edition, revised, corrected, and enlarged; with an Appendix relating to the Books of Literary and Scientific Societies. By HENRY G. BOHN.

Now Ready, in 4to. £1 11s. 6d., an Illustrated and Enlarged Edition of

WEBSTER'S COMPLETE DICTIONARY OF THE ENGLISH LANGUAGE. Revised by C. A. GOODRICH, D.D., LL.D., and N. PORTER, D.D., Professors in Yale College. In announcing an entirely new and revised edition of this Dictionary, the proprietors desire to call attention to its peculiar features, and to point out those improvements which render it the most complete and best Dictionary for constant use that has yet been issued.

1. **Fulness and completeness.**—The number of words is about 114,000, being more by 10,000 than those in any other dictionary.
2. The Scientific and Technical Words are incorporated in the body of the dictionary, are largely augmented, and revised by professional gentlemen eminent in their several departments.
3. **Accuracy of Definition.**—Dr. Webster's definitions are remarkable for precision and nice discrimination, and they have been pronounced by competent authority to be models of condensation and purity.
4. **Pronunciation.**—It is believed that the pronunciation is more correctly presented than in any other dictionary.
5. **Etymology.**—The eminent philologist, Dr. C. A. F. Mahn, of Berlin, has been engaged five years in bringing into the dictionary the recent results of philological investigation.
6. **Uniformity in Spelling.**—Words that from caprice have been spelt differently are here brought to one standard.
7. Quotations helping to illustrate the signification of a word, or happily indicating its application, are largely used. This distinguishes this complete dictionary from all the abridgments.
8. **Synonyms.**—The Synonyms are given under the words to which they belong, and will be found very useful to speakers and writers.
9. **Illustrations.**—The value of the dictionary is further enhanced by the addition of nearly 3,000 pictorial illustrations, arranged under the words to which they refer.
10. **Cheapness.**—The volume contains 1,768 pages, sold in cloth for £1 11s. 6d. It will be found on comparison to be one of the cheapest books ever issued, containing as much as thirty octavo volumes.

LONDON: BELL AND DALDY, 186, FLEET STREET.

GEORGE ELIOT'S WORKS.

I.
In 1 vol. crown 8vo. 6s.,
ADAM BEDE.

In 1 vol. crown 8vo., 6s.,
THE MILL ON THE FLOSS.

In 1 vol. crown 8vo., 6s.,
SCENES OF CLERICAL LIFE, AND SILAS MARNER.

ALSO,
ADAM BEDE. 2 vols. fcap. 8vo. cloth, 12s.
THE MILL ON THE FLOSS. 2 vols. fcap. 8vo. cloth, 12s.
SCENES OF CLERICAL LIFE. 2 vols. fcap. 8vo. cloth, 12s.
SILAS MARNER. 1 vol. fcap. 8vo. cloth, 6s.

II.
A New Edition, being the Seventeenth, in small 8vo. cloth, 7s. 6d.,
THE LAYS of the SCOTTISH CAVALIERS.
By W. EDMONDSTOUNE AYTOUN, D.C.L., Professor of Rhetoric and Belles Lettres in the University of Edinburgh.

III.
A New and Cheap Edition, complete in 1 vol., with Map, 5s., of
CAPTAIN SHERARD OSBORN'S STRAY LEAVES from an ARCTIC JOURNAL.
Or, Eighteen Months in the Polar Regions in search of Sir John Franklin's Expedition in 1850-51.
To which is added,
The Career, Last Voyage, and Fate of Captain Sir John Franklin.

IV.
In post 8vo. cloth, 6s.,
FAUST: a Dramatic Poem by Goethe.
Translated into English verse by THEODORE MARTIN.

V.
In 2 vols. 8vo., 28s., in ornamental cloth,
THE GREAT GOVERNING FAMILIES OF ENGLAND.
By J. LANGTON SANFORD and MEREDITH TOWNSEND.

VI.
In post 8vo. cloth, 9s., uniform with the First Series,
A SECOND SERIES OF ESSAYS ON SOCIAL SUBJECTS,
FROM THE SATURDAY REVIEW.

VII.
In 4 vols. 8vo. cloth, 48s.,
LECTURES on METAPHYSICS and LOGIC.
By Sir WILLIAM HAMILTON, Bart. Edited by the Rev. H. L. MANSEL, B.D., LL.D., and JOHN VEITCH, M.A.

VIII.
In imperial folio, half-bound morocco, £5 15s. 6d.,
THE ROYAL ATLAS OF MODERN GEOGRAPHY.
A Series of entirely original and authentic Maps. By ALEX. KEITH JOHNSTON, F.R.S.E., &c.

IX.
In imperial 8vo., pp. 676, 21s.,
INDEX GEOGRAPHICUS:
Being a List, Alphabetically arranged, of the principal Places on the Globe, with the Countries and Subdivisions of the Countries, and their Latitude and Longitude; applicable to all modern Atlases and Maps.

WILLIAM BLACKWOOD AND SONS,
EDINBURGH AND LONDON.

THE UNITED LIBRARIES.

BOOTH'S, CHURTON'S, HODGSON'S, AND SAUNDERS AND OTLEY'S.

307, Regent Street, London, W., next the Royal Polytechnic Institution.

SINGLE SUBSCRIPTION, ONE GUINEA.
Family Subscriptions, Three, Five, and Ten Guineas.
Country Subscribers, Book Clubs, &c., from Two Guineas to any amount, according to the supply required.
Great advantages are offered by this Library to Country Subscribers, in the large number of volumes supplied at one time.
All the New Books taken, as soon as published, in large numbers.
The best French, German, and Italian Books also added immediately on publication.
All the Magazines and Reviews: "Revue des Deux Mondes," "Revue Contemporaine," "Rivista Contemporanea," "Preussischer Jahrbucher," &c.
The collection of Standard Works in English and Foreign Literature is large, and has been accumulating since 1786.
Catalogues and terms for the coming season sent on application.
** A Catalogue of Surplus Copies (withdrawn from circulation) of books of the past season, being clean and perfect copies of the most popular works of the day, at very reduced prices.

307, REGENT STREET, W.

EDUCATIONAL WORKS OF DR. CORNWELL, F.R.C.S.

MAP BOOK FOR BEGINNERS. 70 Maps, large and small. 1s. 6d.; 2s. 6d. coloured.

BOOK OF BLANK MAPS. 1s.

BOOK OF MAP PROJECTIONS. 1s.

GEOGRAPHY FOR BEGINNERS. 18th Edition. 1s.

SCHOOL GEOGRAPHY. 36th Edition. 3s. 6d.; or with Thirty Maps on Steel, 5s. 6d.
** Enlarged and revised, bringing down the information to the present time.

SCHOOL ATLAS. 2s. 6d. plain; 4s. coloured.

THE YOUNG COMPOSER; or, Progressive Exercises in English Composition. 27th Edition. 1s. 6d.

KEY TO THE YOUNG COMPOSER: with Hints as to the Mode of Using the Book. 3s.

ALLEN AND CORNWELL'S SCHOOL GRAMMAR. 36th Edition. 2s. red leather; 1s. 9d. cloth.

GRAMMAR FOR BEGINNERS. 44th Edition. 1s. cloth; 9d. sewed.

SELECT ENGLISH POETRY for the Use of Schools and Young Persons in general. Edited by the late Dr. ALLEN. 13th Edition. 4s.

DR. ALLEN'S EUTROPIUS. With Dictionary. 3s.

SCHOOL ARITHMETIC: a First Book of Practical Arithmetic, with an Inductive Explanation of each Rule. 7th Edition. 1s. 6d.

KEY TO SCHOOL ARITHMETIC; with numerous Suggestions, special and general, for teaching Arithmetic. 4s. 6d.

THE SCIENCE OF ARITHMETIC. By JAMES CORNWELL, Ph.Dr., and JOSHUA G. FITCH, M.A. 9th Edition. 4s. 6d.

London: SIMPKIN, MARSHALL & Co.; HAMILTON, ADAMS & Co.
Edinburgh: OLIVER & BOYD.

In four Volumes, fcap. 8vo. cloth, 10s. 6d.

DANTE'S DIVINE COMEDY, translated in the Original Ternary Rhyme. By C. B. CAYLEY, B.A.
Each volume may be had separately: *Hell*, 3s. *Purgatory*, 2s. 6d. *Paradise*, 2s. 6d. NOTES, 2s. 6d.

London: LONGMAN, GREEN & Co., Paternoster Row.

THE FARM HOMESTEADS OF ENGLAND.
A New Edition will be ready in a few days.

CHAPMAN AND HALL, 193, Piccadilly.

New Books

ALEXANDER STRAHAN, Publisher.

IDYLS AND LEGENDS OF INVERBURN. By ROBERT BUCHANAN, Author of "Undertones." Small 8vo., 5s. [*Ready.*

HENRY HOLBEACH, Student in Life and Philosophy. A Narrative and a Discussion. With Letters to Mr. Alexander Bain, Mr. Thomas Carlyle, Mr. Arthur Helps, Mr. G. H. Lewes, Rev. H. Mansel, Rev. F. D. Maurice, Mr. John Stuart Mill, Rev. Dr. J. H. Newman, Mr. Matthew Arnold, and others. 2 vols. post 8vo., 14s. [*Ready.*

HEADS AND HANDS IN THE WORLD OF LABOUR. By W. G. BLAIKIE, D.D., F.R.S.E., Author of "Better Days for Working People." Crown 8vo., 3s. 6d. [*Ready.*

SIX MONTHS AMONG THE CHARITIES OF EUROPE. By JOHN DE LIEFDE, London. With Illustrations. 2 vols. post 8vo., 16s. [*Nearly Ready.*

THE FOURTH VOLUME OF THE COLLECTED WRITINGS OF EDWARD IRVING. Edited by his Nephew, the Rev. G. CARLYLE, M.A. Demy 8vo., 12s. [*Ready.*
Vol. V., completing the work, will be ready immediately.

ESSAYS ON WOMAN'S WORK. By BESSIE RAYNER PARKES. Small 8vo., 4s. [*Ready.*

JUDAS ISCARIOT; a Dramatic Poem. Small 8vo., 5s. [*Nearly Ready.*

LETTERS FROM ABROAD in 1864. By HENRY ALFORD, D.D., Dean of Canterbury. Second Edition. Crown 8vo., 7s. 6d. [*Ready.*

CHRIST AND HIS SALVATION, in Sermons variously related thereto. By HORACE BUSHNELL, D.D., Author of "Nature and the Supernatural," &c. Crown 8vo., 6s. [*Ready.*

OUTLINES OF THEOLOGY. By ALEXANDER VINET. Post 8vo., 8s. [*Ready.*

OUTLINES OF PHILOSOPHY AND LITERATURE. By ALEXANDER VINET. Post 8vo., 8s. [*Ready.*

THE REGULAR SWISS ROUND. In Three Trips. By the Rev. HARRY JONES, Incumbent of St. Luke's, London. With Illustrations. Small 8vo., 5s. [*Immediately.*

STUDIES FOR STORIES, FROM GIRLS' LIVES. Cheap Edition. Complete in One Volume. Crown 8vo., 6s. [*Immediately.*

A YEAR AT THE SHORE. By P. H. GOSSE, F.R.S. With 36 Illustrations by the Author, printed in colours by Leighton Brothers. Crown 8vo., 9s. [*Ready.*

PLAIN WORDS ON CHRISTIAN LIVING. By C. J. VAUGHAN, D.D., Vicar of Doncaster. Small 8vo., 4s. 6d. [*Ready.*

A SUMMER IN SKYE. 2 Vols. By ALEXANDER SMITH, Author of "A Life Drama," &c. [*Nearly ready.*

HYMNS AND HYMN WRITERS OF GERMANY. By WILLIAM FLEMING STEVENSON, Author of "Praying and Working." 2 Vols. [*Nearly ready.*

TRAVELS IN TURKEY IN EUROPE. By G. MUIR MACKENZIE and A. P. IRBY. [*Shortly.*

DAYS OF YORE. By Sarah Tytler, Author of "Papers for Thoughtful Girls." 2 Vols. [*Shortly.*

UNDERTONES. By Robt. Buchanan. Revised and enlarged. [*Shortly.*

POEMS. By Henry Alford, D.D., Dean of Canterbury. A new and enlarged edition. [*Nearly ready.*

THE AUTOCRAT OF THE BREAKFAST TABLE. By OLIVER WENDELL HOLMES. New Edition. [*Shortly.*

148, STRAND, *May*, 1865.

MUDIE'S SELECT LIBRARY.

BOOKS FOR ALL READERS.
See MUDIE's List of New Books for May.

BOOKS FOR ALL BUYERS.
See MUDIE's List of Cheap Books for May.

MUDIE'S SELECT LIBRARY (LIMITED), NEW OXFORD STREET, LONDON.

PROFESSOR CRAIK'S HISTORY OF THE ENGLISH
LITERATURE and the ENGLISH LANGUAGE. A New Edition. In two very handsome volumes royal 8vo., 25s.

"The great value of the book is its thorough comprehensiveness. . . . Eminently distinguished by good sense."—*Saturday Review.*

DR. AITKEN'S SCIENCE AND PRACTICE OF MEDICINE.
The Third Edition, revised and portions re-written. Numerous Diagrams and Illustrations. 2 vols. 8vo. cloth, 31s. 6d. [*Now ready.*

* The *Lancet* says:—"A book in which the work of collection, arrangement, and exposition of all the new things in our calling is done to our hand."

REV. FREDERICK DENNISON MAURICE'S MORAL AND
METAPHYSICAL PHILOSOPHY. Fourteenth Century to the French Revolution. With a Glimpse into the Nineteenth Century. Crown 8vo. cloth, 10s. 6d.

"This great book is one of the most characteristic fruits of Mr. Maurice's genius, and is of a kind to exercise, if not directly, a very wide influence on the history of English Philosophy."—*Spectator.*
"It abounds in passages of great richness and truth."—*Westminster Review.*

LONDON: CHARLES GRIFFIN AND CO.

Dedicated by permission to the Lord Bishop of Oxford.

This day, beautifully printed on toned paper, cloth, antique, 5s., with Frontispiece by JOHN LEIGHTON, F.S.A.

ENGLISH LYRICS. A Collection of English Poetry of the
Present Day. Arranged by the Rev. R. H. BAYNES, M.A., Editor of the "Lyra Anglicana."

Contributions from the following Writers will be found in this Volume:—

HIS GRACE THE LORD ARCHBISHOP OF DUBLIN.	THE VERY REV. THE DEAN OF CANTERBURY.
THE RIGHT REV. THE LORD BISHOP OF OXFORD.	THE VERY REV. THE DEAN OF ELY.
SIR E. BULWER LYTTON, BART.	REV. CANON WORDSWORTH, D.D., &c. &c.

LONDON: HOULSTON AND WRIGHT, 65, PATERNOSTER ROW.

Dedicated by permission to the Very Rev. the Dean of Canterbury.

This day, beautifully printed on toned paper, cloth antique, 3s. 6d.

LYRA SABBATICA; Hymns and Poems for Sundays and
Holy Days. By BENJAMIN GOUGH.

LONDON: HOULSTON AND WRIGHT, 65, PATERNOSTER ROW.

NEW NOVEL.

This day is published, 3 vols., crown 8vo. cloth, price £1 11s. 6d.,

THE HILLYARS AND THE BURTONS:
A STORY OF TWO FAMILIES.
By HENRY KINGSLEY,
Author of "Austin Elliot," "Ravenshoe," &c.

MACMILLAN AND CO., LONDON AND CAMBRIDGE.

EDMONSTON AND DOUGLAS' NEW PUBLICATIONS.

NEW WORK BY MR. J. F. CAMPBELL.

Next week will be published, in 2 Vols., demy 8vo., with Maps and numerous Illustrations,

FROST & FIRE NATURAL ENGINES, TOOL-MARKS & CHIPS.

With Sketches taken at Home and Abroad by a TRAVELLER.

NOW READY.
MYSTIFICATIONS.

By CLEMENTINA STIRLING GRAHAME. Edited by JOHN BROWN, M.D. In 1 vol. small 4to., 5s.

"None but dull beings, devoid of a particle of humour in their composition, will reject the amusement of mystification as distinct from practical joking. It is only to the sour, the inferior, or the pragmatically vain, who will bristle up in offence at a good-humoured joke, or in vengeance if their sagacity has been imposed on. The merriest people are apt to make as rare sport of themselves as of any among those whom they have the good fortune to mystify. There is too little harmless laughter in this care-worn world. Fancies like these have been recalled to us by this book from Edinburgh, in which we are told how a lady, by her dramatic assumption of old world types and manners, contrived entirely to deceive some of the shrewdest and most intellectual men of Edinburgh society. We could fill columns showing the audacious, yet probable, readiness of this whimsical woman in more eccentric characters than one. It is a racy little book, well worth reading by Northern or Southern."—*Abridged from Athenæum.*

A SHORT AMERICAN TRIP IN THE FALL OF 1864.

By the Editor of "Life in Normandy." 1 vol. 8vo., 12s.

"We desire to call attention to a sparkling and pleasant book by the editor of 'Life in Normandy.' Having read it, we may say that it is one which will well repay perusal. We believe, too, that this genial book is but an earnest of one of a much more scientific character, only a sparkling splinter, or flint flake, off a much grander rock; and we hope at no distant period to welcome the author in his graver, as we have laughed with him in his lighter mood."—*Times.*

LIFE IN NORMANDY.

Sketches of French Fishing, Farming, Cooking, Natural History, and Politics. Drawn from Nature. By an ENGLISH RESIDENT. Third Edition, 1 vol. 8vo., with a Portrait of the Author, 6s.

ODDS AND ENDS, GRAVE OR HUMOROUS.

A Series. 6d. each.

Now ready,
No. 1. SKETCHES OF HIGHLAND CHARACTER. Sheep Farmers and Drovers.
No. 2. CONVICTS. By a PRACTICAL HAND.
No. 3. WAYSIDE THOUGHTS. By Professor D'ARCY THOMPSON.
 No. 1, Rainy Weather, or the Philosophy of Melancholy; Goose Skin, or the Philosophy of Horror; Te Deum Laudamus, or the Philosophy of Joy.
No. 4. THE ENTERKIN. By JOHN BROWN, M.D.

TRAVELS.

By UMBRA. 1 vol. 8vo., 10s. 6d.

"The fun of this book is good wholesome fun; it may not be sufficiently spicy for those whose palates have long been habituated to highly-peppered condiments. There is no *double entendre* in it, no suggestion that could bring a blush upon a modest cheek: it is quiet and gentlemanly; just the form and sparkle of a refined and cordial disposition, but with all the best qualities of real humour."—*Daily News.*

POPULAR GENEALOGISTS;

Or, The Art of Pedigree-Making. In 1 vol. crown 8vo., 4s.

"We have here an agreeable little treatise of a hundred pages from an anonymous but evidently competent hand on the ludicrous and fraudulent sides of genealogy, which we commend to those who want a bit of instructive and amusing reading."—*Pall Mall Gazette.*

FOREST SKETCHES:

Deer Stalking and other Sports in the Highlands Fifty Years Ago. With Illustrations by Gourlay Steell, R.S.A. 1 vol. demy 8vo., 15s.

THE SALMON.

By ALEX. RUSSEL.

CONTENTS.—Chap. I. Value of the Salmon—II. Natural History of the Salmon—III. Decay of the Salmon—IV. Salmon Legislation—V. Future Salmon Legislation—VI. Non-Legislative Remedies. In 1 Vol. 8vo., 7s. 6d.

"This important work is the greatest effort of one of our foremost and best writers upon the salmon and all that pertains to it. Mr. Russel has so high a reputation as a writer, that we had a right to expect (on a theme upon which he has clearly wrought *con amore*) a work of considerable power and interest, and we are not disappointed. In fact, our expectations are far more than realised, for, after reading Mr. Russel's work, we put down the book, feeling that there is really no more to be said on the subject, that the author has seen through every phase of every argument that bears upon it, and has fairly exhausted them. No book has ever yet appeared which so entirely and thoroughly deals with the subject. We must strongly commend its perusal to all our readers, of whatever section, who are interested in the salmon. The general reader need fear no dry polemics and weary wailing for the book, though on a special subject, is written in such a pleasant and lucid manner that the public at large can hardly fail to be deeply interested in its perusal."—*Field.*

EDMONSTON AND DOUGLAS, 88, PRINCES STREET, EDINBURGH.

MR. CHARLES DICKENS'S WORKS.

THE ILLUSTRATED LIBRARY EDITION,
Beautifully printed in Post Octavo, and carefully revised by the Author. With the Original Illustrations.

PICKWICK PAPERS	43 Illustrations		2 vols. 15s.
NICHOLAS NICKLEBY	39	ditto	2 vols. 15s.
MARTIN CHUZZLEWIT	40	ditto	2 vols. 15s.
OLD CURIOSITY SHOP	36	ditto	2 vols. 15s.
BARNABY RUDGE	36	ditto	2 vols. 15s.
SKETCHES BY BOZ	39	ditto	1 vol. 7s. 6d.
OLIVER TWIST	24	ditto	1 vol. 7s. 6d.
DOMBEY AND SON	39	ditto	2 vols. 15s.
DAVID COPPERFIELD	40	ditto	2 vols. 15s.
PICTURES FROM ITALY, AND AMERICAN NOTES	8	ditto	1 vol. 7s. 6d.
BLEAK HOUSE	40	ditto	2 vols. 15s.
LITTLE DORRIT	40	ditto	2 vols. 15s.
CHRISTMAS BOOKS	17	ditto	1 vol. 7s. 6d.
A TALE OF TWO CITIES	16	ditto	1 vol. 7s. 6d.

MR. THOMAS CARLYLE'S WORKS.

HISTORY OF FRIEDRICH THE SECOND, called FREDERICK THE GREAT. By THOMAS CARLYLE. With Portraits and Maps. Third Edition. 6 vols. 20s. each.

UNIFORM EDITION,
Handsomely printed in Crown Octavo, price Six Shillings per Volume.

THE FRENCH REVOLUTION: A HISTORY. In Two Volumes. 12s.
OLIVER CROMWELL'S LETTERS AND SPEECHES. With Elucidations and Connecting Narrative. In 3 Volumes. 18s.
LIFE OF JOHN STERLING. } One Volume. 6s.
LIFE OF SCHILLER.
CRITICAL AND MISCELLANEOUS ESSAYS. In 4 Volumes. 24s.
SARTOR RESARTUS. } One Volume. 6s.
HERO WORSHIP.
LATTER-DAY PAMPHLETS. One Volume. 6s.
CHARTISM. } One Volume. 6s.
PAST AND PRESENT.
TRANSLATIONS OF GERMAN ROMANCE. One Volume. 6s.
WILHELM MEISTER. By Goethe. A Translation. In 2 Volumes. 12s.

MR. ANTHONY TROLLOPE'S WORKS.

CAN YOU FORGIVE HER? A new Serial, with Illustrations, uniform with "Orley Farm." Publishing in Monthly Parts.
RACHEL RAY. Seventh Edition. 5s.
ORLEY FARM. With Forty Illustrations by J. E. MILLAIS. Handsomely bound in cloth. 2 vols. demy 8vo. £1 2s.
TALES OF ALL COUNTRIES. 1 vol. post 8vo. } New Edition. 5s.
—————— Second Series.
DR. THORNE. Eighth Edition. 5s.
THE BERTRAMS. Sixth Edition. 5s.
WEST INDIES AND THE SPANISH MAIN. Fifth Edition. 5s.
THE KELLYS AND THE O'KELLYS. Fifth Edition. 5s.
THE MACDERMOTS OF BALLYCLORAN. Third Edition. 5s.
CASTLE RICHMOND. Fourth Edition. 5s.
NORTH AMERICA. New Edition. 2 vols. post 8vo. 16s.

CHAPMAN AND HALL, 193, PICCADILLY.

LONDON LIBRARY, 12, ST. JAMES'S SQUARE, S.W.

A NEW EDITION OF THE CATALOGUE,

Comprising the Old Catalogue and Supplements incorporated into one Alphabetical List, with many additional Cross References, an Index to the Collection of Tracts, and a Classified Index of Subjects, in one volume of 1000 pages, royal 8vo. Price 10s. 6d. to members of the Library; 15s. to non-members. Terms of admission to the Library, £3 a-year; £2 a-year, with Entrance Fee of £6; or Life Subscription, £26. [*Early in May.*]

Immediately, in crown 8vo., cloth extra, 6s.,

CHARACTERS AND CRITICISMS.

By JAMES HANNAY,
Author of "Essays from the *Quarterly Review*," "Singleton Fontenoy," &c. &c.

EDINBURGH: WILLIAM P. NIMMO. LONDON: SIMPKIN, MARSHALL, & CO.

Just published, 7s. 6d., in crown 8vo., cloth extra,

PICTURES OF THE PERIODS:

A SKETCH-BOOK OF OLD ENGLISH LIFE.

By WILLIAM FRANCIS COLLIER, LL.D.,
Author of "History of English Literature," "History of England," &c. &c.

CONTENTS.

I. ICILIUS THE CENTURION: A Tale of the early Roman Period.
II. THE WERE-GILD OF EARL ALFGAR: A Tale of the Saxon Period.
III. How SIR EUSTACE CRISPIN LOST AND FOUND HIS HAWK: A Tale of the Norman Period.
IV. ALICE DALE'S LESSON: A Christmas Tale of the Tudor Period.
V. SATIN AND SAD-COLOUR: A Tale of the Stuart Period.
VI. SQUIRE HAZELRIG'S INVESTMENT IN SOUTH SEA STOCK: A Tale of the early Brunswick Period.

EDINBURGH: WILLIAM P. NIMMO. LONDON: SIMPKIN, MARSHALL & CO.

In the Press, and shortly will be published, 8vo. cloth, with numerous Illustrations from Original Sketches, drawn on Wood by R. P. Leitch, and engraved by J. D. Cooper and W. J. Linton, price 21s.,

THE NORTH-WEST PASSAGE BY LAND; being the

History of an Expedition from the Atlantic to the Pacific through British Territory, by one of the thern Passes in the Rocky Mountains.

By VISCOUNT MILTON, F.R.G.S., F.G.S., &c. &c., and W. B. CHEADLE, B.A., M.B. CANTAB., F.R.G.S.

CASSELL, PETTER, AND GALPIN, LONDON, E.C.

IMPORTANT  ANNOUNCEMENT.

JOSEPH GILLOTT,
METALLIC PEN MAKER TO THE QUEEN,

BEGS to inform the Commercial World, Scholastic Institutions, and the Public generally, that, by a novel application of his unrivalled Machinery for making Steel Pens, he has introduced a NEW SERIES of his useful productions, which, for EXCELLENCE of TEMPER, QUALITY of MATERIAL, and, above all, CHEAPNESS in PRICE, must ensure universal approbation, and defy competition.

Each Pen bears the impress of his name as a guarantee of quality. They are put up in boxes containing one gross each, with label outside, and the fac-simile of his signature.

At the request of numerous persons engaged in tuition, J. G. has introduced his WARRANTED SCHOOL and PUBLIC PENS, which are especially adapted to their use, being of different degrees of flexibility, and with fine, medium, and broad points, suitable for the various kinds of writing taught in Schools.

Sold retail by all Stationers and Booksellers. Merchants and Wholesale Dealers can be supplied at the Works, Graham Street, Birmingham; at 91, John Street, New York; and at 37, Gracechurch Street, London.

Now ready, MAY, No. IX. Price 4s. (Annually, post free, 13s. 4d.)

THE ANTHROPOLOGICAL REVIEW, and JOURNAL of the ANTHROPOLOGICAL SOCIETY of LONDON.

Contents.

1. ON the SCIENCE of RELIGION.
2. POUCHET on the PLURALITY of the HUMAN RACE.
3. ZIMMERMANN'S L'HOMME.
4. SOUTH AFRICAN and ESKIMO FABLES.
5. ON the THINKING SUBSTANCE in MAN. By T. Collyns Simon.
6. LACUSTRINE HABITATIONS and PRIMEVAL ANTIQUITIES.
7. PROCEEDINGS of the ANTHROPOLOGICAL SOCIETY of PARIS.
8. FAREWELL DINNER to CAPTAIN R. F. BURTON.
9. CORRESPONDENCE.
10. ANTHROPOLOGICAL NEWS.

THE JOURNAL of the ANTHROPOLOGICAL SOCIETY contains:—The Address of the President, Dr. James Hunt, on the History and Meaning of the Words Anthropology, Ethnography, and Ethnology—and Papers of Mr. E. Seldon, Mr. W. T. Pritchard, Dr. E. Lund, Dr. G. W. Gibb, Dr. T. B. Peacock, Mr. K. R. H. Mackenzie, Dr. J. Shortt, and M. Vámbéry.

London; TRÜBNER & Co., 60, Paternoster Row.

SHAKESPEARE, 1623.

The exact Reprint of this 'Famous Folio' Edition is now completed.
Price £1 11s. 6d. cloth bound.

LONDON: L. BOOTH, 307, REGENT STREET, W.

SHAKESPEARE, 1623, REPRINTED.

The COMEDIES . . . . Price 10s. 6d.
The HISTORIES . . . . Price 10s. 6d.
The TRAGEDIES . . . . Just out. Price 10s. 6d.

LONDON: L. BOOTH, 307, REGENT STREET, W.

Now ready, price 2s. 6d.

PERICLES, PRINCE OF TYRE.

Reprinted from the Third Folio, 1664, to range with the above.

LONDON: L. BOOTH, 307, REGENT STREET, W.

D. NUTT'S DEPOT FOR FOREIGN LITERATURE.

FOREIGN BOOKS IN EVERY DEPARTMENT OF LITERATURE.
WEEKLY AND SEMI-WEEKLY IMPORTATIONS FROM THE CONTINENT.
Orders for Books not in Stock executed as quickly as possible.
PERIODICALS AND NEWSPAPERS SUPPLIED BY POST.
CATALOGUES GRATIS.

LONDON: D. NUTT, 270, STRAND, W.C.

This day, in 1 vol., crown 8vo., beautifully printed on toned paper, cloth extra, price 6s.,

LIKE UNTO CHRIST: a New Translation of the "De Imitatione Christi," usually ascribed to Thomas à Kempis, with a Vignette from an Original Drawing by Sir Thomas Lawrence.
SAMPSON LOW, SON, and MARSTON, Milton House, Ludgate Hill.

This day, in 1 vol., fcap. 8vo., cloth, 3s. 6d., with numerous Maps and Illustrations,

MISSIONARY GEOGRAPHY: a Manual for all persons interested in Missions, and especially adapted for School Teachers and Missionary Teachers.
SAMPSON LOW, SON, and MARSTON, Milton House, Ludgate Hill.

This day, to be obtained at every Library,

A WINTER IN ALGERIA in 1863-4. By Mrs. GEORGE ALBERT ROGERS. With Illustrations, 8vo., cloth, 12s.
SAMPSON LOW, SON, and MARSTON, Milton House, Ludgate Hill.

This day, at all the Libraries,

HELEN FELTON'S QUESTION: a Problem in a Novel. By AGNES WYLDE. One Volume.

"I hold it truth, with him who sings,
To one clear harp in divers tones,
That men may rise on stepping stones
Of their dead selves to higher things."

SAMPSON LOW, SON, and MARSTON, Milton House, Ludgate Hill.

THE
FORTNIGHTLY REVIEW.

THE ENGLISH CONSTITUTION.

No. I. The Cabinet.

"On all great subjects," says Mr. Mill, "much remains to be said," and of none is this more true than of the English Constitution. The literature which has accumulated upon it is very considerable. The books are many, and the writers of those books very various; the aims of the treatises are as opposite as the tenets of their authors, or their natures. But a writer who looks close at the living reality will see there much that is different from any description which he can discover on paper. He will find in the life much that is not in the books; and he will hardly find in the rough practice many of the refinements that are treated as essential in the literary theory.

I wish, in the present series of papers, to look at the English Constitution *as it is;* and this narrowly restricts the entire novelty of what I have to say. Of course no free people is, or can be, unacquainted with the general working of its actual institutions. Politics teach politics, and teach much else by teaching them. A free people knows its political constitution vaguely and generally, as an active man knows his physical constitution vaguely and generally; but he does not know it precisely. The sensations are distinct, but their explanation is indistinct. The English nation has before it all manner of political facts and figures, but it has not *added them up.* It has all the items and particulars out of which a summary description could be made, but it has never made that description. Popular ideas remain always loose and disjointed, until some distinct composition defines their outline, and confirms their coherence. The odd book writing as to the British Constitution, derived from old times, augments the confusion. You may find a writer in one sentence speaking what is real, and derived from life; in the next what is unreal, and derived from tradition. Scarcely any one keeps clearly before him the simple facts which he knows when he is aroused to consider them. Extinct formulæ hang like an old cloak about the bare reality; and we must get rid of them, and cast them aside, before we can seize the simple fact.

It is very natural—indeed, by the constitution of human nature, inevitable—that such an undergrowth of irrelevant ideas should have gathered round the British Constitution. Language is the tradition of nations; each generation describes what it sees, but it describes in words inherited from the last. When a great entity like the British Constitution has continued in connected outward sameness, but hidden inner change, during many generations, every generation inherits a series of inapt words—of maxims once true, but of which the truth is ceasing or has ceased. As a man's family continue to repeat about his manhood traditional phrases derived from a just observation of his immature youth, so, in the full activity of an historical constitution, its subjects continue to repeat phrases true in the time of their fathers, inherited from those fathers, but now true no longer. Or, to speak perhaps better, an ancient and ever-altering constitution is like an old man who still wears with attached fondness clothes in the fashion of his youth: what you see of him is the same; what you do not see is wholly altered.

The theories about a constitution are not, indeed, so important as the working of that constitution, but they are very important. Every change is both encouraged and discouraged by reference to one theory or another. We are incited by doctrines, and we are retarded by doctrines; and we should carefully look to see which doctrine accords with visible reality, and which is a fancy of philosophers, or a legacy from a by-gone age. To many countries, too, the theory of the English Constitution is even more important than its practice. Constitution-making is the necessary misfortune of new nations—of nations whom an unsuitable set of inherited institutions compels to break with their past. And all nations who have to make a constitution look to England. The most successful specimen of a free government presents itself necessarily before their minds. They want to know about it, to consider it, to judge of it. They wish to see what parts are peculiar, insular, incapable of exportation,—the produce of exceptional circumstances, the result of a special and individual national character; and, on the other hand, which parts are communicable, applicable, part of the general stock of useful political instruments, the special addition of England to the common political capital of mankind. It will be easy to show that, in the imitation of English institutions, erroneous theories of their structure and nature have caused the gravest mistakes; that *Anglo-mania* has seldom been a wise taste; that it has often been a wild and ignorant dream; that even in nations speaking our own language, the misconception of our practical institutions has been fundamental; that if, as seems probable, the English colonies will, one after another, have to model for themselves a constitution, it is necessary they should know exactly what the constitution of their mother-country was—that they should be free from the grave errors which misled Washington and Hamilton—that they should escape the misconceptions which even now hamper the intelligence and impede the development of the great American people.

There are two descriptions of the English Constitution which have exercised a great and wide influence, but which are substantially erroneous. First, it is laid down as an essential principle of the English polity, and a main source of its good working, that in it the legislative, the executive, and the judicial powers, are entirely divided, —that each is entrusted to a separate person or set of persons—that neither of these can interfere with the work of the other, but that each is solely charged with, and is exclusively responsible for, its own functions. There has been much eloquence expended in explaining how the rough genius of the English people, even in the middle ages, when it was especially rude, carried into life and practice that elaborate division of functions which philosophers had suggested on paper, but which they had hardly hoped to see except on paper.

Secondly, it is said even more generally, and with even greater eloquence, that the peculiar excellence of the British Constitution depends on its being a balanced union of three powers. It is alleged that the monarchical element, the aristocratic element, and the democratic element, have each a representative part in the structure of the supreme sovereignty, and that the assent of each of these elements is necessary to the action of the ultimate authority. Kings, lords, and commons, by this theory, are alleged to be not only the outward form, but the inner moving essence, the vitality of the constitution. A great theory, called the theory of "Checks and Balances," pervades an immense part of political literature, and much of it is collected from or supported by English experience. Monarchy, it is said, has some faults, some bad tendencies, aristocracy others, democracy, again, others; but England has shown that a government can be constructed in which these evil tendencies exactly check, balance, and destroy one another—in which a good whole is constructed not simply in spite of, but by means of, the counteracting defects of the constituent parts. It is believed, first, that the structure of the English sovereign authority is, in truth, very complicated; and secondly, that its merit is a consequence of its complexity—that it is good because it is heterogeneous, and would certainly become bad if it were made more simple.

On this account it is very generally believed, that the principal characteristics of the English Constitution are inapplicable in countries where the materials for a monarchy or an aristocracy do not exist. That constitution is conceived as the best imaginable or possible use of the political elements which the great majority of states in modern Europe inherited from the mediæval period. It is believed that out of these materials nothing better can be made than the English Constitution. But it is also believed that the essential parts of the English Constitution cannot be made except from these materials. These materials are the accidents of a period and a place; they belong only to one or two centuries in human history, and to a few countries. The United States could not have become monarchical, even if the constituent convention had decreed it—even if the component states had ratified it. The mystic reverence, the religious allegiance, which are essential to a true monarchy, to a monarchy in which the characteristic part preserves inherent vigour, are imaginative sentiments that no legislature can manufacture in any people. These semi-filial feelings in government are inherited just as the true filial feelings in common life. You might as well adopt a father as make a monarchy; the special sentiment belonging to the one is as incapable of voluntary creation as the peculiar affection belonging to the other. It is, however, not difficult to prove, that the theory which limits the characteristic action which confines the imitability of the English Constitution to nations which have received a special *capital*, a singular accumulation of mediæval materials, is superficial and erroneous, and that the experience of England is far more generally applicable, and her real government far more widely attainable, than this theory would lead us to suppose.

No one can approach to an understanding of the English institutions, or, indeed, of any others which are the growth of many centuries, and which exercise a wide sway over mixed populations, unless he divide those institutions into two classes. In every such constitution there are always two parts, not necessarily separable with microscopic or precise accuracy; for the genius of great political structures, the nature of great affairs, abhors extreme nicety of division. All great things of human creation are very mixed in their nature, complex in their qualities, and various in the classifications which, for the changing purposes of human thought, they admit and need. Only a pedant hopes in any one division to make his separating lines too exact; divide his classes where he may, an objector will always be able to bring him a specimen just outside his definition which ought apparently to be within, so little does it differ from others which *are* within. Broad and rough classifications are all which the most important affairs of life admit of, if they are to be spoken of shortly and concisely. Popular literature—literature, we may say, as such—is only a first approximation to the truth. It would tire men to hear—they would not stop to read—the elaborate and painful disquisitions which alone would track out the minuter details of truth in all their little crevices. All political argument omits much because it needs be brief; and political distinctions and definitions therefore only need to be vague and general: for it would be idle to prepare a fine material of definition when its argumentative manufacture is to be so coarse, and its mental use so hasty. If, however, we bear in mind this fundamental and inseparable difficulty of political distinctions and definitions, if we do not expect to discern too clearly or distinguish too sharply, we shall find the English Constitution, and most old ones like it, to be divisible into two great parts: first, the parts which excite and preserve the reverence of the population,—the *dignified* parts, if I may so call them; and next, the *efficient* parts,—those parts by which it, in fact, works and rules. There are two great objects which every constitution must attain to be successful, which every old and celebrated constitution must have remarkably attained or it could not have survived, much less gained renown:—every constitution must first *gain* authority, and then *use* authority; it must first win the loyalty, obedience, and confidence of mankind, then employ that confidence, that trust, that homage, in the actual work of life and government.

There is a whole race of rude speculators, with practical aims and common sense, who strike out the dignified parts of government as useless. They say, we want only to attain certain results, to do certain business; a constitution is a collection of political means for political ends; and if you admit that any part of a constitution does no business, or that a simple machine would do equally well what business it does, you admit that this part of the constitution, however dignified it may be, however awful it may seem, is nevertheless in truth useless. Another class of reasoners, who feel that there is more in the complicated politics of life than finds a place in this bare utilitarian philosophy, have frequently propounded subtle arguments to prove that these dignified parts of old governments are cardinal components of the essential apparatus, great pivots of substantial utility; and they have, in so doing, put forth fallacies which the plainer and more practical school have been delighted to expose. But both schools are in error. The dignified parts of government are those which bring its force, which attract its motive power. The so-called useful parts only employ that power. The comely parts of a government *have* need, for they are those upon which its vital strength depends. They do not, indeed, do any definite work[1] that justifies their existence, that a simpler thing would not do better; but they

---

(1) It is to be observed that I here speak of the direct business of government, of the actual work of law-making and law-executing. The indirect and social effects of the dignified parts of government are, as I hope to show hereafter, very considerable.

are the preliminaries, the needful prerequisites of *all* work—they raise the army, though they do not win the battle.

Doubtless, if all subjects of the same government thought only of what was useful to them—if they all took the same view of what was useful to them, and if they were unanimous as to the most sure and speedy means of getting what was useful to them, the more efficient parts of a constitution would suffice, no dignified parts would be required. But the world in which we live is organised far otherwise.

The most strange fact, though the most certain in nature, is the unequal development of the human race. If we look back to the early ages of mankind, such as we seem in the faint distance to see them—if we call up the image of that obscure past in lake villages, or wretched beaches,—scarcely equal to the most common material needs and employments, cutting down trees slowly and painfully with stone tools, scarcely resisting the attacks of huge, fierce animals,—without culture, without leisure, without poetry, almost without thought,—destitute of morality, with only a sort of magic for religion,—if we try to think what the life of early Europe was at the first period, we begin to see it vague and with the mind's eye; and if we compare that imagined life with the actual life of Europe now, we are struck, overwhelmed, surprised at the huge transition—we can scarcely conceive ourselves as of the same race as those we seem in the far distance to perceive. They began and we end; but it is difficult to believe that the chain is consecutive, that the progress has been gradual, so long is the interposed interval, so contrasted are the two sides. But when we look deeper and more thoroughly, we shall find that the immensity of the transition is scarcely so wonderful as the *inequality* of the transition. Looking at the vast transitions of history, remembering the possible contrasts of mankind, we can dismiss the lurking tradition that human nature being always the same, its varieties are casual, momentary, transient. There used to be a notion—not so much widely asserted as deeply implanted, rather pervadingly latent than commonly apparent in political philosophy—that in a little while, ten years, more or less, all human beings might without inaccessible or extraordinary appliances be brought to the same level. But when we now see by the painful history of mankind at what point we began, by what slow toil, what favourable circumstances, what accumulated achievements, civilised man has become at all worthy in any degree so to call himself—when we realise the tedium of history and the painfulness of results, our perceptions are sharpened as to the relative steps of our long and gradual progress. If it has taken so many ages to make some men civilised, may it not need as many ages wholly to civilise those now half civilised? We have in a great community like England crowds of people scarcely more civilised than those of two thousand years ago and longer; we have others even more numerous—such the best people were a thousand years ago. The lower orders, the middle orders, almost every one, are still, when tried by what is the standard of the educated "ten thousand," narrow-minded, unintelligent, ignorant, incurious. It is useless to pile up abstract words. Those who doubt should go out into their kitchens: let an accomplished man try what seems to him most obvious, most certain, most palpable in intellectual matters, upon the housemaid and the footman, and he will find that what he says seems unintelligible, confused, and erroneous —that his audience think him mad and wild when he is speaking what is in his own sphere of thought the dullest platitude of cautious soberness. Great communities are like great mountains—they have in them the primary, secondary, and tertiary strata of human progress; the characteristics of the lower regions resemble the life of old times rather than the present life of the higher regions. And a philosophy which does not ceaselessly remember, which does not continually obtrude the palpable differences of the various parts, will be a theory radically false, because it has omitted a capital reality—will be a theory essentially misleading, because it will lead men to expect what does not exist, and not to anticipate that which they will find.

Every one knows these plain facts, but by no means every one has traced their political importance. When a state is thus constituted,— when it is composed of several sections of population, in several distinct stages of intellectual development,—it by no means follows that the less instructed will at all perceive the utility of much which the more instructed know to be useful; or even when all are agreed on ends, that the less instructed will appreciate the refined means which the more instructed perceive to be the very best means of attaining the admitted object. It is not even true that the lower classes will be absorbed in anything so homely as the useful; they do not like to hear of anything so poor. Even using the word as we here use it as denoting the attainable good, not of the particular nation only, but of mankind at large, it is not certain, or even likely, that the lowest classes will think much of it. They are still mostly in the imaginative state of development. No orator ever made an impression by appealing to men as to their plainest physical wants, except when he could allege or prove that those wants were caused by the tyranny of some other class. But thousands have made the greatest impression by appealing to some vague dream of glory, or empire, or nationality. The ruder sort of men—that is, men at *one* stage of rudeness—will sacrifice all they hope for, all they have, *themselves*, for what is called an idea,—for some attraction which seems to transcend reality, which aspires to elevate men by an interest higher, deeper, wider than that of ordinary life. But this order of men care nothing for the common, plain, palpable ends of government; they do not much think of them; they do not in the least comprehend how they should be attained. It is very natural, therefore, that the most useful parts of the structure of government should by no means be those which excite the most reverence. The elements which excite the most easy reverence will be the *theatrical* elements; those which appeal to the senses, which claim to be embodiments of the greatest human ideas—which boast in some cases of far more than human origin. That which is mystic in its claims; that which is occult in mode of action; that which is brilliant to the eye; that which is seen vividly for a moment, and then is seen no more; that which is hidden and unhidden; that which is specious, and yet interesting—palpable in its seeming, and yet professing to be more than palpable in its results; that which is half of glaring "this world," and half of what is more than this world;—this, howsoever its form may change, or however we may define it or describe it, is the sort of thing—the only sort which yet comes home to the mass of men. So far from the dignified parts of a constitution being necessarily the most useful, they are likely, according to *primâ facie* and outside presumption, to be the least useful—that is, they are likely to be suitable for, and adjusted to, the lowest orders—the orders of most showy and theatrical taste; those likely to care the least and judge the worst about what *is* useful.

There is another reason which, in an old constitution like that of England, is hardly less important. The most intellectual of men are moved quite as much by what they are used to as by what they think best. The active voluntary part of man is very small, and if it were not economised by a sleepy kind of habit, its results would be null. We could not do every day out of our own heads all we have to do. We should accomplish nothing; for all our energies would be frittered away in minor attempts at petty improvement. One man, too, would go off from the known track in one direction, and one in another; so that when a crisis requiring massed combination should arise, no two men would be found near enough to act together. It is the dull traditional habit of mankind that guides most men's actions—which is the steady frame in which the higher artist may set the new picture that he paints—which is the material in which such as would improve others must work. And all this traditional part of human nature is, *ex vi termini*, most easily impressed and acted on by that which is handed down—by that which *was*, as well as *is*—by what is customary. Other things being equal, yesterday's institutions are by far the best for to-day; they are the most ready, the most influential, the most easy to get obeyed, the most likely to retain the reverence which they alone inherit, and which all other institutions have to win. The most imposing institutions of mankind are the oldest; and yet so changing is the world,—so fluctuating are its needs,—so apt to lose inward force, though retaining outward strength, are its best instruments, that we must not expect the oldest institutions to be now the most efficient. We must expect what is venerable to acquire influence because of its inherent dignity; but we must not expect it to use that influence so well as new creations more apt for the modern world, more instinct with its spirit, more closely fitting to its life.

The brief description of the characteristic merit of the English Constitution is, that its dignified parts are very complicated and somewhat imposing, very old and rather venerable; while its efficient part, at least when in great and critical action, is decidedly simple and rather modern. We have contrived to make, or, rather, we have stumbled on, a constitution which, though certainly subject to all manner of objections of detail—though full of every species of incidental defect—though of the worst *workmanship* in all out-of-the-way matters of any constitution in the world, yet has two capital merits:—yet contains a simple efficient part which, on occasion, and when wanted, *can* work more simply, and easily, and better than any instrument of government that has yet been tried; and it contains likewise historical, complex, august, theatrical parts, which it has inherited from a long past,—which *take* the multitude,—which guide by an insensible but omnipotent influence the associations of its subjects. Its essence is strong with the strength of modern simplicity; its exterior is august with the Gothic grandeur of a more imposing age. Its simple essence may, *mutatis mutandis*, be transplanted to many very various countries, but its august outside—what most men think it is—is narrowly confined to nations with an analagous history and similar political relics.

The efficient secret of the English Constitution may be described as the close union, the nearly complete fusion, of the executive and legislative powers. So far from its being true, according to the traditional theory formerly stated, that the goodness of our constitution consists in the entire separation of the legislative and executive authorities, its real merit consists in their singular approximation. The connecting link is *the cabinet*. By that comparatively new word we mean a certain committee of the legislative body selected to be the executive body. The legislature has many committees, but this is its greatest committee. It chooses for this, its greatest committee, the set of men in whom it has most confidence. It does not, it is true, choose them directly; but it is nearly omnipotent in choosing them indirectly. A century ago the crown had a real choice of ministers, though it had no longer a choice in policy. During the long reign of Sir R. Walpole he was obliged not only to manage parliament but to manage the palace. He was obliged to take care that some court intrigue did not expel him from his place. The nation then selected the English policy, but the crown chose the English ministers. They were not only in name, as now, but in fact, the Queen's servants. Remnants, important remnants of this great prerogative still remain. The discriminating favour of William IV. made Lord Melbourne head of the Whig party, when he was only one of several rivals, when he had no conclusive title to ascendency. At the death of Lord Palmerston it is very likely that the Queen may have the opportunity of freely choosing between two, if not three statesmen. But, as a rule, the nominal prime minister is chosen by the legislature—and the real prime minister for most purposes—the leader of the House of Commons almost without exception is so. There is nearly always some one man plainly selected by the voice of the predominant party in the predominant house of the legislature, to head that party, and consequently to rule the nation. We have in England an elective first magistrate as truly as the Americans have an elective first magistrate. The Queen is only at the head of the dignified part of the constitution. The prime minister is at the head of the efficient part. The Crown is, according to the saying, the "fountain of honour;" but the treasury is the spring of business. But our first magistrate differs from the American. He is not elected directly by the people; he is elected by the representatives of the people. He is an example of "double election." The legislature chosen, nominally at least, to make laws, in fact finds its principal business—its main function—to be to make an executive, and to keep an executive.

The leading minister so selected has to choose his associates, but he only chooses among a charmed circle. The position of most men in parliament forbids their being invited to the cabinet; the position of a few men ensures their being invited. Between the compulsory list whom he must take, and the impossible list whom he cannot take, a prime minister's independent choice in the formation of a cabinet is not very large; it extends rather to the division of the cabinet offices than to the choice of cabinet ministers. Parliament and the nation have pretty well settled who shall have the first places; but they have not discriminated with the same accuracy which man shall have which place. The highest patronage of a prime minister is, of course, a considerable power, though it is exercised under close and imperative restrictions; though it is far less than it seems to be when stated in theory, or regarded from a distance.

The cabinet, in a word, is a board of control chosen by the legislature out of persons whom it trusts and knows to rule the nation. The particular mode in which the English ministers are selected; the fiction that they are, in any political sense, the Queen's servants; the rule which limits the choice of the cabinet to the members of the legislature,—are accidents unessential to its definition—historical incidents separable from its nature. Its characteristic is that it should be chosen by the legislature out of persons agreeable to and trusted by the legislature. Naturally these are principally its own members—but they need not be exclusively so. A cabinet which included persons not members of the legislative assembly might still perform all useful duties. Indeed the peers, who constitute a large element in modern cabinets, are members, now-a-days, only of a subordinate assembly. The House of Lords still exercises several useful functions; but the ruling influence—the deciding faculty—has passed to what, using the language of old times, we still call the lower house—to an assembly which, though inferior as a dignified institution, is superior as an efficient institution. A principal advantage of the House of Lords during the present age consists in its acting as a *reservoir* of cabinet ministers. Unless the composition of the House of Commons were improved, or unless the rules requiring cabinet ministers to be members of the legislature were relaxed, or both, it would undoubtedly be difficult to find, within these narrow boundaries, a sufficient supply of chief ministers. But the detail of the composition of a cabinet, and the precise method of its choice, are not much to the purpose now. The first and cardinal consideration is the definition of a cabinet. We must not bewilder ourselves with the separable accidents until we know the necessary essence. A cabinet is a combining committee,—a *hyphen* which joins, a *buckle* which fastens, the legislative part of the state to the executive part of the state. In its origin it belongs to the one, in its functions it belongs to the other.

The most curious point about the cabinet is that so very little is known about it. The meetings are not only secret in theory, but secret in reality. No official minute is ever kept of them. Even a private note is discouraged and disliked. The House of Commons, even in its most inquisitive and turbulent moments, would not permit a note of a cabinet meeting to be read. No minister who respected the fundamental usages of political practice would attempt to read such a note. The committee which unites the law-making power to the law-executing power—which, by virtue of that combination, is, while it lasts and holds together, the most powerful body in the state —is a committee wholly secret. No description of it, at once graphic and authentic, has ever been given. It is said to be sometimes like a rather disorderly board of directors, where many speak and few listen—but no one knows.[1]

But a cabinet, though it is a committee of the legislative assembly,

(1) It is *said*, at the end of the cabinet which agreed to propose a fixed duty on corn, Lord Melbourne put his back to the door and said, "Now is it to lower the price of corn or isn't it? It is not much matter which we say, but mind, we must all say *the same*." This is the most graphic story of a cabinet I ever heard, but I cannot vouch for its truth. Lord Melbourne's is a character about which men make stories.

is a committee with a power which no assembly would—unless for singular historical accidents, and till by experience its advantages had been discovered—have been persuaded to entrust to any committee. It is a committee which can dissolve the assembly which appointed it; it is a committee with a suspensive veto—a committee with a power of appeal. Though appointed by one parliament, it can appeal if it chooses to the next parliament. Theoretically, indeed, the power to dissolve parliament is entrusted to the sovereign only; and there remain some vestiges of doubt whether in *all* cases a sovereign is bound to dissolve parliament if his existing cabinet wish him to do so. But these possible cases are very rare, and perhaps it would be a more perfect constitutional usage if there were no such doubts and no such cases. But leaving apart these small and dubious exceptions, and speaking roughly and generally, we may say that the cabinet which was chosen by one House of Commons has an appeal to the next House of Commons. The chief committee of the legislature has the power of dissolving the predominant part of that legislature,—we might say, on critical occasions, the legislature itself. The English system, therefore, is not an absorption of the executive power by the legislative power; it is a fusion of the two. The cabinet can act and it can legislate; if it cannot, it can dissolve, and some one who can act, who can legislate, is put into its place. It is a creature, but it has the power of destroying its creators. It is an executive which can annihilate the legislature, as well as an executive which is the nominee of the legislature. It *was* made, but it *can* unmake; it was dependent in its origin, but it is independent in its action.

This fusion of the legislative and executive functions may, to those who have not much considered it, seem but a dry and small matter to be the latent essence and effectual secret of the English Constitution; but we can only judge of its real importance by looking at a few of its principal effects, and contrasting it very shortly with its great competitor, which seems likely, unless care be taken and the real nature of the two understood, to outstrip and supersede it in the progress of the world. That competitor is the Presidential system: the characteristic of it is that the President—the executive—is elected by the people by one process, and that the House of Representatives is elected by a different process. The independence of the two powers is the specific quality of Presidential Government, just as their fusion and combination is the precise principle of Cabinet Government.

First, compare the two in quiet times. The essence of a civilised age is that administration requires the continued aid of legislation. One principal kind of legislation, and a necessary kind, is financial legislation, is *taxation*. The expense of civilised government is continually varying. It must vary if the government does its duty.

The miscellaneous estimates of the English Government contain an inevitable medley of changing items. Education, prison discipline, art, science, civil contingencies of a hundred kinds, require more money one year and more another. The expense of defence—the naval and military estimates—vary still more as the danger of attack seems more or less imminent, as the means of retarding such danger become more or less costly. If the persons who have to do the work are not the same as those who have to give the authority, to make the laws, and grant the money, there is sure to be a controversy between two sets of persons. The law-makers and tax-imposers are sure to quarrel with the tax-requirers. The executive is crippled by not getting the laws it needs, and the legislature is spoiled by having to act without responsibility, by having to refuse money which some one else will have to do without, but which that some one else says is essential; the executive becomes unfit for its name since it cannot execute what it decides on: the legislature is demoralised by liberty, by taking decisions of which others, but not itself, will suffer the effects.

So much has this difficulty been felt in America—where, as every one knows, the legislative and executive bodies are rigidly divided—that a sort of semi-connection unknown to the law has grown up between them. When the Secretary of the Treasury of the Federal Government wants a tax he consults upon it with the Chairman of the Financial Committee of Congress. He cannot go down to Congress himself and propose what he wants; he can only write a letter and send it. But he tries to get a chairman of the finance committee who likes his tax, and through that chairman he hopes to persuade the committee to recommend such tax; by that committee he hopes to induce the house to adopt that tax. But this chain of communications is liable to continual interruption; it may do for a single tax on a fortunate occasion, but will scarcely suffice for a complicated budget—we do not say in cases of war or rebellion —we are now comparing the cabinet system and the presidential system in quiet times—but in cases of financial difficulty. Two clever men never exactly agreed about a budget. We have had lately an Indian Chancellor of the Exchequer talking English finance at Calcutta, and an English one talking Indian finance in England. But the figures are never the same, and the views of policy are rarely the same. One most angry controversy has amused the world, and probably others scarcely less interesting are hidden in the copious stores of our Anglo-Indian correspondence.

But something like these are sure to be the relations of the head of a finance committee in the legislature, and a finance minister in the executive.[1] They are sure to quarrel, and the result is sure to be a

---

(1) It is worth observing that even during the short existence of the Confederate

compromise. And when the taxes do not yield as they were expected to yield, who is responsible? Very likely the secretary of the treasury could not persuade the chairman—very likely the chairman could not persuade his committee—very likely the committee could not persuade the assembly. Whom, then, can you punish—whom can you turn out, when your taxes run short? You have nobody to punish but the legislature, a vast miscellaneous body difficult to punish, and the very persons to inflict the punishment.

Nor is financial administration the sole part of administration which requires in a civilised age the constant support and accompaniment of facilitating legislation. How can a Home Secretary be really responsible for the prison discipline of the country if some one else makes the laws by which that discipline is regulated? In England, on all vital occasions, the cabinet can compel legislation by the threat of resignation, by the threat of dissolution; but neither of these can be used under the presidential system of government— under the system where the executive is one thing, and the legislature another thing. In such a government the legislature cannot be dissolved by the executive government; it does not care for the resignation of the executive government, for it will not have to find a successor. Accordingly, when a difference of opinion arises, the legislature is forced to fight the executive, and the executive is forced to fight the legislature; and so very likely they contend to the conclusion of their respective terms. There is, indeed, one condition of things in which this description, though still approximately true, is, nevertheless, not exactly true; and that is, when there is nothing to fight about. Before the rebellion in America, owing to the vast distance of other states, and the favourable economical condition of the country, there were very few considerable subjects of contention; but if that government had been tried by the English legislation of the last thirty years, or by any consecutive series of important and exciting acts,—such as an old country needs, and a complicated, unequal, existing law demands—the inherent vices of the system, the discordant action of the two powers whose constant accordant action is essential to the best government, would have shown itself much more distinctly.

Nor is this the worst. Cabinet governments educate the nation; the presidential does not educate it, and may corrupt it. It has been said that England invented the phrase, "Her Majesty's Opposition;" that it was the first government which made a criticism of administration as much a part of the polity as administration itself. This critical opposition is the consequence of cabinet government. The great scene of debate, the great engine of popular instruction and

government these evils distinctly showed themselves. Almost the last incident at the Richmond Congress was an angry financial correspondence with Jefferson Davis.

political controversy, is the legislative assembly. A speech there by an eminent statesman, a party movement by a great political combination, are the best means yet known for arousing, awakening, *teaching* a people. The cabinet system ensures that there shall be such debates, for it makes them the means by which statesmen advertise themselves for future government, and confirm themselves in popular estimation as fit members of existing governments. It brings forward men eager to speak, and gives them occasion to speak—occasions when every one is ready to hear. The deciding catastrophes of cabinet governments are critical divisions preceded by fine discussions. Everything which is worth saying, everything which can be said, everything which ought to be said, most certainly *will* be said. Conscientious men think they ought to persuade others; selfish men think they would like to obtrude themselves. The nation is forced to hear two sides—all the sides, perhaps, of that which most concerns it. And it likes to hear—it is eager to know. Human nature cares little for long arguments which come to nothing, —heavy speeches which precede no motion—abstract disquisitions which leave visible things as it found them. But all men care for great results, and a change of government is a great result. It has a hundred ramifications; it runs through society; it gives hope to many, and it takes away hope from many. It is one of those marked events which, by its suddenness, its greatness, its *theatricalness*, impresses man more even than it should. And debates, which have this catastrophe at the end of them—which may so have it—which may be the small beginning to a great series of which it is the end, are sure to be regarded, sure to be listened to, sure to sink deep into the national mind.

Travellers in presidential countries,—even in the Northern States of America, which is the greatest and best of them,—have noticed that they were a nation " not specially addicted to politics;" a nation which has not a public opinion finished and chastened as that of the English has been finished and chastened. A great many hasty writers have charged this defect on the " Yankee race," on the Anglo-American character: but English people, if they had no motive to attend to politics, certainly would not attend to politics. At present there is *business* in their attention. They assist at the determining crisis; they retard or help it; whether the government will go out or remain is determined by the debate, and by the division in parliament, and the opinion out of doors. The secret pervading decision of society has a great influence on that division. The nation feels that its opinion is important, and it strives to form one. It succeeds in forming one because the debates and the discussions give it the facts and the arguments. But under a presidential government a nation has, except at the stated period of presidential election, no motive to attend to political matters, for it has no influence; it has not the ballot-box before it; its virtue is gone out of it, and it must wait till its passing moment of despotism returns again. It is not incited or urged to form an opinion like a nation under a cabinet government; nor is it instructed like such a nation. There are doubtless debates in the legislature, but they are prologues without a play. There is nothing of a catastrophe about them; you cannot turn out the government: the prize of power is not in the gift of the legislature, and no one cares for the legislature. The executive, the great centre of power and place, sticks irremovable; you cannot turn it out, say what you will. The teaching apparatus which has educated our public mind, which prepares our resolutions, which shapes our opinions, does not exist in any presidential country. No such country needs to form careful, daily, delicate opinions, or is helped in forming them.

It might be thought beforehand that the discussions in the press would supply the deficiencies of the constitution; that by a reading people especially the conduct of their government would be as carefully watched, that their opinions about it would be as consistent, as accurate, as well considered, under a presidential as under a cabinet polity. But the same difficulty oppresses the press which oppresses the legislature. It can *do nothing*. It cannot turn out the government; the government was elected for such and such years, and for such and such years it must stay. People wonder that so literary a people as the Americans—a people who read more than any people who ever lived—who read so many newspapers—should have such bad newspapers. The papers are not as good as the English papers, because they have not the same motive to be good as the English papers. At a political "crisis," as we say—that is, when the fate of an administration is unfixed, when it depends on a few votes, yet unsettled, upon a wavering and veering opinion—effective articles in newspapers become of essential moment. The *Times* has made many governments. When, as of late, there has been a long continuance of divided parliaments, of governments which were without "brute voting power," which were only half supported by an almost imperceptible majority, which depended on intellectual strength, the support of the most influential organ of English opinion has been of critical moment to Lord Palmerston. If a Washington newspaper could have turned out Mr. Lincoln, there would have been good writing and fine argument in the Washington newspapers. But the Washington newspapers can no more remove a president during his term of place than the *Times* can remove a lord mayor during his year of office. Nobody cares for a debate in Congress which "comes to nothing;" no one reads long articles which have no influence on events. The Americans glance at the heads of news, and through the paper. They do not enter upon a discussion. They do not *think* of entering on a discussion which would be useless.

After saying that the division of the legislative and executive characteristic of presidential governments weakens the legislative power, it may seem a contradiction to say that it also weakens the executive power. But it is not a contradiction. The division weakens the whole aggregate force of government—the entire imperial power; and therefore it weakens both its halves. The executive is weakened in a very plain way. A strong cabinet can obtain the concurrence of the legislature in all acts which facilitate its administration; it is itself, so to say, the legislature. But a president may be hampered by the parliament, and is likely to be hampered. The natural tendency of the members of every legislature is to make themselves conspicuous. They wish to gratify an ambition laudable or blameable; they wish to promote the measures they think best for the public welfare; they wish to make their *will* felt in great affairs. All these mixed motives urge them to oppose the executive. They are embodying the purposes of others if they aid; they are advancing their own opinions if they defeat: they are first if they vanquish; they are auxiliaries if they support. The weakness of the American executive used to be the great theme of all critics before the Confederate rebellion. Congress and committees of Congress of course interfered and impeded when there was no absorbing public sentiment, no coercive public opinion, to check and rule them.

But the presidential system not only gives the executive power an antagonist in the legislative power, and so makes it weaker; it not only absorbs its strength by providing a competitor; but it likewise enfeebles it by impairing its quality, by making it worse. A cabinet is elected by a legislature; and when that legislature is composed of persons fit for political life, and competent to the work of legislation, this mode of electing the executive is the best mode. It is an instance of secondary election, under the only condition in which secondary election is preferable to primary election. Generally speaking, in an electioneering country (I mean in a country full of political life, and used to the manipulation of popular institutions), the election of certain men to elect certain other men is a farce. The Electoral College of America is so. It was intended that the deputies when assembled should exercise a real discretion—should make a substantial choice—should select the president. But the primary electors take too much interest in the matter for that. They only elect a deputy to vote for Mr. Lincoln or Mr. Breckenridge, and the deputy, when he meets his fellow deputies, only deposits his ticket in a box. He is but a messenger—a transmitter: the real decision is in those who chose him; who chose him because they knew what he would do.

It is undeniably true that the British House of Commons is in some degree subject to the same influences. Members are mostly, perhaps, elected because they will vote for a particular ministry, because they will select a specified executive, rather than for purely legislative reasons, because they will promote this or that act of parliament. But—and here is the capital distinction—the functions of the House of Commons are important and *continuous*. It does not, like the electoral college in the United States, separate when it has elected its ruler; it sits, legislates, watches ministers, tries to unseat, and perhaps unseats ministries, from day to day. Accordingly it is a *real* electoral body. The parliament of 1857, which, more than any other parliament of late years, was a parliament elected to support a particular premier—which was chosen, as Americans might say, upon the "Palmerston ticket"—before it had been in existence two years dethroned Lord Palmerston. Though selected as much as perhaps is possible in the interest of a particular ministry, it, in fact, after a brief interval, destroyed that ministry.

A *good* parliament is a capital choosing body. If it is fit to make laws for a country, its majority ought to represent the general average intelligence of that country; its various members ought to represent the various special interests, special opinions, special prejudices, to be found in that community. There ought to be an advocate for every particular sect, and a vast neutral body of no sect —homogeneous and judicial like the nation itself. Such a body, when it can be found, in a country which can elect it, is the best selecting body for an executive that can be imagined. It is full of political activity; it is close to political life; it feels the responsibility of affairs which are brought as it were to its threshold; it has as much intelligence as the society in question chances to contain. It is, what Washington and Hamilton strove to create, an electoral college of the picked men of the nation.

The best mode of appreciating its advantages is to look at the alternative. The competing constituency is the nation itself, and this is, according to theory and experience, in all but the rarest cases, a bad constituency. Mr. Lincoln, at his second election, being elected when all the Federal states had set their united hearts on one single object, was re-elected by the nation, really represented the nation. He embodied the object in which every one was absorbed. But this is almost the only presidential election of which so much can be said. In almost all cases the President is chosen by a machinery of caucuses and combinations too complicated to be perfectly known, and too familiar to require description. He is not the choice of the nation, he is the choice of the wire-pullers. A very large constituency in quiet times is the necessary, almost the legitimate, subject of electioneering management: a man cannot know that he does not throw his vote away except he votes as part of some great organisation; and if he votes as a part, he abdicates his electoral function in favour of the managers of that association. The nation, even if it chose for itself, would, in some degree, be an unskilled body; but when it does not choose for itself, but only as latent agitators wish, it is like a large, lazy man, with a small, vicious mind,—it moves slowly and heavily, but it moves at the bidding of a bad intention; it "means *little*, but it means that little *ill*."

And, as the nation is less able to choose than a parliament, so it has worse people to choose out of. The American legislature of the last century have been much blamed for not permitting the ministers of the President to be members of the assembly. But, with reference to the specific end which they had in view, they judged wisely, they saw clearly. They wished to keep "the legislative branch absolutely distinct from the executive branch;" they believed that such a separation was essential to a good constitution; they believed that such a separation, in fact, existed in the English, which the wisest of them, though imperfectly understanding it, believed the best constitution which had as yet existed. And, to the effectual maintenance of such a separation, the exclusion of the President's ministers from the legislature is essential. If they are not excluded they become the executive, they eclipse the President himself. A great legislative body is, as has been said before, as must never be forgotten, a perpetual absorbent: it takes all it can; it gives up nothing it can help. The passions of its members are its rulers; the law-making faculty, the most comprehensive of the imperial faculties, is its instrument; it will *take* the administration if it can take it. Estimated by their own criterion, judged by their own objects, the founders of the American Republic were wise in excluding the ministers from Congress.

But though this exclusion is essential to the presidential system of government, it is not for that reason an inconsiderable evil. It causes the degradation of public life. Unless a member of the legislature be sure of something more than speech, unless he is incited by the hope of action, and chastened by the chance of responsibility, a first-rate man will not care to take the place, and will not do much if he does take it. To belong to a debating society adhering to an executive (and this is no inapt description of a congress under a presidential constitution), is not an object to stir a noble ambition, and is a position to encourage idleness. The members of a parliament excluded from office can never be comparable, much less equal, to those of a parliament excluded from office. The presidential government, by its nature, divides political life into two halves, an executive half and a legislative half; and, by so dividing it, makes neither half worth a man having—worth his making it a continuous career—worthy to absorb, as cabinet government absorbs, his whole soul. The statesmen from whom a nation chooses under a presidential system, are much inferior to those from whom it chooses under a cabinet system, while the selecting apparatus is also far less discerning.

All these advantages are more important at critical periods, because government itself is more important. A formed public opinion, a respected, able, and disciplined legislature, a well-chosen executive, a parliament and an administration not thwarting each other, but co-operating with each other, are of greater consequence when great affairs are in progress than when small affairs are in progress—when there is much to do than when there is little to do. But in addition to this, a parliamentary or cabinet constitution possesses an additional or special advantage in very dangerous times. It has what we may call a reserve of power fit for and needed by extreme exigencies.

The principle of popular government is that the supreme power, the determining efficacy in matters political, resides in the people—not necessarily or commonly in the whole people, in the numerical majority, but in a *chosen* people, a picked and selected people. It is so in England; it is so in all free countries. Under a cabinet constitution at a sudden emergency this people can choose a ruler for the occasion. It is quite possible and even likely that he would not be ruler *before* the occasion. The great qualities, the imperious will, the rapid energy, the eager nature fit for a great crisis are not required—are impediments—in common times. A Lord Liverpool is better in every-day politics than a Chatham—a Louis Philippe far better than a Napoleon. By the structure of the world we often want at the sudden occurrence of a grave tempest to change the helmsman—the pilot of the calm is not the helmsman of the storm. In England we have had so few severe storms since our constitution attained maturity that we hardly appreciate this latent excellence which it keeps in reserve. We do not know what it is to have a Cavour to rule our revolution—a representative man above all men fit for a great occasion, and by a legal, natural, obvious use of a free constitution brought in to rule that occasion. But even in England, at what was the nearest to a great sudden crisis which we have had of late years—at the Crimean difficulty, which was in truth a sudden crisis, though a small one, we used this inherent latent constitutional power. We abolished the Aberdeen cabinet, the ablest we have had, perhaps, since the Reform Act—a cabinet not only adapted, but eminently adapted for every sort of difficulty save the particular difficulty which it had to meet—which abounded in pacific discretion, which was wanting in but one element, yet that one in warlike times the most necessary, the "dæmonic element:" we chose a statesman who had the sort of merit then wanted, when he feels the power of England behind him, when he is conscious of the steady support of a consistent opinion, will advance without reluctance, and will strike without restraint. As was said at the time, "we turned out the Quaker, and put in the pugilist."

But under a presidential government you can do nothing of the kind. The American government calls itself a government of the supreme people. But at a quick crisis, the time when a sovereign power is most needed, you cannot *find* the supreme people. You have got a Congress elected for one fixed period, going out by fixed instalments, which cannot be accelerated or retarded—you have a President chosen for a fixed period, and immovable during that period: all the arrangements are for *stated* times. There is no *elastic* element, everything is rigid, specified, dated. Come what may, you can quicken nothing and can retard nothing. You have bespoken your government in advance, and whether it suits you or not, whether it works well or works ill, whether it is what you want or not, by law you must keep it. In a country of complex foreign relations it would be the ordinary law, the common rule, that the first and most critical year of every war would be managed by a peace premier, and the first and most critical years of peace by a war premier. ' In each case the period of transition would be irrevocably governed by a man selected not for the things he was to introduce, but for the things he was to change—for the policy he was to abandon, not for the policy he was to administer.

The whole history of the American civil war—a history which has thrown an intense light on the working of a presidential government at the time when government is most important—is but a vast continuous commentary on these reflections. It would, indeed, be absurd to press against presidential government *as such* the singular defect by which Vice-president Johnson has become President—by which a man elected to a sinecure is fixed in what is for the moment the most important administrative part in the political world. This defect, though most characteristic of the expectations[1] of the framers of the constitution and of its working, is but an accident of this particular case of presidential government, and no necessary ingredient in that government itself. But the first election of Mr. Lincoln is liable to no such objection. It was a characteristic instance of the natural working of such a government upon a great occasion. And what was that working for it may be summed up in a word, and it is easy to say it was government by an unknown quantity. No one in Europe, hardly any one in America, had any living idea what Mr. Lincoln was like, any definite notion what sort of thing he would do. The leading statesmen under the system of cabinet government are

---

(1) The framers of the constitution expected that the *vice*-president would be elected by the electoral college as the *second* wisest man in the country. The vice-presidentship being a sinecure a second-rate man agreeable to the wire-pullers is always smuggled in. The chance of succession to the presidentship is too distant to be thought of.

not only household words, but household *ideas*. An idea not, perhaps, in all respects a true idea, but a most vivid idea—what Mr. Gladstone is like, or what Lord Palmerston is like, runs through society. We have simply no notion what it would be to be left with the visible sovereignty in the hands of an unknown man. The notion of employing a man of unknown smallness at a crisis of unknown greatness is to our minds simply ludicrous. Mr. Lincoln, it is true, happened to be a man, if not of eminent ability, yet of eminent justness. There was an inner heart of Puritan nature which came out under suffering, and was very attractive. But success in a lottery is no argument for lotteries. What were the chances against a person of Lincoln's antecedents, elected as he was, proving to be what he was?

Such an incident is, however, natural to a presidential government. The President is elected by processes which forbid the election of known men, except at peculiar conjunctures, and in moments when public opinion is excited, overruling, and compulsory; and consequently, if a crisis comes upon us soon after he is elected, inevitably we have government by an unknown quantity—the superintendence of that crisis by what our great satirist would have called "Statesman X." Even in quiet times, government by a president is, for the several various reasons which have been stated, inferior to government by a cabinet; but the difficulty of quiet times is nothing as compared with the difficulty of unquiet times. The comparative deficiencies of the regular, common operation of a presidential government, are far less than the comparative deficiencies in time of sudden trouble— the want of elasticity, the impossibility of a dictatorship, the total absence of a *revolutionary reserve*.

But if presidential governments have all these disadvantages, why do nations *make* presidential governments? They certainly do make them: out of Europe it is the only government which *is* made. When the Southern States of America revolted, and tried to set up a government, not only did they in fact set up a presidential government, but they never considered whether they should set up any other instead of that. They assumed it as a necessity; they thought they had no practical option. Nor was the conviction that presidential government was natural and inevitable for them confined to themselves, or to America. If you remarked upon it, the almost universal answer was but a vague inquiry, What *else* could they have done?

Several subsidiary reasons may be assigned for this odd anomaly, but there are three principal reasons:—

First. The general and natural notion has been that a government by a cabinet is only possible under a monarchy. It is supposed that a king, or a colonial governor, a king's representative, at least, is necessary to choose the cabinet. The distinction between the *dignified* parts and the *efficient* parts of the English government is, indeed, vaguely seen, but it is not distinctly apprehended, nor its consequences consistently deduced. Everybody knows that the real choice is not in the monarch; that his selection is, in all but rare cases, apparent only; that the real selection is elsewhere; that the notion of the real rulers of the nation being the "servants" of a nominal sovereign is only one of the convenient fictions by which a nation which has changed from mediæval life to modern life without a break has contrived to expedite and smooth the transition. But we do not wake ourselves up to the consequences of what we know. If the real choice is in the assembly, it is—must be—possible, by proper arrangements, for the assembly to exercise it without so cumbrous an adjunct as a king "to say he does it without doing it."

Secondly. The precedent of the United States has deceived mankind. They thought, and justly thought, they could not make a monarchy, just as they could not make an aristocracy. They made a presidential government, and they cleave to it with that loyalty to law which is their characteristic merit, and that love of what is *theirs* as such, and because it is theirs, which is their characteristic defect. They are so natural an example, that a nation which cannot become monarchical at once degrades itself, and becomes presidential, as if by fate, and of necessary sequence. Nothing rules mankind like a conspicuous example, and in this matter America so rules them.

These, however, are but subordinate reasons; there is a third and greater. The presidential government, though an inferior sort of government, even *because* it is an inferior sort is possible where a government by a cabinet is not possible. A cabinet government assumes a good legislative assembly—an assembly fit to elect a cabinet. The existence of such an assembly, again, assumes the existence of a competent political people, of an adequate supply of decent constituencies. But this condition cannot always be satisfied—this people and these constituencies cannot always be found; and where the condition is not satisfied, a real presidential government is better than an ineffectual pretence at cabinet government. An inferior form of government is better than no government at all; and an attempt at a species of government too high for the attempting country commonly ends in no government at all. *Corruptio optimi pessima:* a spoiled refinement which will not work is much worse than a common, mean thing which will work.

In the next chapter I hope to investigate carefully what are the conditions under which cabinet government is possible, what nations can have it, and what others cannot. As I have remarked before, for the numerous colonies of the English race, this may be a practical question before long.

WALTER BAGEHOT.

THE BELTON ESTATE.

CHAPTER I.

THE REMNANTS OF THE AMEDROZ FAMILY.

Mrs. AMEDROZ, the wife of Bernard Amedroz, Esq., of Belton Castle, and mother of Charles and Clara Amedroz, died when those children were only eight and six years old, thereby subjecting them to the greatest misfortune which children born in that sphere of life can be made to suffer. And, in the case of this boy and girl the misfortune was aggravated greatly by the peculiarities of the father's character. Mr. Amedroz was not a bad man,—as men are held to be bad in the world's esteem. He was not vicious,—was not a gambler or a drunkard,—was not self-indulgent to a degree that brought upon him any reproach; nor was he regardless of his children. But he was an idle, thriftless man, who, at the age of sixty-seven, when the reader will first make his acquaintance, had as yet done no good in the world whatever. Indeed he had done terrible evil; for his son Charles was now dead,—had perished by his own hand, —and the state of things which had brought about this woful event had been chiefly due to the father's neglect.

Belton Castle is a pretty country seat, standing in a small but beautifully wooded park, close under the Quantock hills in Somersetshire; and the little town of Belton clusters round the park gates. Few Englishmen know the scenery of England well, and the prettinesses of Somersetshire are among those which are the least known. But the Quantock hills are very lovely, with their rich valleys lying close among them, and their outlying moorlands running off towards Dulverton and the borders of Devonshire,—moorlands which are not flat, like Salisbury Plain, but are broken into ravines and deep watercourses and rugged dells hither and thither; where old oaks are standing, in which life seems to have dwindled down to the last spark; but the last spark is still there, and the old oaks give forth their scanty leaves from year to year.

In among the hills, somewhat off the high road from Minehead to Taunton, and about five miles from the sea, stands the little town, or village, of Belton, and the modern house of Mr. Amedroz, which is called Belton Castle. The village,—for it is in truth no more though it still maintains a charter for a market, and there still exists on Tuesdays some pretence of an open sale of grain and butcher's meat in the square before the church-gate,—contains about two thousand persons. That and the whole parish of Belton did once,—and that not long ago,—belong to the Amedroz family. They had inherited it from the Beltons of old, an Amedroz having married the heiress of the family. And as the parish is large, stretching away to Exmoor on one side, and almost to the sea on the other, containing the hamlet of Redicote, lying on the Taunton high road,—Redicote, where the post-office is placed, a town almost in itself, and one which is now much more prosperous than Belton,—as the property when it came to the first Amedroz had limits such as these, the family had been considerable in the county. But these limits had been straightened in the days of the grandfather and the father of Bernard Amedroz; and he, when he married a Miss Winterfield of Taunton, was thought to have done very well, in that mortgages were paid off the property with his wife's money to such an extent as to leave him in clear possession of an estate that gave him two thousand a year. As Mr. Amedroz had no grand neighbours near him, as the place is remote and the living therefore cheap, and as with this income there was no question of annual visits to London, Mr. and Mrs. Amedroz might have done very well with such of the good things of the world as had fallen to their lot. And had the wife lived such would probably have been the case; for the Winterfields were known to be prudent people. But Mrs. Amedroz had died young, and things with Bernard Amedroz had gone badly.

And yet the evil had not been so much with him as with that terrible boy of his. The father had been nearly forty when he married. He had then never done any good; but as neither had he done much harm, the friends of the family had argued well of his future career. After him, unless he should leave a son behind him, there would be no Amedroz left among the Quantock hills; and by some arrangement in respect to that Winterfield money which came to him on his marriage,—the Winterfields having a long dated connection with the Beltons of old,—the Amedroz property was, at Bernard's marriage, entailed back upon a distant Belton cousin, one Will Belton, whom no one had seen for many years, but who was by blood nearer to the squire, in default of children of his own, than any other of his relatives. And now Will Belton was the heir to Belton Castle; for Charles Amedroz, at the age of twenty-seven, had found the miseries of the world to be too many for him, and had put an end to them and to himself.

Charles had been a clever fellow,—a very clever fellow in the eyes of his father. Bernard Amedroz knew that he himself was not a clever fellow, and admired his son accordingly; and when Charles had been expelled from Harrow for some boyish freak,—in his vengeance against a neighbouring farmer, who had reported to the school authorities the doings of a few beagles upon his land, Charles had cut off the heads of all the trees in a young fir plantation,—his father was proud of the exploit. When he was rusticated a second time from Trinity, and when the father received an intimation that his son's name had better be taken from the College books, the squire was not so well pleased; but even then he found some delight in the stories which reached him of his son's vagaries; and when the young man commenced Bohemian life in London, his father did nothing to restrain him. Then there came the old story—debts, endless debts; and lies, endless lies. During the two years before his death, his father paid for him, or undertook to pay, nearly ten thousand pounds, sacrificing the life assurances which were to have made provision for his daughter; sacrificing, to a great extent, his own life income,—sacrificing everything, so that the property might not be utterly ruined at his death. That Charles Amedroz should be a brighter, greater man than any other Amedroz, had still been the father's pride. At the last visit which Charles had paid to Belton his father had called upon him to pledge himself solemnly that his sister should not be made to suffer by what had been done for him. Within a month of that time he had blown his brains out in his London lodgings, thus making over the entire property to Will Belton at his father's death. At that last pretended settlement with his father and his father's lawyer, he had kept back the mention of debts as heavy nearly as those to which he had owned; and there were debts of honour, too, of which he had not spoken, trusting to the next event at Newmarket to set him right. The next event at Newmarket had set him more wrong than ever, and so there had come an end to everything with Charles Amedroz.

This had happened in the spring, and the afflicted father,—afflicted with the double sorrow of his son's terrible death and his daughter's ruin,—had declared that he would turn his face to the wall and die. But the old squire's health, though far from strong, was stronger than he had deemed it, and his feelings, sharp enough, were less sharp than he had thought them; and when a month had passed by, he had discovered that it would be better that he should live, in order that his daughter might still have bread to eat and a house of her own over her head. Though he was now an impoverished man, there was still left to him the means of keeping up the old home; and he told himself that it must, if possible, be so kept that a few pounds annually might be put by for Clara. The old carriage horses were sold, and the park was let to a farmer, up to the hall door of the castle. So much the squire could do; but as to the putting by of the few pounds, any dependence on such exertion as that on his part would, we may say, be very precarious.

Belton Castle was not in truth a castle. Immediately before the front door, so near to the house as merely to allow of a broad road running between it and the entrance porch, there stood an old tower, which gave its name to the residence,—an old square tower, up which the Amedroz boys for three generations had been able to climb by means of the ivy and broken stones in one of the inner corners,—and this tower was a remnant of a real castle that had once protected the village of Belton. The house itself was an ugly residence, three stories high, built in the time of George II., with low rooms and long passages, and an immense number of doors. It was a large, unattractive house, —unattractive, that is, as regarded its own attributes,—but made interesting by the beauty of the small park in which it stood. Belton Park did not, perhaps, contain much above a hundred acres, but the land was so broken into knolls and valleys, in so many places was the rock seen to be cropping up through the verdure, there were in it so many stunted old oaks, so many points of vantage for the lover of scenery, that no one would believe it to be other than a considerable domain. The farmer who took it, and who would not, under any circumstances, undertake to pay more than seventeen shillings an acre for it, could not be made to think that it was in any way considerable. But Belton Park, since first it was made a park, had never before been regarded after this fashion. Farmer Stovey, of the Grange, was the first man of that class who had ever assumed the right to pasture his sheep in Belton Chace,—as the people around were still accustomed to call the woodlands of the estate.

It was full summer at Belton, and four months had now passed since the dreadful tidings had reached the castle. It was full summer, and the people of the village were again going about their ordinary business; and the shop-girls, with their lovers from Redicote, were again to be seen walking among the oaks in the park on a Sunday evening; and the world in that district of Somersetshire was getting itself back into its old grooves. The fate of the young heir had disturbed the grooves greatly, and had taught many in those parts to feel that the world was coming to an end. They had not loved young Amedroz, for he had been haughty when among them, and there had been wrongs committed by the dissolute young squire, and grief had come from his misdoings upon more than one household; but to think that he should have destroyed himself with his own hand! And then, to think that Miss Clara would become a beggar when the old squire should die! All the neighbours around understood the whole history of the entail, and knew that the property was to go to Will Belton. Now Will Belton was not a gentleman! So, at least, said the Belton folk, who had heard that the heir had been brought up as a farmer somewhere in Norfolk. Will Belton had once been at the Castle as a boy, now some fifteen years ago, and then there had sprung up a great quarrel between him and his distant cousin Charles;—and Will, who was rough and large of stature, had thrashed the smaller boy severely; and the thing had grown to have dimensions larger than those which generally attend the quarrels of boys; and Will had said something which had shown how well he understood his position in reference to the estate;—and Charles had hated him. So Will had gone, and had been no more seen among the oaks whose name he bore. And the people, in spite of his name, regarded him as an interloper. To them, with their short memories and scanty knowledge of the past, Amedroz was more honourable than Belton, and they looked upon the coming man as an intruder. Why should not Miss Clara have the property? Miss Clara had never done harm to any one!

Things got back into their old grooves, and at the end of the third month the squire was once more seen in the old family pew at church. He was a large man, who had been very handsome, and who now, in his yellow leaf, was not without a certain beauty of manliness. He wore his hair and his beard long; before his son's death they were grey, but now they were very white. And though he stooped, there was still a dignity in his slow step,—a dignity that came to him from nature rather than from any effort. He was a man who, in fact, did little or nothing in the world,—whose life had been very useless; but he had been gifted with such a presence that he looked as though he were one of God's nobler creatures. Though always dignified he was ever affable, and the poor liked him better than they might have done had he passed his time in searching out their wants and supplying them. They were proud of their squire, though he had done nothing for them. It was something to them to have a man who could so carry himself sitting in the family pew in their parish church. They knew that he was poor, but they all declared that he was never mean. He was a real gentleman,—was this last Amedroz of the family; therefore they curtseyed low, and bowed on his reappearance among them, and made all those signs of reverential awe which are common to the poor when they feel reverence for the presence of a superior.

Clara was there with him, but she had shown herself in the pew for four or five weeks before this. She had not been at home when the fearful news had reached Belton, being at that time with a certain lady who lived on the farther side of the county, at Perivale,—a certain Mrs. Winterfield, born a Folliott, a widow, who stood to Miss Amedroz in the place of an aunt. Mrs. Winterfield was, in truth, the sister of a gentleman who had married Clara's aunt,—there having been marriages and intermarriages between the Winterfields and the Folliotts, and the Belton-Amedroz families. With this lady in Perivale, which I maintain to be the dullest little town in England, Miss Amedroz was staying when the news reached her father, and when it was brought direct from London to herself. Instantly she had hurried home, making the journey with all imaginable speed, though her heart was all but broken within her bosom. She had found her father stricken to the ground, and it was the more necessary, therefore, that she should exert herself. It would not do that she also should yield to that longing for death which terrible calamities often produce for a season.

Clara Amedroz, when she first heard the news of her brother's fate, had felt that she was for ever crushed to the ground. She had known too well what had been the nature of her brother's life, but she had not expected or feared any such termination to his career as this which had now come upon him—to the terrible affliction of all belonging to him. She felt at first, as did also her father, that she and he were annihilated as regards this world, not only by an enduring grief, but also by a disgrace which would never allow her again to hold up her head. And for many a long year much of this feeling clung to her;—clung to her much more strongly than to her father. But strength was hers to perceive, even before she had reached her home, that it was her duty to repress both the feeling of shame and the sorrow, as far as they were capable of repression. Her brother had been weak, and in his weakness had sought a coward's escape from the ills of the world around him. She must not also be a coward! Bad as life might be to her henceforth, she must endure it with such fortitude as she could muster. So resolving she returned to her father, and was able to listen to his railings with a fortitude that was essentially serviceable both to him and to herself.

"Both of you! Both of you!" the unhappy father had said in his woe. "The wretched boy has destroyed you as much as himself!"

"No, sir," she had answered, with a forbearance in her misery, which, terrible as was the effort, she forced herself to accomplish for his sake. "It is not so. No thought of that need add to your grief. My poor brother has not hurt me;—not in the way you mean."

"He has ruined us all," said the father; "root and branch, man and woman, old and young, house and land. He has brought the family to an end;—ah me, to such an end!" After that the name of him who had taken himself from among them was not mentioned between the father and daughter, and Clara settled herself to the duties of her new life, striving to live as though there was no great sorrow around her,—as though no cloud-storm had burst over her head.

The family lawyer, who lived at Taunton, had communicated the fact of Charles's death to Mr. Belton, and Belton had acknowledged the letter with the ordinary expressions of regret. The lawyer had alluded to the entail, saying that it was improbable that Mr. Amedroz would have another son. To this Belton had replied that for his cousin Clara's sake he hoped that the squire's life might be long spared. The lawyer had smiled as he read the wish, thinking to himself that luckily no wish on the part of Will Belton could influence his old client either for good or evil. What man, let alone what lawyer, will ever believe in the sincerity of such a wish as that expressed by the heir to a property? And yet where is the man who will not declare to himself that such, under such circumstances, would be his own wish?

Clara Amedroz at this time was not a very young lady. She had already passed her twenty-fifth birthday, and in manners, appearance, and habits was, at any rate, as old as her age. She made no pretence to youth, speaking of herself always as one whom circumstances required to take upon herself age in advance of her years. She did not dress young, or live much with young people, or correspond with other girls by means of crossed letters; nor expect that, for her, young pleasures should be provided. Life had always been serious with her; but now, we may say, since the terrible tragedy in the family, it must be solemn as well as serious. The memory of her brother must always be upon her; and the memory also of the fact that her father was now an impoverished man, on whose behalf it was her duty to care that every shilling spent in the house did its full twelve pennies' worth of work. There was a mixture in this of deep tragedy and of little care, which seemed to destroy for her the poetry as well as the pleasure of life. The poetry and tragedy might have gone hand in hand together; and so might the cares and pleasures of life have done, had there been no black sorrow of which she must be ever mindful. But it was her lot to have to scrutinise the butcher's bill as she was thinking of her brother's fate; and to work daily among small household things while the spectre of her brother's corpse was ever before her eyes.

A word must be said to explain how it had come to pass that the life led by Miss Amedroz had been more than commonly serious before that tragedy had befallen the family. The name of the lady who stood to Clara in the place of an aunt has been already mentioned. When a girl has a mother, her aunt may be little or nothing to her. But when the mother is gone, if there be an aunt unimpeded with other family duties, then the family duties of that aunt begin,—and are assumed sometimes with great vigour. Such had been the case with Mrs. Winterfield. No woman ever lived, perhaps, with more conscientious ideas of her duty as a woman than Mrs. Winterfield, of Prospect Place, Perivale. And this, as I say it, is intended to convey no scoff against that excellent lady. She was an excellent lady,—unselfish, given to self-restraint, generous, pious, looking to find in her religion a safe path through life,—a path as safe as the facts of Adam's fall would allow her feet to find. She was a woman fearing much for others, but fearing also much for herself, striving to maintain her house in godliness, hating sin, and struggling with the weakness of her humanity so that she might not allow herself to hate the sinners. But her hatred for the sin she found herself bound at all times to pronounce,—to show it by some act at all seasons. To fight the devil was her work,—was the appointed work of every living soul, if only living souls could be made to acknowledge the necessity of the task. Now an aunt of that kind, when she assumes her duties towards a motherless niece, is apt to make life serious.

But, it will be said, Clara Amedroz could have rebelled; and Clara's father was hardly made of such stuff that obedience to the aunt would be enforced on her by parental authority. Doubtless Clara could have rebelled against her aunt. Indeed, I do not know that she had hitherto been very obedient. But there were family facts about these Winterfield connections which would have made it difficult for her to ignore her so-called aunt, even had she wished to do so. Mrs. Winterfield had twelve hundred a year at her own disposal, and she was the only person related to the Amedroz family from whom Mr. Amedroz had a right to have expectations on his daughter's behalf. Clara had, in a measure, been claimed by the lady, and the father had made good the lady's claim, and Clara had acknowledged that a portion of her life was due to the demands of Perivale. These demands had undoubtedly made her life serious.

Life at Perivale was a very serious thing. As regards amusement, ordinarily so called, the need of any such institution was not acknowledged at Prospect House. Food, drink, and raiment were acknowledged to be necessary to humanity, and, in accordance with the rules of that house, they were supplied in plenty, and good of their kind. Such ladies as Mrs. Winterfield generally keep good tables, thinking no doubt that the eatables should do honour to the grace that is said for them. And Mrs. Winterfield herself always wore a thick black silk dress,—not rusty or dowdy with age,—but with some gloss of the silk on it; giving away, with secret, underhand, undiscovered charity, her old dresses to another lady of her own sort, on whom fortune had not bestowed twelve hundred a year. And Mrs. Winterfield kept a low, four-wheeled, one-horsed little phaeton, in which she made her pilgrimages among the poor of Perivale, driven by the most solemn of stable-boys, dressed up in a white great coat, the most priggish of hats, and white cotton gloves. At the rate of five miles an hour was she driven about, and this driving was to her the amusement of life. But such an occupation to Clara Amedroz assisted to make life serious.

In person Mrs. Winterfield was tall and thin, wearing on her brow thin braids of false hair. She had suffered much from acute ill health, and her jaws were sunken, and her eyes were hollow, and there was a look of woe about her which seemed ever to be telling of her own sorrows in this world and of the sorrows of others in the world to come. Ill-nature was written on her face, but in this her face was a false face. She had the manners of a cross, peevish woman; but her manners also were false, and gave no proper idea of her character. But still, such as she was, she made life very serious to those who were called upon to dwell with her.

I need, I hope, hardly say that a young lady such as Miss Amedroz, even though she had reached the age of twenty-five,—for at the time to which I am now alluding she had nearly done so,—and was not young of her age, had formed for herself no plan of life in which her aunt's money figured as a motive power. She had gone to Perivale when she was very young, because she had been told to do so, and had continued to go, partly from obedience, partly from habit, and partly from affection. An aunt's dominion, when once well established in early years, cannot easily be thrown altogether aside, —even though a young lady have a will of her own. Now Clara Amedroz had a strong will of her own, and did not at all,—at any rate in these latter days,—belong to that school of divinity in which her aunt shone almost as a professor. And this circumstance, also, added to the seriousness of her life. But in regard to her aunt's money she had entertained no established hopes; and when her aunt opened her mind to her on that subject, a few days before the arrival of the fatal news at Perivale, Clara, though she was somewhat surprised, was by no means disappointed. Now there was a certain Captain Aylmer in the question, of whom in this opening chapter it will be necessary to say a few words.

Captain Frederic Folliott Aylmer was, in truth, the nephew of Mrs. Winterfield, whereas Clara Amedroz was not, in truth, her niece. And Captain Aylmer was also Member of Parliament for the little borough of Perivale, returned altogether on the Low Church interest,—for a devotion to which, and for that alone, Perivale was noted among boroughs. These facts together added not a little to Mrs. Winterfield's influence and professorial power in the place, and gave a dignity to the one-horse chaise which it might not otherwise have possessed. But Captain Aylmer was only the second son of his father, Sir Anthony Aylmer, who had married a Miss Folliott, sister of our Mrs. Winterfield. On Frederic Aylmer his mother's estate was settled. That and Mrs. Winterfield's property lay in the neighbourhood of Perivale; and now, on the occasion to which I am alluding, Mrs. Winterfield thought it necessary to tell Clara that the property must all go together. She had thought about it, and had doubted about it, and had prayed about it, and now she found that such a disposition of it was her duty.

"I am quite sure you're right, aunt," Clara had said. She knew very well what had come of that provision which her father had attempted to make for her, and knew also how great were her father's expectations in regard to Mrs. Winterfield's money.

"I hope I am; but I have thought it right to tell you. I shall feel myself bound to tell Frederic. I have had many doubts, but I think I am right."

"I am sure you are, aunt. What would he think of me if, at some future time, he should have to find that I had been in his way?"

"The future time will not be long now, my dear."

"I hope it may; but long or short, it is better so."

"I think it is, my dear; I think it is. I think it is my duty."

It must be understood that Captain Aylmer was member for Perivale on the Low Church interest, and that, therefore, when at Perivale he was decidedly a Low Churchman. I am not aware that the peculiarity stuck to him very closely at Aylmer Castle, in Yorkshire, or among his friends in London; but there was no hypocrisy in this, as the world goes. Women in such matters are absolutely false if they be not sincere; but men, with political views, and with much of their future prospects in jeopardy also, are allowed to dress themselves differently for different scenes. Whatever be the peculiar interest on which a man goes into Parliament, of course he has to live up to that in his own borough. Whether malt, the franchise, or teetotallism be his rallying point, of course he is full of it when among his constituents. But it is not desirable that he should be full of it also at his club. Had Captain Aylmer become Prime Minister, he would, no doubt, have made Low Church bishops. It was the side to which he had taken himself in that matter,—not without good reasons. And he could say a sharp word or two in season about vestments; he was strong against candles, and fought for his side fairly well. No one had good right to complain of Captain Aylmer as being insincere; but had his aunt known the whole history of her nephew's life, I doubt whether she would have made him her heir, —thinking that in doing so she was doing the best for the good cause.

The whole history of her niece's life she did know, and she knew that Clara was not with her, heart and soul. Had Clara left the old woman in doubt on this subject, she would have been a hypocrite. Captain Aylmer did not often spend a Sunday at Perivale, but when he did, he went to church three times, and submitted himself to the yoke. He was thinking of the borough votes quite as much as of his aunt's money, and was carrying on his business after the fashion of men. But Clara found herself compelled to maintain

VOL. I. D

some sort of a fight, though she also went to church three times on Sunday. And there was another reason why Mrs. Winterfield thought it right to mention Captain Aylmer's name to her niece on this occasion.

"I had hoped," she said, "that it might make no difference in what way my money was left."

Clara well understood what this meant, as will, probably, the reader also. "I can't say but what it will make a difference," she answered, smiling; "but I shall always think that you have done right. Why should I stand in Captain Aylmer's way?"

"I had hoped your ways might have been the same," said the old lady, fretfully.

"But they cannot be the same."

"No; you do not see things as he sees them. Things that are serious to him are, I fear, only light to you. Dear Clara, would I could see you more in earnest as to the only matter that is worth our earnestness." Miss Amedroz said nothing as to the Captain's earnestness, though, perhaps, her ideas as to his ideas about religion were more correct than those held by Mrs. Winterfield. But it would not have suited her to raise any argument on that subject. "I pray for you, Clara," continued the old lady; "and will do so as long as the power of prayer is left to me. I hope,—I hope you do not cease to pray for yourself?"

"I endeavour, aunt."

"It is an endeavour which, if really made, never fails."

Clara said nothing more, and her aunt also remained silent. Soon afterwards, the four-wheeled carriage, with the demure stable-boy, came to the door, and Clara was driven up and down through the streets of Perivale in a manner which was an injury to her. She knew that she was suffering an injustice, but it was one of which she could not make complaint. She submitted to her aunt, enduring the penances that were required of her; and, therefore, her aunt had opportunity enough to see her shortcomings. Mrs. Winterfield did see them, and judged her accordingly. Captain Aylmer, being a man and a Member of Parliament, was called upon to bear no such penances, and, therefore, his shortcomings were not suspected.

But, after all, what title had she ever possessed to entertain expectations from Mrs. Winterfield? When she thought of it all in her room that night, she told herself that it was strange that her aunt should have spoken to her in such a way on such a subject. But, then, so much had been said to her on the matter by her father, so much, no doubt, had reached her aunt's ears also, the hope that her position with reference to the rich widow at Perivale might be beneficial to her had been so often discussed at Belton as a make-weight against the extravagance of the heir, there had already been so much of this mistake, that she taught herself to perceive that the communication was needed. "In her honesty she has not chosen to leave me with false hopes," said Clara to herself. And at that moment she loved her aunt for her honesty.

Then, on the day but one following this conversation as to the destiny of her aunt's property, came the terrible tidings of her brother's death. Captain Aylmer, who had been in London at the time, hurried down to Perivale, and had been the first to tell Miss Amedroz what had happened. The words spoken between them then had not been many, but Clara knew that Captain Aylmer had been kind to her; and when he had offered to accompany her to Belton, she had thanked with a degree of gratitude which had almost seemed to imply more of regard between them than Clara would have acknowledged to exist. But in moments such as those, soft words may be spoken and hands may be pressed without any of that meaning which soft words and the grasping of hands generally carry with them. As far as Taunton Captain Aylmer did go with Miss Amedroz, and there they parted, he on his journey up to town, and she for her father's desolate house at Belton.

CHAPTER II.

THE HEIR PROPOSES TO VISIT HIS COUSINS.

IT was full summer at Belton, and the sweet scent of the new hay filled the porch of the old house with fragrance, as Clara sat there alone with her work. Immediately before the house door, between that and the old tower, there stood one of Farmer Stovey's hay-carts, now empty, with an old horse between the shafts looking as though he were asleep in the sun. Immediately beyond the tower the men were loading another cart, and the women and children were chattering as they raked the scattered remnants up to the rows. Under the shadow of the old tower, but in sight of Clara as she sat in the porch, there lay the small beer-barrels of the haymakers, and three or four rakes were standing erect against the old grey wall. It was now eleven o'clock, and Clara was waiting for her father, who was not yet out of his room. She had taken his breakfast to him in bed, as was her custom; for he had fallen into idle ways, and the luxury of his bed was, of all his remaining luxuries, the one that he liked the best. After a while he came down to her, having an open letter in his hand. Clara saw that he intended either to show it to her or to speak of it, and asked him therefore, with some tone of interest in her voice, from whom it had come. But Mr. Amedroz was fretful at the moment, and instead of answering her began to complain of his tenant's ill-usage of him.

"What has he got his cart there for? I haven't let him the road up to the hall door. I suppose he'll bring his things into the parlour next."

"I rather like it, papa."

"Do you? I can only say that you're lucky in your tastes. I don't like it, I can tell you."

"Mr. Stovey is out there. Shall I ask him to have the things moved farther off?"

"No, my dear,—no. I must bear it, as I do all the rest of it. What does it matter? There'll be an end of it soon. He pays his rent, and I suppose he is right to do as he pleases. But I can't say that I like it."

"Am I to see the letter, papa?" she asked, wishing to turn his mind from the subject of the hay-carts.

"Well, yes. I brought it for you to see; though perhaps I should be doing better if I burned it, and said nothing about it. It is a most impudent production; and heartless,—very heartless."

Clara was accustomed to such complaints as these from her father. Everything that everybody did around him he would call heartless. The man pitied himself so much in his own misery, that he expected to live in an atmosphere of pity from others; and though the pity doubtless was there, he misdoubted it. He thought that Farmer Stovey was cruel in that he had left the hay-cart near the house, to wound his eyes by reminding him that he was no longer master of the ground before his own hall door. He thought that the women and children were cruel to chatter so near his ears. He almost accused his daughter of cruelty, because she had told him that she liked the contiguity of the haymaking. Under such circumstances as those which enveloped him and her, was it not heartless in her to like anything? It seemed to him that the whole world of Belton should be drowned in woe because of his misery.

"Where is it from, papa?" she asked.

"There, you may read it. Perhaps it is better that you should know that it has been written." Then she read the letter, which was as follows:—

"Plaistow Hall, — July, 186—."

Though she had never before seen the handwriting, she knew at once from whence came the letter, for she had often heard of Plaistow Hall. It was the name of the farm at which her distant cousin, Will Belton, lived, and her father had more than once been at the trouble of explaining to her, that though the place was called a hall, the house was no more than a farmhouse. He had never seen Plaistow Hall, and had never been in Norfolk; but so much he could take upon himself to say, "They call all the farms halls down there." It was not wonderful that he should dislike his heir; and, perhaps, not unnatural that he should show his dislike after this fashion. Clara, when she read the address, looked up into her father's face. "You know who it is now," he said. And then she read the letter.

"Plaistow Hall, — July, 186—.

"MY DEAR SIR,

"I have not written to you before since your bereavement, thinking it better to wait awhile; but I hope you have not taken me to be unkind in this, or have supposed me to be unmindful of your sorrow. Now I take up my pen, hoping that I may make you understand how greatly I was distressed by what has occurred. I believe I am now the nearest male relative that you have, and as such I am very anxious to be of service to you if it may be possible. Considering the closeness of our connection, and my position in reference to the property, it seems bad that we should never meet. I can assure you that you would find me very friendly if we could manage to come together.

"I should think nothing of running across to Belton, if you would receive me at your house. I could come very well before harvest, if that would suit you, and would stay with you for a week. Pray give my kindest regards to my cousin Clara, whom I can only just remember as a very little girl. She was with her aunt at Perivale when I was at Belton as a boy. She shall find a friend in me if she wants a friend. "Your affectionate cousin,

"W. BELTON."

Clara read the letter very slowly, so that she might make herself sure of its tone and bearing before she was called upon by her father to express her feeling respecting it. She knew that she would be expected to abuse it violently, and to accuse the writer of vulgarity, insolence, and cruelty; but she had already learned that she must not allow herself to accede to all her father's fantasies. For his sake, and for his protection, it was necessary that she should differ from him, and even contradict him. Were she not to do so, he would fall into a state of wailing and complaining that would exaggerate itself almost to idiotcy. And it was imperative that she herself should exercise her own opinion on many points, almost without reference to him. She alone knew how utterly destitute she would be when he should die. He, in the first days of his agony, had sobbed forth his remorse as to her ruin; but, even when doing so, he had comforted himself with the remembrance of Mrs. Winterfield's money, and Mrs. Winterfield's affection for his daughter. And the aunt, when she had declared her purpose to Clara, had told herself that the provision made for Clara by her father was sufficient. To neither of them had Clara told her own position. She could not inform her aunt that her father had given up to the poor reprobate who had destroyed himself all that had been intended for her. Had she done so she would have been asking her aunt for charity. Nor would she bring herself to add to her father's misery, by destroying the hopes which still supported him. She never spoke of her own position in regard to money, but she knew that it had become her duty to live a wary, watchful life, taking much upon herself in their impoverished household, and holding her own opinion against her father's when her doing so became expedient. So she finished the letter in silence, and did not speak at the moment when the movement of her eyes declared that she had completed the task.

"Well," said he.

"I do not think my cousin means badly."

"You don't! I do, then. I think he means very badly. What business has he to write to me, talking of his position?"

"I can't see anything amiss in his doing so, papa. I think he wishes to be friendly. The property will be his some day, and I don't see why that should not be mentioned, when there is occasion."

"Upon my word, Clara, you surprise me. But women never understand delicacy in regard to money. They have so little to do with it, and think so little about it, that they have no occasion for such delicacy."

Clara could not help the thought that to her mind the subject was present with sufficient frequency to make delicacy very desirable, if only it were practicable. But of this she said nothing. "And what answer will you send to him, papa?" she asked.

"None at all. Why should I trouble myself to write to him?"

"I will take the trouble off your hands."

"And what will you say to him?"

"I will ask him to come here, as he proposes."

"Clara!"

"Why not, papa? He is the heir to the property, and why should he not be permitted to see it? There are many things in which his co-operation with you might be a comfort to you. I can't tell you whether the tenants and people are treating you well, but he can do so; and, moreover, I think he means to be kind. I do not see why we should quarrel with our cousin because he is the heir to your property. It is not through any doing of his own that he is so."

This reasoning had no effect upon Mr. Amedroz, but his daughter's resolution carried the point against him in spite of his want of reason. No letter was written that day, or on the next; but on the day following a formal note was sent off by Clara, in which Mr. Belton was told that Mr. Amedroz would be happy to receive him at Belton Castle. The letter was written by the daughter, but the father was responsible for the formality. He sat over her while she wrote it, and nearly drove her distracted by discussing every word and phrase. At last, Clara was so annoyed with her own production, that she was almost tempted to write another letter unknown to her father; but the formal note went.

"My dear Sir,

"I am desired by my father to say that he will be happy to receive you at Belton Castle, at the time fixed by yourself.

"Yours truly,
"Clara Amedroz."

There was no more than that, but that had the desired effect; and by return of post there came a rejoinder, saying that Will Belton would be at the Castle on the fifteenth of August. "They can do without me for about ten days," he said in his postscript, writing in a familiar tone, which did not seem to have been at all checked by the coldness of his cousin's note,—" as our harvest will be late; but I must be back for a week's work before the partridges."

"Heartless! quite heartless!" Mr. Amedroz said as he read this. "Partridges! to talk of partridges at such a time as this!"

Clara, however, would not acknowledge that she agreed with her father; but she could not altogether restrain a feeling on her own part that her cousin's good humour towards her and Mr. Amedroz should have been repressed by the tone of her letter to him. The man was to come, however, and she would not judge of him until he was there.

In one house in the neighbourhood, and in only one, had Miss Amedroz a friend with whom she was intimate; and as regarded even this single friend, the intimacy was the effect rather of circumstances than of real affection. She liked Mrs. Askerton, and saw her almost daily; but she could hardly tell herself that she loved her neighbour.

In the little town of Belton, close to the church, there stood a pretty, small house, called Belton Cottage. It was so near the church that strangers always supposed it to be the parsonage; but the rectory stood away out in the country, half a mile from the town, on the road to Redicote, and was a large house, three stories high, with grounds of its own, and very ugly. Here lived the old bachelor rector, seventy years of age, given much to long absences when he could achieve them, and never on good terms with his bishop. His two curates lived at Redicote, where there was a second church. Belton Cottage, which was occupied by Colonel Askerton and Mrs Askerton, was on the Amedroz property, and had been hired some two years since by the Colonel, who was then a stranger in the country and altogether unknown to the Belton people. But he had come there for shooting, and therefore his coming had been understood. Even as long ago as two years since, there had been neither use nor propriety in keeping the shooting for the squire's son, and it had been let with the cottage to Colonel Askerton. So Colonel Askerton had come there with his wife, and no one in the neighbourhood had known anything about them. Mr. Amedroz, with his daughter, had called upon them, and gradually there had grown up an intimacy between Clara and Mrs. Askerton. There was an opening from the garden of Belton Cottage into the park, so that familiar intercourse was easy, and Mrs. Askerton was a woman who knew well how to make herself pleasant to such another woman as Miss Amedroz.

The reader may as well know at once that rumours prejudicial to the Askertons reached Belton before they had been established there for six months. At Taunton, which was twenty miles distant, these rumours were very rife, and there were people there who knew with accuracy,—though probably without a grain of truth in their accuracy, —every detail in the history of Mrs. Askerton's life. And something, too, reached Clara's ears,—something from old Mr. Wright, the rector, who loved scandal, and was very ill-natured. "A very nice woman," the rector had said; "but she does not seem to have any belongings in particular." "She has got a husband," Clara had replied with some little indignation, for she had never loved Mr. Wright. "Yes; I suppose she has got a husband." Then Clara had, in her own judgment, accused the rector of lying, evil-speaking, and slandering, and had increased the measure of her cordiality to Mrs. Askerton. But something more she had heard on the same subject at Perivale. "Before you throw yourself into close intimacy with the lady, I think you should know something about her," Mrs. Winterfield had said to her. "I do know something about her; I know that she has the manners and education of a lady, and that she is living affectionately with her husband, who is devoted to her. What more ought I to know?" "If you really do know all that, you know a great deal," Mrs. Winterfield had replied.

"Do you know anything against her, aunt?" Clara asked, after a pause.

There was another pause before Mrs. Winterfield answered. "No, my dear; I cannot say that I do. But I think that young ladies, before they make intimate friendships, should be very sure of their friends."

"You have already acknowledged that I know a great deal about her," Clara replied. And then the conversation was at an end. Clara had not been quite ingenuous, as she acknowledged to herself. She was aware that her aunt would not permit herself to repeat rumours as to the truth of which she had no absolute knowledge. She understood that the weakness of her aunt's caution was due to the old lady's sense of charity and dislike of slander. But Clara had buckled on her armour for Mrs. Askerton, and was glad, therefore, to achieve her little victory. When we buckle on our armour in any cause, we are apt to go on buckling it, let the cause become as weak as it may; and Clara continued her intimacy with Mrs. Askerton, although there was something in the lady's modes of speech, and something also in her modes of thinking, which did not quite satisfy the aspirations of Miss Amedroz as to a friend.

Colonel Askerton himself was a pleasant, quiet man, who seemed to be contented with the life which he was leading. For six weeks in April and May he would go up to town, leaving Mrs. Askerton at the cottage,—as to which, probably jovial, absence in the metropolis there seemed to be no spirit of grudging on the part of the wife. On the first of September a friend would come to the cottage and remain there for six weeks' shooting; and during the winter the Colonel and his wife always went to Paris for a fortnight. Such had been their life for the last two years; and thus,—so said Mrs. Askerton to Clara,—did they intend to live as long as they could keep the cottage at Belton. Society at Belton they had none, and,—as they said,—desired none. Between them and Mr. Wright there was only a speaking acquaintance. The married curate at Redicote would not let his wife call on Mrs. Askerton, and the unmarried curate was a hard-worked, clerical hack,—a parochial minister at all times and seasons, who went to no houses except the houses of the poor, and who would hold communion with no man, and certainly with no woman, who would not put up with clerical admonitions for Sunday backslidings. Mr. Amedroz himself neither received guests nor went as a guest to other men's houses. He would occasionally stand for a while at the gate of the Colonel's garden, and repeat the list of his own woes as long as his neighbour would stand there to hear it. But there was no society at Belton, and Clara, as far as she herself was aware, was the only person with whom Mrs. Askerton held any social intercourse, except what she might have during her short annual holiday in Paris.

"Of course, you are right," she said, when Clara told her of the proposed coming of Mr. Belton. "If he turn out to be a good fellow, you will have gained a great deal. And should he be a bad fellow, you will have lost nothing. In either case you will know him, and considering how he stands towards you, that itself is desirable."

"But if he should annoy papa?"

"In your papa's condition, my dear, the coming of any one will annoy him. At least, he will say so; though I do not in the least doubt that he will like the excitement better even than you will."

"I can't say there will be much excitement to me."

"No excitement in a young man's coming into the house! Without shocking your propriety, allow me to say that that is impossible. Of course, he is coming to see whether he can't make matters all right by marrying you."

"That's nonsense, Mrs. Askerton."

"Very well. Let it be nonsense. But why shouldn't he? It's just what he ought to do. He hasn't got a wife; and, as far as I know, you haven't got a lover."

"I certainly have not got a lover."

"Our religious nephew at Perivale does not seem to be of any use."

"I wish, Mrs. Askerton, you would not speak of Captain Aylmer in that way. I don't know any man whom I like so much, or at any rate better, than Captain Aylmer; but I hate the idea that no girl can become acquainted with an unmarried man without having her name mentioned with his, and having to hear ill-natured remarks of that kind."

"I hope you will learn to like this other man much better. Think how nice it will be to be mistress of the old place after all. And then to go back to the old family name! If I were you I would make up my mind not to let him leave the place till I had brought him to my feet."

"If you go on like that I will not speak to you about him again."

"Or rather not to my feet,—for gentlemen have laid aside the humble way of making love for the last twenty years at least; but I don't know whether the women haven't gained quite as much by the change as the men."

"As I know nothing will stop you when you once get into a vein of that kind, I shall go," said Clara. "And till this man has come and gone I shall not mention his name again in your presence."

"So be it," said Mrs. Askerton; "but as I will promise to say nothing more about him, you need not go on his account." But Clara had got up, and did leave the cottage at once.

ANTHONY TROLLOPE.

THE INFLUENCE OF RATIONALISM.[1]

THERE is a valuable class of books on great subjects which have something of the character and functions of good popular lecturing. They are not original, not subtle, not of close logical texture, not exquisite either in thought or style; but by virtue of these negatives they are all the more fit to act on the average intelligence. They have enough of organising purpose in them to make their facts illustrative, and to leave a distinct result in the mind even when most of the facts are forgotten; and they have enough of vagueness and vacillation in their theory to win them ready acceptance from a mixed audience. The vagueness and vacillation are not devices of timidity; they are the honest result of the writer's own mental character, which adapts him to be the instructor and the favourite of "the general reader." For the most part, the general reader of the present day does not exactly know what distance he goes; he only knows that he does not go "too far." Of any remarkable thinker, whose writings have excited controversy, he likes to have it said that "his errors are to be deplored," leaving it not too certain what those errors are; he is fond of what may be called disembodied opinions, that float in vapoury phrases above all systems of thought or action; he likes an undefined Christianity which opposes itself to nothing in particular, an undefined education of the people, an undefined amelioration of all things: in fact, he likes sound views—nothing extreme, but something between the excesses of the past and the excesses of the present. This modern type of the general reader may be known in conversation by the cordiality with which he assents to indistinct, blurred statements: say that black is black, he will shake his head and hardly think it; say that black is not so very black, he will reply, "Exactly." He has no hesitation, if you wish it, even to get up at a public meeting and express his conviction that at times, and within certain limits, the radii of a circle have a tendency to be equal; but, on the other hand, he would urge that the spirit of geometry may be carried a little too far. His only bigotry is a bigotry against any clearly-defined opinion; not in the least based on a scientific scepticism, but belonging to a lack of coherent thought—a spongy texture of mind, that gravitates strongly to nothing. The one thing he is staunch for is, the utmost liberty of private haziness.

But precisely these characteristics of the general reader, rendering him incapable of assimilating ideas unless they are administered in a highly diluted form, make it a matter of rejoicing that there are

[1] HISTORY OF THE RISE AND INFLUENCE OF THE SPIRIT OF RATIONALISM IN EUROPE. By W. E. H. LECKY, M.A. Longman & Co., London.

clever, fair-minded men, who will write books for him—men very much above him in knowledge and ability, but not too remote from him in their habits of thinking, and who can thus prepare for him infusions of history and science, that will leave some solidifying deposit, and save him from a fatal softening of the intellectual skeleton. Among such serviceable writers, Mr. Lecky's "History of the Rise and Influence of the Spirit of Rationalism in Europe" entitles him to a high place. He has prepared himself for its production by an unusual amount of well-directed reading; he has chosen his facts and quotations with much judgment; and he gives proof of those important moral qualifications, impartiality, seriousness, and modesty. This praise is chiefly applicable to the long chapter on the history of Magic and Witchcraft, which opens the work, and to the two chapters on the antecedents and history of Persecution, which occur, the one at the end of the first volume, the other at the beginning of the second. In these chapters Mr. Lecky has a narrower and better-traced path before him than in other portions of his work; he is more occupied with presenting a particular class of facts in their historical sequence, and in their relation to certain grand tide-marks of opinion, than with disquisition; and his writing is freer than elsewhere from an apparent confusedness of thought and an exuberance of approximative phrases, which can be serviceable in no other way than as diluents needful for the sort of reader we have just described.

The history of magic and witchcraft has been judiciously chosen by Mr. Lecky as the subject of his first section on the Declining Sense of the Miraculous, because it is strikingly illustrative of a position with the truth of which he is strongly impressed, though he does not always treat of it with desirable clearness and precision, namely, that certain beliefs become obsolete, not in consequence of direct arguments against them, but because of their incongruity with prevalent habits of thought. Here is his statement of the two "classes of influences," by which the mass of men, in what is called civilised society, get their beliefs gradually modified:—

"If we ask why it is that the world has rejected what was once so universally and so intensely believed, why a narrative of an old woman who had been seen riding on a broomstick, or who was proved to have transformed herself into a wolf, and to have devoured the flocks of her neighbours, is deemed so entirely incredible, most persons would probably be unable to give a very definite answer to the question. It is not because we have examined the evidence and found it insufficient, for the disbelief always precedes, when it does not prevent, examination. It is rather because the idea of absurdity is so strongly attached to such narratives, that it is difficult even to consider them with gravity. Yet at one time no such improbability was felt, and hundreds of persons have been burnt simply on the two grounds I have mentioned.

"When so complete a change takes place in public opinion, it may be ascribed to one or other of two causes. It may be the result of a controversy which has conclusively settled the question, establishing to the satisfaction of all parties a clear preponderance of argument or fact in favour of one opinion, and making that opinion a truism which is accepted by all enlightened men, even though they have not themselves examined the evidence on which it rests. Thus, if any one in a company of ordinarily educated persons were to deny the motion of the earth, or the circulation of the blood, his statement would be received with derision, though it is probable that some of his audience would be unable to demonstrate the first truth, and that very few of them could give sufficient reasons for the second. They may not themselves be able to defend their position; but they are aware that, at certain known periods of history, controversies on those subjects took place, and that known writers then brought forward some definite arguments or experiments, which were ultimately accepted by the whole learned world as rigid and conclusive demonstrations. It is possible, also, for as complete a change to be effected by what is called the spirit of the age. The general intellectual tendencies pervading the literature of a century profoundly modify the character of the public mind. They form a new tone and habit of thought. They alter the measure of probability. They create new attractions and new antipathies, and they eventually cause as absolute a rejection of certain old opinions as could be produced by the most cogent and definite arguments."

Mr. Lecky proceeds to some questionable views concerning the evidences of witchcraft, which seem to be irreconcilable even with his own remarks later on; but they lead him to the statement, thoroughly made out by his historical survey, that "the movement was mainly silent, unargumentative, and insensible; that men came gradually to disbelieve in witchcraft, because they came gradually to look upon it as absurd; and that this new tone of thought appeared, first of all, in those who were least subject to theological influences, and soon spread through the educated laity, and, last of all, took possession of the clergy."

We have rather painful proof that this "second class of influences" with a vast number go hardly deeper than Fashion, and that witchcraft to many of us is absurd only on the same ground that our grandfathers' gigs are absurd. It is felt preposterous to think of spiritual agencies in connection with ragged beldames soaring on broomsticks, in an age when it is known that mediums of communication with the invisible world are usually unctuous personages dressed in excellent broadcloth, who soar above the curtain-poles without any broomstick, and who are not given to unprofitable intrigues. The enlightened imagination rejects the figure of a witch with her profile in dark relief against the moon and her broomstick cutting a constellation. No undiscovered natural laws, no names of "respectable" witnesses, are invoked to make us feel our presumption in questioning the diabolic intimacies of that obsolete old woman, for it is known now that the undiscovered laws, and the witnesses qualified by the payment of income-tax, are all in favour of a different conception—the image of a heavy gentleman in boots and black coat-tails foreshortened against the cornice. Yet no less a person than Sir Thomas Browne once wrote that those who denied there were witches, inasmuch as they thereby denied spirits also, were "obliquely and upon consequence a sort, not of infidels, but of atheists." At present, doubtless, in certain circles, unbelievers in heavy gentlemen who float in the air by means of undiscovered laws are also taxed with atheism; illiberal as it is not to admit that mere weakness of understanding may prevent one from seeing how that phenomenon is necessarily involved in the Divine origin of things. With still more remarkable parallelism, Sir Thomas Browne goes on: "Those that, to refute their incredulity, desire to see apparitions, shall questionless never behold any, nor have the power to be so much as witches. The devil hath made them already in a heresy as capital as witchcraft, *and to appear to them were but to convert them.*" It would be difficult to see what has been changed here but the mere drapery of circumstance, if it were not for this prominent difference between our own days and the days of witchcraft, that instead of torturing, drowning, or burning the innocent, we give hospitality and large pay to—the highly-distinguished medium. At least we are safely rid of certain horrors; but if the multitude—that "farraginous concurrence of all conditions, tempers, sexes, and ages"—do not roll back even to a superstition that carries cruelty in its train, it is not because they possess a cultivated Reason, but because they are pressed upon and held up by what we may call an external Reason—the sum of conditions resulting from the laws of material growth, from changes produced by great historical collisions shattering the structures of ages and making new highways for events and ideas, and from the activities of higher minds no longer existing merely as opinions and teaching, but as institutions and organisations with which the interests, the affections, and the habits of the multitude are inextricably interwoven. No undiscovered laws accounting for small phenomena going forward under drawing-room tables are likely to affect the tremendous facts of the increase of population, the rejection of convicts by our colonies, the exhaustion of the soil by cotton plantations, which urge even upon the foolish certain questions, certain claims, certain views concerning the scheme of the world, that can never again be silenced. If right reason is a right representation of the co-existences and sequences of things, here are co-existences and sequences that do not wait to be discovered, but press themselves upon us like bars of iron. No séances at a guinea a head for the sake of being pinched by "Mary Jane" can annihilate railways, steam-ships, and electric telegraphs, which are demonstrating the inter-dependence of all human interests, and making self-interest a duct for sympathy. These things are part of the external Reason to which internal silliness has inevitably to accommodate itself.

Three points in the history of magic and witchcraft are well brought out by Mr. Lecky. First, that the cruelties connected with it did not begin until men's minds had ceased to repose implicitly in a sacramental system which made them feel well armed against evil spirits; that is, until the eleventh century, when there came a sort of morning dream of doubt and heresy, bringing on the one side the terror of timid consciences, and on the other the terrorism of authority or zeal bent on checking the rising struggle. In that time of comparative mental repose, says Mr. Lecky—

"All those conceptions of diabolical presence; all that predisposition towards the miraculous, which acted so fearfully upon the imaginations of the fifteenth and sixteenth centuries, existed; but the implicit faith, the boundless and triumphant credulity with which the virtue of ecclesiastical rites was accepted, rendered them comparatively innocuous. If men had been a little less superstitious, the effects of their superstition would have been much more terrible. It was firmly believed that any one who deviated from the strict line of orthodoxy must soon succumb beneath the power of Satan; but as there was no spirit of rebellion or doubt, this persuasion did not produce any extraordinary terrorism."

The Church was disposed to confound heretical opinion with sorcery; false doctrine was especially the devil's work, and it was a ready conclusion that a denier or innovator had held consultation with the father of lies. It is a saying of a zealous Catholic in the sixteenth century, quoted by Maury in his excellent work, "De la Magie"—"*Crescit cum magia hæresis, cum hæresi magia.*" Even those who doubted were terrified at their doubts, for trust is more easily undermined than terror. Fear is earlier born than hope, lays a stronger grasp on man's system than any other passion, and remains master of a larger group of involuntary actions. A chief aspect of man's moral development is the slow subduing of fear by the gradual growth of intelligence, and its suppression as a motive by the presence of impulses less animally selfish; so that in relation to invisible Power, fear at last ceases to exist, save in that interfusion with higher faculties which we call awe.

Secondly, Mr. Lecky shows clearly that dogmatic Protestantism, holding the vivid belief in Satanic agency to be an essential of piety, would have felt it shame to be a whit behind Catholicism in severity against the devil's servants. Luther's sentiment was that he would not suffer a witch to live (he was not much more merciful to Jews); and, in spite of his fondness for children, believing a certain child to have been begotten by the devil, he recommended the parents to throw it into the river. The torch must be turned on the worst errors of heroic minds—not in irreverent ingratitude, but for the sake of measuring our vast and various debt to all the influences which have concurred, in the intervening ages, to make us recognise as detestable errors the honest convictions of men who, in mere individual capacity and moral force, were very much above us. Again, the

Scotch Puritans, during the comparatively short period of their ascendency, surpassed all Christians before them in the elaborate ingenuity of the tortures they applied for the discovery of witchcraft and sorcery, and did their utmost to prove that if Scotch Calvinism was the true religion, the chief "note" of the true religion was cruelty. It is hardly an endurable task to read the story of their doings; thoroughly to imagine them as a past reality is already a sort of torture. One detail is enough, and it is a comparatively mild one. It was the regular profession of men called "prickers" to thrust long pins into the body of a suspected witch in order to detect the insensible spot which was the infallible sign of her guilt. On a superficial view one would be in danger of saying that the main difference between the teachers who sanctioned these things and the much-despised ancestors who offered human victims inside a huge wicker idol, was that they arrived at a more elaborate barbarity by a longer series of dependent propositions. We do not share Mr. Buckle's opinion that a Scotch minister's groans were a part of his deliberate plan for keeping the people in a state of terrified subjection; the ministers themselves held the belief they taught, and might well groan over it. What a blessing has a little false logic been to the world! Seeing that men are so slow to question their premises, they must have made each other much more miserable, if pity had not sometimes drawn tender conclusions not warranted by Major and Minor; if there had not been people with an amiable imbecility of reasoning which enabled them at once to cling to hideous beliefs, and to be conscientiously inconsistent with them in their conduct. There is nothing like acute deductive reasoning for keeping a man in the dark: it might be called the *technique* of the intellect, and the concentration of the mind upon it corresponds to that predominance of technical skill in art which ends in degradation of the artist's function, unless new inspiration and invention come to guide it.

And of this there is some good illustration furnished by that third node in the history of witchcraft, the beginning of its end, which is treated in an interesting manner by Mr. Lecky. It is worth noticing, that the most important defences of the belief in witchcraft, against the growing scepticism in the latter part of the sixteenth century and in the seventeenth, were the productions of men who in some departments were among the foremost thinkers of their time. One of them was Jean Bodin, the famous writer on government and jurisprudence, whose "Republic," Hallam thinks, had an important influence in England, and furnished "a store of arguments and examples that were not lost on the thoughtful minds of our countrymen." In some of his views he was original and bold; for example, he anticipated Montesquieu in attempting to appreciate the relations of government and climate. Hallam inclines to the opinion that he was a Jew, and attached Divine authority only to the Old Testament. But this was enough to furnish him with his chief data for the existence of witches and for their capital punishment; and in the account of his "Republic" given by Hallam, there is enough evidence that the sagacity which often enabled him to make fine use of his learning was also often entangled in it, to temper our surprise at finding a writer on political science of whom it could be said that, along with Montesquieu, he was "the most philosophical of those who had read so deeply, the most learned of those who had thought so much," in the van of the forlorn hope to maintain the reality of witchcraft. It should be said that he was equally confident of the unreality of the Copernican hypothesis, on the ground that it was contrary to the tenets of the theologians and philosophers and to common sense, and therefore subversive of the foundations of every science. Of his work on witchcraft, Mr. Lecky says:—

"The 'Démonomanie des Sorciers' is chiefly an appeal to authority, which the author deemed on this subject so unanimous and so conclusive, that it was scarcely possible for any sane man to resist it. He appealed to the popular belief in all countries, in all ages, and in all religions. He cited the opinions of an immense multitude of the greatest writers of pagan antiquity, and of the most illustrious of the Fathers. He showed how the laws of all nations recognised the existence of witchcraft; and he collected hundreds of cases which had been investigated before the tribunals of his own or of other countries. He relates with the most minute and circumstantial detail, and with the most unfaltering confidence, all the proceedings at the witches' Sabbath, the methods which the witches employed in transporting themselves through the air, their transformations, their carnal intercourse with the Devil, their various means of injuring their enemies, the signs that lead to their detection, their confessions when condemned, and their demeanour at the stake."

Something must be allowed for a lawyer's affection towards a belief which had furnished so many "cases." Bodin's work had been immediately prompted by the treatise "De Prestigiis Dæmonum," written by John Wier, a German physician, a treatise which is worth notice as an example of a transitional form of opinion for which many analogies may be found in the history both of religion and science. Wier believed in demons, and in possession by demons, but his practice as a physician had convinced him that the so-called witches were patients and victims, that the devil took advantage of their diseased condition to delude them, and that there was no consent of an evil will on the part of the women. He argued that the word in Leviticus translated "witch" meant "poisoner," and besought the princes of Europe to hinder the further spilling of innocent blood. These heresies of Wier threw Bodin into such a state of amazed indignation that if he had been an ancient Jew instead of a modern economical one, he would have rent his garments. "No one had ever heard of pardon being accorded to sorcerers;" and probably the reason why Charles IX. died young was because he had pardoned the sorcerer, Trois Echelles! We must remember that this was in 1581, when the great scientific movement of the Renaissance had hardly begun—when Galileo was a youth of seventeen, and Kepler a boy of ten.

But directly afterwards, on the other side, came Montaigne, whose sceptical acuteness could arrive at negatives without any apparatus of method. A certain keen narrowness of nature will secure a man from many absurd beliefs which the larger soul, vibrating to more manifold influences, would have a long struggle to part with. And so we find the charming, chatty Montaigne—in one of the brightest of his essays, "Des Boiteux," where he declares that, from his own observation of witches and sorcerers, he should have recommended them to be treated with curative hellebore—stating in his own way a pregnant doctrine, since taught more gravely. It seems to him much less of a prodigy that men should lie, or that their imaginations should deceive them, than that a human body should be carried through the air on a broomstick, or up a chimney by some unknown spirit. He thinks it a sad bus'ness to persuade oneself that the test of truth lies in the multitude of believers—"en une presse où les fols surpassent de tant les sages en nombre." Ordinarily, he has observed, when men have something stated to them as a fact, they are more ready to explain it than to inquire whether it is real: "ils passent par-dessus les propositions, mais ils examinent les conséquences; *ils laissent les choses, et courent aux causes.*" There is a sort of strong and generous ignorance which is as honourable and courageous as science—"ignorance pour laquelle concevoir il n'y a pas moins de science qu'à concevoir la science." And *à propos* of the immense traditional evidence which weighed with such men as Bodin, he says —"As for the proofs and arguments founded on experience and facts, I do not pretend to unravel these. What end of a thread is there to lay hold of? I often cut them as Alexander did his knot. *Après tout, c'est mettre ses conjectures à bien haut prix, que d'en faire cuire un homme tout vif.*"

Writing like this, when it finds eager readers, is a sign that the weather is changing; yet much later, namely, after 1665, when the Royal Society had been founded, our own Glanvil, the author of the "Scepsis Scientifica," a work that was a remarkable advance towards a true definition of the limits of inquiry, and that won him his election as fellow of the society, published an energetic vindication of the belief in witchcraft, of which Mr. Lecky gives the following sketch:—

"The 'Sadducismus Triumphatus,' which is probably the ablest book ever published in defence of the superstition, opens with a striking picture of the rapid progress of the scepticism in England. Everywhere, a disbelief in witchcraft was becoming fashionable in the upper classes; but it was a disbelief that arose entirely from a strong sense of its antecedent improbability. All who were opposed to the orthodox faith united in discrediting witchcraft. They laughed at it, as palpably absurd, as involving the most grotesque and ludicrous conceptions, as so essentially incredible that it would be a waste of time to examine it. This spirit had arisen since the Restoration, although the laws were still in force, and although little or no direct reasoning had been brought to bear upon the subject. In order to combat it, Glanvil proceeded to examine the general question of the credibility of the miraculous. He saw that the reason why witchcraft was ridiculed was, because it was a phase of the miraculous and the work of the devil; that the scepticism was chiefly due to those who disbelieved in miracles and the devil; and that the instances of witchcraft or possession in the Bible were invariably placed on a level with those that were tried in the law courts of England. That the evidence of the belief was overwhelming, he firmly believed; and this, indeed, was scarcely disputed; but, until the sense of *à priori* improbability was removed, no possible accumulation of facts would cause men to believe it. To that task he accordingly addressed himself. Anticipating the idea and almost the words of modern controversialists, he urged that there was such a thing as a credulity of unbelief; and that those who believed so strange a concurrence of delusions, as was necessary on the supposition of the unreality of witchcraft, were far more credulous than those who accepted the belief. He made his very scepticism his principal weapon; and, analysing with much acuteness the *à priori* objections, he showed that they rested upon an unwarrantable confidence in our knowledge of the laws of the spirit world; that they implied the existence of some strict analogy between the faculties of men and of spirits; and that, as such analogy most probably did not exist, no reasoning based on the supposition could dispense men from examining the evidence. He concluded with a large collection of cases, the evidence of which was, as he thought, incontestible."

We have quoted this sketch because Glanvil's argument against the *à priori* objection of absurdity is fatiguingly urged in relation to other alleged marvels which, to busy people seriously occupied with the difficulties of affairs, of science, or of art, seem as little worthy of examination as aëronautic broomsticks. And also because we here see Glanvil, in combating an incredulity that does not happen to be his own, wielding that very argument of traditional evidence which he had made the subject of vigorous attack in his "Scepsis Scientifica." But perhaps large minds have been peculiarly liable to this fluctuation concerning the sphere of tradition, because, while they have attacked its misapplications, they have been the more solicited by the vague sense that tradition is really the basis of our best life. Our sentiments may be called organised traditions; and a large part of our actions gather all their justification, all their attraction and aroma, from the memory of the life lived, of the actions done, before we were born. In the absence of any profound research into psychological functions or into the mysteries of inheritance, in the absence of any comprehensive view of man's historical development and the dependence of one age on another, a mind at all rich in sensibilities must always have had an indefinite uneasiness in an undistinguishing attack on the coercive influence of tradition. And this may be the apology for the apparent inconsistency of Glanvil's acute criticism on the one side, and his indignation at the "looser gentry," who laughed at the evidences for witchcraft, on the other. We have already taken up too much space with this subject of witchcraft, else we should be tempted to dwell on Sir Thomas Browne, who far surpassed Glanvil in magnificent incongruity of opinion, and whose works are the most remarkable combination existing, of witty sarcasm against ancient nonsense and modern obsequiousness, with indications of a capacious credulity. After all, we may be sharing what seems to us the hardness of these men, who sat in their studies and argued at their ease about a belief that would be reckoned to have caused more misery and bloodshed than any other superstition, if there had been no such thing as persecution on the ground of religious opinion.

On this subject of Persecution, Mr. Lecky writes his best: with clearness of conception, with calm justice, bent on appreciating the necessary tendency of ideas, and with an appropriateness of illustration that could be supplied only by extensive and intelligent reading. Persecution, he shows, is not in any sense peculiar to the Catholic Church; it is a direct sequence of the doctrines that salvation is to be had only within the Church, and that erroneous belief is damnatory—doctrines held as fully by Protestant sects as by the Catholics; and in proportion to its power, Protestantism has been as persecuting as Catholicism. He maintains, in opposition to the favourite modern notion of persecution defeating its own object, that the Church, holding the dogma of exclusive salvation, was perfectly consequent, and really achieved its end of spreading one belief and quenching another, by calling in the aid of the civil arm. Who will say that governments, by their power over institutions and patronage, as well as over punishment, have not power also over the interests and inclinations of men, and over most of those external conditions into which subjects are born, and which make them adopt the prevalent belief as a second nature? Hence, to a sincere believer in the doctrine of exclusive salvation, governments had it in their power to save men from perdition; and wherever the clergy were at the elbow of the civil arm, no matter whether they were Catholic or Protestant, persecution was the result. "Compel them to come in" was a rule that seemed sanctioned by mercy, and the horrible sufferings it led men to inflict seemed small to minds accustomed to contemplate, as a perpetual source of motive, the eternal unmitigated miseries of a hell that was the inevitable destination of a majority amongst mankind.

It is a significant fact, noted by Mr. Lecky, that the only two leaders of the Reformation who advocated tolerance were Zuinglius and Socinus, both of them disbelievers in exclusive salvation. And in corroboration of other evidence that the chief triumphs of the Reformation were due to coercion, he commends to the special attention of his readers the following quotation from a work attributed without question to the famous Protestant theologian, Jurieu, who had himself been hindered, as a Protestant, from exercising his professional functions in France, and was settled as pastor at Rotterdam. It should be remembered that Jurieu's labours fell in the latter part of the seventeenth century and in the beginning of the eighteenth, and that he was the contemporary of Bayle, with whom he was in bitter controversial hostility. He wrote, then, at a time when there was warm debate on the question of Toleration; and it was his great object to vindicate himself and his French fellow-Protestants from all laxity on this point.

"Peut on nier que le paganisme est tombé dans le monde par l'autorité des empereurs Romains? On peut assurer sans temerité que le paganisme seroit encore debout, et que les trois quarts de l'Europe seroient encore payens si Constantin et ses successeurs n'avaient employé leur autorité pour l'abolir. Mais, je vous prie, de quelles voies Dieu s'est il servi dans ces derniers siècles pour rétablir la veritable religion dans l'Occident? *Les rois de Suède, ceux de Danemarck, ceux d'Angleterre, les magistrats souverains de Suisse, des Païs Bas, des villes libres d'Allemagne, les princes électeurs, et autres princes souverains de l'empire, n'ont ils pas employé leur autorité pour abbattre le Papisme?*"

Indeed, wherever the tremendous alternative of everlasting torments is believed in—believed in so that it becomes a motive determining the life—not only persecution, but every other form of severity and gloom are the legitimate consequences. There is much ready declamation in these days against the spirit of asceticism and against zeal for doctrinal conversion; but surely the macerated form of a Saint Francis, the fierce denunciations of a Saint Dominic, the groans and prayerful wrestlings of the Puritan who seasoned his bread with tears and made all pleasurable sensation sin, are more in keeping with the contemplation of unending anguish as the destiny of a vast multitude whose nature we share, than the rubicund cheerfulness of some modern divines, who profess to unite a smiling liberalism with a well-bred and tacit but unshaken confidence in the reality of the bottomless pit. But, in fact, as Mr. Lecky maintains, that awful image, with its group of associated dogmas concerning the inherited curse, and the damnation of unbaptised infants, of heathens, and of heretics, has passed away from what he is fond of calling "the realisations" of Christendom. These things are no longer the objects of practical belief. They may be mourned for in encyclical letters; bishops may regret them; doctors of divinity may sign testimonials to the excellent character of these decayed beliefs; but for the mass of Christians they are no more influential than unrepealed but forgotten statutes. And with these dogmas has melted away the strong basis for the defence of persecution. No man now writes eager vindications of himself and his colleagues from the suspicion of adhering to the principle of toleration. And this momentous change, it is Mr. Lecky's object to show, is due to that concurrence of conditions which he has chosen to call "the advance of the Spirit of Rationalism."

In other parts of his work, where he attempts to trace the action of the same conditions on the acceptance of miracles and on other chief phases of our historical development, Mr. Lecky has laid himself open to considerable criticism. The chapters on the Miracles of the Church, the æsthetic, scientific, and moral Development of Rationalism, the Secularisation of Politics, and the Industrial history of Rationalism, embrace a wide range of diligently gathered facts; but they are nowhere illuminated by a sufficiently clear conception and statement of the agencies at work, or the mode of their action, in the gradual modification of opinion and of life. The writer frequently impresses us as being in a state of hesitation concerning his own standing-point, which may form a desirable stage in private meditation but not in published exposition. Certain epochs in theoretic conception, certain considerations, which should be fundamental to his survey, are introduced quite incidentally in a sentence or two, or in a note which seems to be an after-thought. Great writers and their ideas are touched upon too slightly and with too little discrimination, and important theories are sometimes characterised with a rashness which conscientious revision will correct. There is a fatiguing use of vague or shifting phrases, such as "modern civilisation," "spirit of the age," "tone of thought," "intellectual type of the age," "bias of the imagination," "habits of religious thought," unbalanced by any precise definition; and the spirit of rationalism is sometimes treated of as if it lay outside the specific mental activities of which it is a generalised expression. Mr. Curdle's famous definition of the dramatic unities as "a sort of a general oneness," is not totally false; but such luminousness as it has could only be perceived by those who already knew what the unities were. Mr. Lecky has the advantage of being strongly impressed with the great part played by the emotions in the formation of opinion, and with the high complexity of the causes at work in social evolution; but he frequently writes as if he had never yet distinguished between the complexity of the conditions that produce prevalent states of mind, and the inability of particular minds to give distinct reasons for the preferences or persuasions produced by those states. In brief, he does not discriminate, or does not help his reader to discriminate, between objective complexity and subjective confusion. But the most muddle-headed gentleman who represents the spirit of the age by observing, as he settles his collar, that the development-theory is quite "the thing" is a result of definite processes, if we could only trace them. "Mental attitudes," and "predispositions," however vague in consciousness, have not vague causes, any more than the "blind motions of the spring" in plants and animals.

The word "Rationalism" has the misfortune, shared by most words in this grey world, of being somewhat equivocal. This evil may be nearly overcome by careful preliminary definition; but Mr. Lecky does not supply this, and the original specific application of the word to a particular phase of Biblical interpretation seems to have clung about his use of it with a misleading effect. Through some parts of his book he appears to regard the grand characteristic of modern thought and civilisation, compared with ancient, as a radiation in the first instance from a change in religious conceptions. The supremely important fact, that the gradual reduction of all phenomena within the sphere of established law, which carries us a consequence the rejection of the miraculous, has its determining current in the development of physical science, seems to have engaged comparatively little of his attention; at least, he gives it no prominence. The great conception of universal regular sequence, without partiality and without caprice—the conception which is the most potent force at work in the modification of our faith, and of the practical form given to our sentiments—could only grow out of that patient watching of external fact, and that silencing of preconceived notions, which are urged upon the mind by the problems of physical science.

There is not room here to explain and justify the impressions of dissatisfaction which have been briefly indicated, but a serious writer like Mr. Lecky will not find such suggestions altogether useless. The objections, even the misunderstandings, of a reader who is not careless or ill-disposed, may serve to stimulate an author's vigilance over his thoughts as well as his style. It would be gratifying to see some future proof that Mr. Lecky has acquired juster views than are implied in the assertion that philosophers of the sensational school "can never rise to the conception of the disinterested;" and that he has freed himself from all temptation to that mingled laxity of statement, and ill-pitched elevation of tone, which are painfully present in the closing pages of his second volume.

GEORGE ELIOT.

PERSONAL RECOLLECTIONS OF PRESIDENT LINCOLN.

THERE would seem to be some deep foundation in nature for the ancient custom which sacrificed a victim's blood at the inauguration of any public project. On that Good Friday when President Lincoln called together his Cabinet—when the Confederate capital and the army which had defended it lay at his feet, and the flag of the United States was being formally raised over the fort from which it was first struck down—it was really to lay the foundation of a new nation. And scarcely had he uttered, at this meeting, his resolution that his conquered foes should not be the victims at the beginning of the vast work of construction, ere Fate decrees that nothing less costly than the blood of his own brave heart can consecrate his country's tremendous task.

"Gentlemen of the jury," said the aged chancellor, dying, "the case is now closed. You may retire and bring in your verdict." On the career of the American President, so cruelly closed, the world became a jury, and returned a spontaneous verdict. Only from a right and true man could extend those influences and impressions, so deep and far, which, wherever the fearful tidings could be flashed, were startled into the utterances of lamentation and admiration which even rose above those of amazement and horror. Amid the roar of strife in America, the attentive world had heard the heart-beat of an honest man, and had come to rest upon him its hope for the future of that country in which all are so largely concerned.

It has been my lot to be amongst those Americans who have been, in some degree, politically alienated from the President on account of what they considered his dangerous hesitation to hurl slavery, utterly and for ever, into the pit which it had digged for the Union; and to me this lot has been very painful, because I had rarely seen and known a man whom I could more admire personally.

In June, 1856, when the Republican Convention that nominated Mr. Fremont for the Presidency, was holding its sessions in the city of Philadelphia, there were counted out, on the nominating vote for a candidate for the Vice-presidency, 110 votes for Abraham Lincoln. Mr. Dayton, of New Jersey, late Minister at Paris, was nominated, having received 259; but the large vote for a man whose name comparatively few of the delegates had ever heard, excited attention, and I remember well the surprise with which the question was whispered from seat to seat, "Who is Abraham Lincoln?" "He is one of our Western men," said a delegate, "of whom you are likely to know more one of these days." About two years after this (1858) Mr. Lincoln was indeed brought very prominently before the country.

Those two years had been crowded with portentous events. Slavery, then dominant at Washington, had, in 1853, swept away what was known as the Missouri Compromise, by which a line had been agreed upon, with reference to the territories of the West, north of which slavery could not go. The object of the abolition of this line was the advancement of the "peculiar institution" of the South into that vast portion of the territory, wrested from Mexico by a Southern president, known as Kansas. As the result of the destruction of this compromise emigrants from the North and from the South had poured into Kansas, and that territory had become the theatre of civil war. The man who had introduced the Act abolishing the Missouri Compromise, and who had chiefly secured its adoption, was Mr. S. A. Douglass, a senator from Illinois. When, in 1858, this senator was put forward by his party for re-election, the Republicans resolved to confront him with Abraham Lincoln, who contested his seat on the absorbing issue of the prohibition of slavery in territories by Congress. Illinois thus became the arena of a close political conflict; and, as it involved the one question at issue in the States, the eyes of the nation were fixed upon the contestants. Mr. Lincoln's antagonist, Judge Douglass, was a man who had long been known in the country as a master in debate. The impression which his speeches (the few that I heard) made upon my own mind was that of vigour, of various talent, and of consummate ability in detecting the weak points of his antagonist, and covering up his own. Mr. Douglass was re-elected by a majority of eight in this contest, which was preliminary to the great presidential campaign in which he suffered a defeat under which he seemed to sink, and soon after which he died.

It was during this memorable political struggle, which presently led the champions to address public meetings far beyond the limits of their State, that I first saw and heard Abraham Lincoln. It was at Cincinnati, in the State of Ohio, an important point as being at the very centre of the country, and on the line separating the free from the slave states. Across the Ohio river, narrower than the Thames, rise the hills of Kentucky, and one may (or *could*) stand in the streets of Cincinnati and see slaves at their work. From the towns of Newport and Covington, on the Kentucky side, hundreds of persons were in the habit of coming to the political meetings of the city, or to witness the performances of their favourite actors, among whom may have been Wilkes Booth.[1] To the great delight of the Kentuckians, and of the Democracy, so-called, Mr. Douglass had delivered a public address there advocating what he used to call his "gur-reat per-

---

(1) I once saw this man on the stage in Cincinnati, and a worse actor, and a face into which more vile passions were distilled, I have not often seen; "aber," as Schiller said of a somewhat similar case, "aber durch welche hand or auch mag gefallen seyn, so muss uns dieses ausserordentliche Schicksal als eine That der grossen Natur erscheinen."

rinciple" that the newborn territories should be allowed to arrange their own institutions—and especially to introduce or exclude slavery—as freely as full-grown States. Mr. Lincoln was soon after invited to the city. The meeting was in a large public square, and two or three thousands of persons were present, possibly more, to hear this new man. Party feeling was running very high, and there were adverse parties in the crowd who had come with the intention of disturbing the meeting. Mr. Lincoln appeared on a balcony in the clear moonlight, and without paying the slightest attention to the perturbations of the multitude, began his address. I had at first paused on the skirts of the crowd, meaning to leave soon; but an indefinable something in the tones of the man's voice induced me to go closer. Surely if there were to be chosen a figure-head for America it must be this! There was something undeniably grotesque about the face, and yet not a coarse line; it was battered and bronzed, but the light of an eye, both gentle and fiery, kept it from being hard. The nose was a good strong buttress—such as Bonaparte would have valued—to a solid brow; and the forehead rose to its greatest height in the region assigned to the benevolent and the conscientious organs, declining along those of firmness and self-esteem into what I should call a decidedly feeble occiput. But never was there a case in which the sage's request—" Speak, that I may see you "—had more need to be repeated; for a voice more flexible, more attuned to every kind of expression, and to carry truth in every tone, was never allotted to mortal. Although he seemed to me oddly different from any other man whom I had seen, he seemed also related to them all, and to have lineaments characteristic of every section of the country; and this is why I thought he might well be taken as its figure-head. His manner of speaking in public was simple, direct, and almost religious; he was occasionally humorous, but rarely told anecdotes as he did in private conversation; and there was no sarcasm, no showing of the teeth. I had not listened to him long, on the occasion to which I refer, before I perceived that there was a certain artistic ability in him as a public speaker, which his audience would least recognise when it was most employed. Early in the address some adverse allusion to slavery brought a surge of hisses, but when it broke at his feet, there was the play of a faint smile on his face as he gathered from it the important knowledge of the exact proportion of Kentucky which he had to deal with on the occasion. I have often wondered that Mr. Lincoln's power as an orator—surpassed as it is by that of only one other American—is so little known or thought of in Europe; and I have even found the impression that he was, as a speaker, awkward, heavy, and ungrammatical. It is a singular misjudgment. For terse, well-pronounced, clear speech; for a careful and easy selection of the fit word for the right place; for perfect tones; for quiet, chaste, and dignified manner,—it would be hard to find the late President's superior. | In those days it was, when slavery was concerned, " a kind of good deed to say well," and sufficiently proved the man who, when the public meeting must give way to the camp,

"With his deed did crown
His word upon you."

He had said with an emphasis which made the proposition seem novel, "Slavery is WRONG!"—then came the hiss. After a moment's pause he continued—each word driven through and clenched—"I acknowledge that you must maintain your opposition just there, if at all. But I find that every man comes into the world with a mouth to be fed and a back to be clothed; that each has also two hands; and I infer that those hands were meant to feed that mouth and to clothe that back. And I warn you, Kentuckians, that whatever institution would fetter those hands from so doing, violates that justice which is the only political wisdom, and is sure to crumble around those who seek to uphold it. This is the constant testimony of the men who founded this Republic. It was this that made Jefferson tremble for his country when he remembered that God is just; and this that made your own great statesman, Henry Clay, pray that his tongue might cleave to the roof of his mouth ere it voted to carry slavery into any territory where it did not exist. Your hisses will not blow down the walls of Justice. Slavery is wrong: the denial of that truth has brought on the angry conflict of brother with brother; it has kindled the fires of civil war in Kansas; it has raised the portents that overhang the future of our nation. And be you sure that no compromise, no political arrangement with slavery will ever last which does not deal with it as A GREAT WRONG." The Kentuckians had no sibilant arguments to bring forward now. How much more serious Mr. Lincoln was than the mass of his party in these views may be estimated by the fact, that when his speeches, with those of Judge Douglass, were afterwards collected for circulation as a campaign document, it was thought prudent to omit the above passage, which I noted down at the time, and probably others of similar import.

The next time that Mr. Lincoln passed through that city it was as the newly-elected President, on his way to take his place as the first Republican President at the Capitol. The ovation was great. Arches of evergreen spanned the streets; the banners of German, Italian, Irish, and Polish societies, so largely represented there, mingled with the stars and stripes; and the streets were lettered with mottoes in every language. When the procession ended, and the President had made his last bow, and turned to enter his hotel, his eyes were filled with tears. The Southern States had already seceded; the city of

Washington, to which he was journeying, was already the arena of angry disputes; and many, it was feared a majority, of the North were already faltering out that a fresh compromise should be offered to Slavery to save the Union. How comfortable to him as an occupant of the presidential mansion, what a relief from the terrible alternative of strife, such a compromise would have been, may be easily understood. But now, while on his way to Washington, he answered those who sought his opinion on this point: "I will suffer death before I will consent or advise my friends to consent to any concession or compromise, which looks like buying the privilege of taking possession of the Government to which we have a constitutional right; because, whatever I might think of the merit of the various propositions before Congress, I should regard any concession, in the face of menace, as the destruction of the government itself, and a consent on all hands that our system shall be brought down to a level with the existing disorganised state of affairs in Mexico. But this thing will hereafter be, as it is now, in the hands of the people; and if they desire to call a Convention to remove any grievances complained of, or to give any guarantees for the permanence of vested rights, it is not mine to oppose." These are his own careful words. As soon as they became known the plan was laid to assassinate him in Baltimore, a fate which he only escaped by passing through that city in disguise.

A friend of mine who was with Mr. Lincoln when he bade adieu to his townsmen in Springfield, where he was universally beloved, and also when he was inaugurated, told me that the two scenes would ever stand in his memory apart as instances of pathos and of moral sublimity. There was a deep hush and a profound emotion in the vast crowd, many of which were angry Southerners, when he made the closing appeal of his inaugural address from the steps of the Capitol. He said, "In your hands, my dissatisfied fellow-citizens, and not in mine is the momentous issue of civil war. The government will not assail you. You can have no conflict without being yourselves the aggressors. You have no oath registered in heaven to destroy the government, while I shall have the most solemn one to 'preserve, protect, and defend' it. I am loth to close. We are not enemies, but friends. We must not be enemies. Though passion may have strained, it must not break our bonds of affection. The mystic chords of memory, stretching from every battlefield and patriot grave to every living heart and hearthstone, all over this broad land, will yet swell the chorus of the Union, when again touched, as they surely will be, by the better angels of our nature."

But the passions of the South were untameable by any persuasions. The one point demanded—that slavery should have equal admission into the territories with freedom—was precisely the one which the President, elected upon that specific issue, would not concede, and the civil war broke out. Early in the war I had the opportunity of a private interview with the President. The hour of eight in the morning was named by him, and I found that even that was not early enough for his work to begin. In the ante-room was a young woman with her child, whose plea the President would hear. Sad and tearful when she presently entered his room, she was radiant enough on her return, and doubtless some poor prisoner was set free that day to return home. My friend and I were also there to plead for prisoners; believing that the hour had come when slavery had earned the right to perish by the sword which it had taken, we came to implore the President to be our deliverer from this fearful demon that had so long harried the land and poisoned life for all who loved their country or justice. The President listened very patiently, and gave us his views fully. The words which remain now most deeply fixed in my memory are these:—"We grow in this direction daily; and I am not without hope that some great thing is to be accomplished. When the hour comes for dealing with slavery I trust I shall be willing to act though it costs my life; and, gentlemen," he added, with a sad smile and a solemn tone, "*lives will be lost.*"

Throughout the conversation the President spoke with profound feeling of the Southerners, who, he said, had become at an early day, when there was at least a feeble conscience against slavery, deeply involved commercially and socially with the institution; he pitied them heartily, all the more that it had corrupted them; and he earnestly advised us to use what influence we might have to impress on the people the feeling that they should be ready and eager to share largely the pecuniary losses to which the South would be subjected if emancipation should occur. It was, he said, the disease of the entire nation, and all must share the suffering of its removal. It was entirely through this urgency of Mr. Lincoln to all whom he met, that all the slaves in the district of Columbia were paid for when liberated (though many thought the slave himself was the real owner to be paid), and a full price offered by Congress to all Slave States that would, even gradually, emancipate their slaves.

Mr. Lincoln answered well Frederick the Great's definition of a prince—"the first of subjects." His confidence in the people was as simple and unhesitating as his loyalty to them was perfect. He believed that there was under all parties a substratum of patriotism; and I never saw his eye shine more than when some one told of a town in Ohio where, up to the time of the war, two party-flags had been flying, and whose inhabitants, when they heard of the attack upon Fort Sumter, cut down the two poles with their flags, and making the two into one, hoisted it with the stars and stripes alone at its head. I believe there is but one instance of the President's losing his temper. Many of the Northern people were scandalised that Kentucky should, in the beginning of the war, declare herself neutral in the contest; and also that, in dealing with slavery, the opinion of that State should be so much consulted by the President. On one occasion, when a senator of very decided opinions was in consultation with the chief magistrate, the latter said, concerning some proposition, "But will Kentucky stand that?" "Damn Kentucky!" exclaimed the senator. "Then damn *you?*" cried Mr. Lincoln with warmth. But, much as he loved his native state, there were points on which he would "put his foot down," even to her. A Kentuckian wishing some governmental aid in recovering his slaves, escaped and escaping, "reminded him," he said, "of a little story. When I was going down the Ohio once on a steamer, a little boy came up to the captain, and said, 'Captain, please stop the boat a little while; I've lost my apple overboard!'"

Mr. Lincoln had much more fortitude than heroism in his temperament, and his slow, gradual political methods seemed at times, when martial law was alone possible, like trying to fire off a gun a little at a time. He invited popular criticism as a means of knowing what measures, especially relating to slavery, the country was "up to;" and no man was ever less spared. Many of the abolitionists criticised him fiercely, for he represented a policy which they had reason to fear would close up the war power before it had crushed the source of the national troubles. The President was generally patient under these criticisms, which he knew were not made in the spirit of personal antagonism. The nearest approach to a complaint I ever heard him utter was to Wendell Phillips and some others, from Boston. "I fear," he said, "that some of the severity with which this administration is criticised, results from the fact that so many of us have had so long to act with minorities that we have got an uncontrollable *habit* of criticising." This was said with an unfeigned humility, and the feeling of all present was fitly expressed by Mr. Phillips, who promptly declared to the President that he knew no one who would prefer any man for the next presidential term to Abraham Lincoln, provided it were certain that the work of emancipation was to be firmly prosecuted. "Oh, Mr. Phillips," exclaimed the President, with a childlike simplicity, "if I have ever indulged *that* hope, and I do not say I have not, it has long ago been beaten out of me." He went to hear that greatest of American orators (Mr. Phillips) at the Smithsonian Institute, and sat calmly to hear the severe review of his own policy. A letter which he wrote to the editors of the *North American Review*, which has not before been published, I believe, in England, is characteristic of his temper. That *Review* had published an article entitled "The President's Policy," containing the following paragraph:—

"Even so long ago as when Mr. Lincoln, not yet convinced of the danger and magnitude of the crisis, was endeavouring to persuade himself of Union majorities at the South, and to carry on a war that was half peace, in hope of a peace that would have been all war, while he was still enforcing the fugitive slave law, under some theory that secession, however it might absolve States from their obligations, could not escheat them of their claims under the constitution, and that slaveholders in rebellion had alone, among mortals, the privilege of having their cake and eating it at the same time—the enemies of free government were striving to persuade the people that the war was an abolition crusade."

To this Mr. Lincoln responded, under date of January, 16, 1864, as follows :—

"GENTLEMEN :

"The number for this year and month of the *North American Review* was duly received, and for it please accept my thanks. Of course I am not the most impartial judge, yet, with due allowance for this, I venture to hope that the article entitled 'The President's Policy' will be of value to the country. I fear I am not quite worthy of all which is therein kindly said of me personally.

"The sentence of twelve lines commencing at the top of page 252 I could wish to be not exactly as it is. In what is there expressed the writer has not correctly understood me. I have never had a theory that secession could absolve States or people from their obligations. Precisely the opposite is asserted in the inaugural address ; and it was because of my belief in the continuance of these obligations that I was puzzled, for a time, as to denying the legal rights of those citizens who remained individually innocent of treason or rebellion. But I mean no more now than to merely call attention to this point. "Yours respectfully,

"A. LINCOLN."

It is natural that in the presence of the grave, wherein questions of individual policy are buried, and on which traits of personal character bloom with fresh beauty, these critics of the President should be harshly judged. It should be remembered, however, that if the President had a heavy burden to bear, so had they who were set to watch the war in the special interest of emancipation. At one time Mr. Lincoln was proposing to send the negroes out of the country, at another to abolish slavery in the year 1900, at another to reconstruct States with a tenth of their former population, and that tenth made up exclusively of the lately disloyal whites, in whose rooted hatred of the Union his patriotic heart found it impossible to believe. But those words "for a time," in the letter to the *North American Review* indicate the fact that Mr. Lincoln grew as the people grew. An able writer has pronounced the truest judgment upon him in saying :

—"He became great—as such natures do become great—by the action of the ennobling duties of such a station, upon a mind honest, courageous, conscientious, and truthful."[1] Mr. Lincoln would be the last to be ungenerous to his reviewers. In a conversation with some western anti-slavery men, when I was present, he said, good-humouredly,—"Well, gentlemen, all I can say is, we shall want all the anti-slavery feeling in the country, and more; go home and screw the people up to it, and you may say anything you like about me, if that will help." There was, indeed, a time when the country was much excited against him, on account of the length of time in which he clung to a general about whose loyalty there were many doubts, but about whose incapacity and devotion to slavery there were none at all. Amongst the many protests which were uttered, some written by Rev. H. W. Beecher were of marked power, and very scathing. Some one clipped these from the *Independent*, in which they first appeared, and sent them to the President, who undertook, on a rainy Sunday, to read them; he had not, however, read very far before he became indignant, and leaping from his chair, exclaimed to some one present, "Am I a dog or a man?" Nevertheless the nation very soon began to realise the good effect of those articles which, in the great rush of war, had the fortune to be read.

If it should be supposed that President Lincoln, growing with his fellow-citizens, and representing them, was a mere sign of the popular breath, it would be an utter misjudgment. On a point of moral conviction he was immovable. When Major-General Fremont proclaimed universal emancipation in his military department of Missouri, the whole country was electrified, and there was scarcely a pulpit or press throughout the North which did not applaud the act, and scarcely a statesman or lawyer who did not regard it as a legitimate exercise of martial power; but the President did not believe it an indispensable military necessity, and consequently held it a violation of his oath to support the constitution to permit it. Profoundly mistaken in his interpretation of the constitution as we all believed him to be, his quiet firmness on this occasion commanded respect for a deed which, had it been done by a mean man, would have produced something approximating to a revolution in the North. But perhaps a more conspicuous instance of this fidelity to himself on the part of the President, is his action in the surrender of Mason and Slidell. It would be difficult for an Englishman to understand the peculiar trials of that case, the least part of which related to England. They can be appreciated only by those who know the history of that political party which, by its alliance with the anti-English prejudices of the Irish in America, and with the slavery interest, had so long ruled at Washington, and which, deprived of its Southern votes, was

(1) Historicus, in the *Times*, May 2.

now madly endeavouring to promote a reaction by raising a storm of popular feeling against England, and of wrath against the party in power for "truckling to England," a storm upon which it hoped to ride into power. The Republicans and their President knew that the accession of that party would be the restoration of slavery to supreme power in the nation. Some idea of the feeling among the Irish at the time may be conveyed by the following expression which I heard from a leading Irishman at a public dinner, given to an Irish colonel, in Ohio:—"Gentlemen," he said, "the opinions which are expressed throughout the country concerning this Trent affair afflict me deeply. I *did* hope that the hour for which we have so long prayed had arrived, and that we were to have a collision with England; but, alas! there seems reason to believe that the act of Wilkes is entirely legal, and that England will not object to it." Undoubtedly many of the foolish expressions among Republicans favourable to the capture were due more to a determination to diminish the party capital which the Democracy was making out of it, than to ignorance of the law, or hostility to England. Nevertheless, Mr. Lincoln had a hurricane to withstand. He was for a few days uncertain as to the law in the case; but there came to him a letter from an old friend in the far West, in whose legal knowledge he had complete faith—Hon. Thomas Ewing—which said simply—*In this affair of the Trent we are in the wrong.* And before any comment on the event had returned from England, the President had arrived at his decision, and was only considering how the surrender could be made with as little risk of a Democratic (pro-slavery) reaction as possible. These facts I have from one who was in intimate relation with the President during that affair.

Mr. Lincoln was a gentleman, he was incapable of rudeness; he was benevolent in small things; and he had humility. In manners and personal bearing he gave the impression of fine blood, which could speak through his cheeks on occasion; and when one looked upon his towering form, moving through the fashionable crowd at his receptions with awkward ease, he might well say—as the Yunani sage said of Zoroaster—"This form and this gait cannot lie, and nothing but truth can proceed from them." His conversational powers were extraordinary, and his wit, with a quaint and fresh way he had of illustrating his ideas, made it a delight to be in his society. The simple Theism, which I believe, without knowing a great deal about his religious opinions, to have been the substance of his faith, was real to him; and it is worthy of remark that all the religious deputations, representing all sects, which have crowded the President's house for four years have not prevailed to evoke any utterance from him savouring of cant or narrowness.

MONCURE D. CONWAY.

THE HEART AND THE BRAIN.

HEART and Brain are the two lords of life. In the metaphors of ordinary speech and in the stricter language of science, we use these terms to indicate two central powers, from which all motives radiate, to which all influences converge. They rule the moral and the physical life: the moral owes to them its continuous supply of feelings and ideas; the physical its continuous supply of food and stimulus. All the composite material which serves to build up the bodily fabric, and repair its daily waste, is only so much "carted material" awaiting the architect, until it has twice passed through the heart—until having been sent by the heart to the lungs it has there received its plastic virtues, and returns to the heart to be thence distributed throughout the organism. So much is familiar to every one; but less familiar is the fact that this transmission of the blood from heart to lungs, and its distribution throughout the organism, are rendered possible and made effective only under the influence of the brain. Life is sustained by Food and Stimulus. The operation of Nutrition itself is indissolubly connected with Sensibility. Life is a plexus of Nutrition and Sensation, the threads of which may ideally be separated, but which in reality are so interwoven as to be indissoluble. This is a paradox which even many physiologists will reject; but it is only a paradox because biological questions have constantly been regarded from a chemical point of view.

To render my proposition free from ambiguity, it is needful to premise that the term Heart, by a familiar device of rhetoric, here expresses the whole of that great circulatory apparatus of which it is only a part; and in like manner the term Brain here expresses the whole of the sensory apparatus. The reader knows perfectly well that in strict anatomical language the heart is only one organ having a definite function; and that the brain—although the term is used with considerable laxity—is only one portion of the complex nervous mechanism, having also its definite functions. But I am not here addressing anatomists, and for purposes of simplification I shall generally speak of the heart as if it were the whole of the vascular system, and of the brain as if it were the whole of the nervous system. And there is a philosophic truth suggested by this departure from the limitations of anatomical definition, namely, that if the brain as a nervous centre requires to be distinguished from all other nervous centres, it also requires to be affiliated on them: it has its special functions as an organ, but it has also a community of property—*i.e.* Sensibility—with all other nervous centres.

In the study of animal organisms, the scientific artifice called Analysis, which separates ideally what Nature has indissolubly united, isolating each portion of a complex whole to study it undisturbed by the influences of other portions, has established a division of Life into Animal and Vegetal. The division is as old as Aristotle, but has become the common property of science only since the days of Bichât. It is not exact, but it is convenient. As an artifice it has proved its utility, but like all such distinctions it has a tendency to divert the mind from contemplation of the real synthesis of Nature. Even as an artifice the classification is not free from ambiguities; and perhaps it would be less exceptionable if instead of Vegetal and Animal we were to substitute Nutritive and Sensitive. All the phenomena of growth, development, and decay—phenomena common to plants as to animals—may range under the laws of Nutrition. All the phenomena of feeling and motion which specially distinguish animals, will range under the laws of Sensibility. Plants, it is true, manifest motion, some few of them even locomotion; but in them it is believed that these phenomena are never due to the stimulus of Sensibility.

Viewing the animal organism as thus differentiated, we see on the one hand a complex system of organs—glands, membranes, vessels—all harmoniously working to one end, which is to build up the body, and silently repair its continual waste. They evolve the successive phases of development. They prepare successive generations. On the other hand we see a complex system of organs—muscles, tendons, bones, nerves, and nerve-centres—also harmoniously co-operative. They stimulate the organs of Nutrition. They work first for the preservation of the individual in the struggle of existence; next for the perfection of the individual in the development of his highest qualities.

But it is important to remember that this division is purely ideal—a scientific artifice, not a reality. Nature knows of none such. In the organism the two lives are one. The two systems interlace, interpenetrate each other, so that the slightest modification of the one is followed by a corresponding change in the other. The brain is nourished by the heart, and were it not for the blood which is momently pumped into it by the heart, its Sensibility would vanish. And the heart in turn depends upon the brain, not for food, but for stimulus, for motive power, without which food is inert. That we may feel, it is necessary we should feed; that we may feed, it is necessary we should feel. Nutrition cannot be dissociated from Sensation. The blood which nourishes the brain, giving it impulse and sustaining power, could never have become arterial blood, could never have reached the brain, had not the heart which sent it there been subjected to influences from the brain. The blood itself has no locomotive impulse. The heart has no spontaneous power: it is a muscle, and like all other muscles must be stimulated into activity. Unless the sensitive mechanism were in action, the lungs could not expand, the blood would not become oxygenated, the heart would not pump. Look on the corpse from which the life has just vanished. Why is it inert? There is food within it. It has blood in abundance. There is air in the lungs. The muscles are contractile, and the tendons elastic. So little is the wondrous mechanism impaired, that if by any means we could supply a stimulus to awaken the dormant Sensibility, the chest would expand, the heart would beat, the blood would circulate, the corpse would revive.

It is unnecessary to point out in detail how dependent the brain is upon the heart; but mention may be made of the fact that more blood is sent to the brain than to any other organ in the body: according to some estimates a fifth of the whole, according to others a third. Not only is a large quantity of blood demanded for the continuous activity of the brain, but such is the peculiar nature of this great nervous centre, that of all organs it is the most delicately susceptible to every variation in the quality of the blood sent to it. If the heart pumps feebly the brain acts feebly. If the blood be vitiated the brain is lethargic; and when the brain is lethargic the heart is weak. Thus do the two great centres interact. They are both lords of life, and both mutually indispensable.

There are two objections which it may be well to anticipate: Nutrition, it may be objected, cannot be so indissolubly blended with Sensation as I have affirmed, because, in the first place, most of the nutritive processes go on without the intervention of Sensibility; and in the second place the Nutritive Life of Plants is confessedly independent of sensation, since in Plants there is no sensitive mechanism whatever. Nutrition is simply a chemical process.

The answers to these objections may be very brief. Nutrition is a biological not a chemical process: it involves the operation of chemical laws, but these laws are themselves subordinated to physiological laws; and one of these laws is the necessary dependence of organic activity on a nervous mechanism wherever such a mechanism exists. Although popular language, and the mistaken views (as I conceive) of physiologists, allow us to say, without any apparent absurdity, that the processes of respiration, digestion, circulation, and secretion go on without feeling or sensation—because these processes do not habitually become distinct in consciousness, but are merged in the general feeling of existence—we have only to replace the word feeling, or sensation, by the phrase "nervous influence," and it then becomes a serious biological error to speak of Nutrition as dissociated from the stimulus of nervous centres, as capable of continuance without the intervention of

Sensibility. The chemical combinations and decompositions do not of course depend on this intervention, but the *transport* of materials does. All the disputes which have been waged on this subject would have been silenced had the disputants borne in mind this distinction between the chemical and organic elements in every nutritive process. It is not the stoker who makes the steam; but if the stoker were not to supply the fire with coals, and the safety-valve were not to regulate the amount of pressure, steam might indeed be generated, but no steam-engine would perform its useful work. In like manner, it is not the vascular system which makes a secretion; but if the blood did not supply the gland with materials, the secreting process would quickly end, and the blood can only be brought to the gland through the agency of muscular contractions stimulated by nervous influence.

Granting that Plants have no Sensibility, and that in them the process of Nutrition must go on without such an intervention, we are able to demonstrate that in Animals in whose organism the sensitive apparatus is an integral portion, the processes of Nutrition are more or less under the influence of this apparatus. In saying "more or less," I indicate the greater or less perfection of the organism; for, as every one knows, the perfection of each type is due to the predominance of its sensitive mechanism. In some of the lowest types no trace of a nervous mechanism can be discovered. A little higher in the scale the mechanism is very slight and simple. Still higher it becomes complex and important. It culminates in man. Corresponding with this scale of complexity in the sensitive life is the scale of complexity in the nutritive life. As the two rise in importance they rise in the scale of dependence. Thus a frog or a triton will live long after its brain is removed. I have kept frogs for several weeks without their brains, and tritons without their heads. Redi, the illustrious Italian naturalist, kept a turtle alive five months after the removal of its brain. Now it is needless to say that in higher animals death would rapidly follow the loss of the brain. A somewhat similar parallelism is seen on the removal of the heart. None of the higher animals can survive a serious injury to the heart; but that organ may be removed from a reptile, and the animal will crawl away seemingly as lively as ever. A frog will live several hours without a heart, and will hop, swim, and struggle as if uninjured. Stilling once removed all the viscera from a frog, which, however, continued for one hour to hop, defend itself, and in various ways manifest its vivacity.[1]

In spite of these evidences of a temporary independence of brain and heart, as individual organs, there is nothing more certain than the intimate interdependence of the sensitive and circulating systems;

---

(1) STILLING, *Untersuchungen über die Functionen des Rückenmarks*, p. 38.

and if in lower animals the interdependence of the two great central organs is less energetic than in the higher, the law of the intervention of Sensibility in all processes of Nutrition is unaffected. In fact, wherever the motor mechanism is muscular, as it is in all but the simplest animals, the necessary intervention of Sensibility is an *à priori* axiom. Every action in the organs of such animals is a manifestation of muscular contractility, and there is no known means of exciting this contractility except by the stimulus of a nerve.

The heart is a muscle. Some years ago there was a school of physiologists advocating the hypothesis that the action of the heart was due to the irritability of its muscular tissue, which was stimulated by the presence of blood. The great Haller was the head of this school, and his "Mémoires sur la nature sensible et irritable des parties"[1] is still worthy the attention of experimentalists. And, indeed, when men saw the heart continue its pulsations some time after death, and even after removal from the body, and saw, moreover, that after pulsation had ceased it could be revived by the injection of warm blood, there seemed the strongest arguments in favour of the hypothesis. Unhappily for the hypothesis, the heart continues to beat long after all the blood has been pumped out of it, consequently its beating cannot be due to the stimulus of the blood.

In our own day the difficulty has to a considerable extent been removed by the discovery of a small nervous system specially allotted to the heart,—nerves and ganglia imbedded in its substance, which there do the work of nerves and ganglia everywhere else. Cut the heart into pieces, and each piece containing a ganglion will beat as before; the other pieces will be still. Besides this special cardiac system which influences the regular pulsations, there is the general nervous system which accelerates and arrests these pulsations at every moment of our lives. The heart is thus connected with the general organism through the intervention of the great sensory apparatus. Filaments of what are called the pneumogastric nerves connect the heart with the spinal chord and cerebral masses; but it is not the influence of these filaments which causes the regular beatings of the heart (as physiologists formerly supposed), and the proof is that these filaments may all be cut, thus entirely isolating the heart from all connection with the great nervous centres, and yet the heart will continue tranquilly beating. What causes this? Obviously the stimulus comes from the heart's own nerves; and these are, presumably, excited by the molecular changes going on within it.

Physiologists, as was said just now, supposed that the filaments of the pneumogastric nerves distributed to the heart caused its beating.

(1) Lausanne, 1756, in 4 vols.

What then was their surprise, a few years since, when Weber announced that the stimulation of these fibres, instead of accelerating the heart's action, arrested it! Here was a paradox. All other muscles, it was said (but erroneously said), are excited to increased action when their nerves are stimulated, and here is a muscle which is paralysed by the stimulation of its nerves. The fact was indisputable; an electric current passed through the pneumogastric did suddenly and invariably arrest the heart. Physiologists were interested. The frogs and rabbits of Europe had a bad time of it, called upon to answer categorically such questions put to their hearts. In a little while it appeared that although a strong electric current arrested the pulsations—and in mammals instantaneously—yet a feeble current accelerated, instead of arresting them. The same opposite results followed a powerful and a gentle excitation of the upper region of the spinal chord.

To these very important and suggestive facts, which throw a strong light on many phenomena hitherto obscure, let us add the interesting facts that in a healthy, vigorous animal, the heart quickly recovers its normal activity after the withdrawal of the electric stimulus; but in a sickly or highly sensitive animal the arrest is final.

Who does not read here the physiological explanation of the familiar fact that powerful mental shocks momently arrest the heart, and sometimes arrest it for ever? That which a powerful current will do applied to the pneumogastric nerve, will be done by a profound agitation of grief or joy—truly called a heart-shaking influence. The agitation of the great centres of thought is communicated to the spinal chord, and from it to the nerves which issue to various parts of the body: the limbs are violently moved, the glands are excited to increased activity, the tears flow, the facial muscles contract, the chest expands, laughter or sobs, dances of delight and shouts of joy, these and the manifold expressions of an agitated emotion are the after results—the first effect is an arrest, more or less fugitive, followed by an increase of the heart's action. If the organism be vigorous, the effect of a powerful emotion is a sudden paleness, indicating a momentary arrest of the heart. This may be but for an instant: the heart pauses, and the lungs pause with it—"the breath is taken away." This is succeeded by an energetic palpitation; the lungs expand, the blood rushes to face and brain with increased force. Should the organism be sickly or highly sensitive, the arrest is of longer duration, and fainting, more or less prolonged, is the result. In a very sensitive or very sickly organism the arrest is final. The shock of joy and the shock of grief have both been known to kill.

The effects of a gentle stimulus we may expect to be very different, since we know that a feeble electric current stimulates the heart's action. The nature of the stimulus is always the same, no matter on what occasion it arises. It may arise from a dash of cold water on the face,—as we see in the revival of the heart's action when we throw water on the face of a fainting person. It may arise from inhaling an irritant odour. It may arise from the pleasurable sight of a dear friend, or the thrill of delight at the new-birth of an idea. In every case the brain is excited, either through an impression on a sensitive nerve, or through the impulses of thought; and the Sensibility thus called into action necessarily discharges itself through one or more of the easiest channels; and among the easiest is that of the pneumo-gastric nerve. But the heart thus acted on in turn reacts. Its increased energy throws more blood into the brain, which draws its sustaining power from the blood.

Experimentalists have discovered another luminous fact connected with this influence of the brain upon the heart, namely, that although a current of a certain intensity (varying of course with the nature of the organism) will infallibly arrest the heart, if applied at once, yet if we begin with a feeble current and go on gradually increasing its intensity, we may at last surpass the degree which would have produced instantaneous arrest, and yet the heart will continue to beat energetically.

The effect of repetition in diminishing a stimulus is here very noticeable. It will serve to explain why, according to the traditions of familiar experience, we are careful to break the announcement of disastrous news, by intimating something much less calamitous, wherewith to produce the first shock, and then, when the heart has withstood that, we hope it may have energy to meet the more agitating emotion. The same fact will also serve, partly, to explain why from repetition the effect of smoking is no longer as it is at first to produce paleness, sweating, and sickness. The heart ceases to be sensibly affected by the stimulus.

Returning to the effects of a gentle stimulus, we can read therein the rationale of change of scene, especially of foreign travel, in restoring the exhausted energies. The gentle excitement of novel and pleasurable sights is not, as people generally suppose, merely a mental stimulus—a pleasure which passes away without a physical influence; on the contrary, it is inseparably connected with an increased activity of the circulation, and *this* brings with it an increased activity of all the processes of waste and repair. If the excitement and fatigue be not too great, even the sickly traveller finds himself stronger and happier, in spite of bad food, irregular hours, and many other conditions which at home would have enfeebled him. I have heard a very distinguished physician (Sir Henry Holland) say that such is his conviction of the beneficial influence of even slight nervous stimulus on the nutritive processes, that when the patient cannot have change of scene, change of room is of some advantage—nay, even change of furniture, if there cannot be change of room!

To those who have thoroughly grasped the principle of the indissoluble conjunction of Nutrition and Sensation, such effects are obvious deductions. They point to the great importance of Pleasure as an element of effective life. They lead to the question whether much of the superior health of youth is not due to the greater amount of pleasurable excitement which life affords to young minds.

Certain it is that much of the marvellous activity of some old men, especially of men engaged in politics or in interesting professions, may be assigned to the greater stimulus given to their bodily functions by the pleasurable excitement of their minds. Men who vegetate sink prematurely into old age. The fervid wheels of life revolve upon excitement. If the excitement be too intense the wheels take fire; but if the mental stimulus be simply pleasurable it is eminently beneficial.

Every impression reacts on the circulation, a slight impression producing a slight acceleration, a powerful impression producing an arrest more or less prolonged. The "shock" of a wound and the "pain" of an operation cause faintness, sometimes death. Indeed it is useful to know that many severe operations are dangerous only because of the shock or pain, and can be performed with impunity if the patient first be rendered insensible by chloroform. On the other hand, the mere irritation of a nerve so as to produce severe pain will produce syncope or death in an animal which is very feeble or exhausted. It is possible to crush the whole of the upper part of the Spinal Chord (the *Medulla oblongata*) without arresting the action of the heart, if the animal has been rendered insensible by chloroform; whereas without such precautions a very slight irritation of the Medulla suffices to arrest the heart.

A moment's reflection will disclose the reason of the remarkable differences observed in human beings in the matter of sensitiveness. The stupid are stupid, not simply because their nervous development is below the average, but also because the connection between the two great central organs, brain and heart, is comparatively languid: the pneumogastric is not in them a ready channel for the discharge of nervous excitement. The sensitive are sensitive because in them the connection is rapid and easy. All nervous excitement must discharge itself through one or more channels; but *what* channels, will depend on the native and acquired tendencies of the organism. In highly sensitive animals a mere prick on the skin can be proved to affect the beating of the heart; but you may lacerate a reptile without sensibly affecting its pulse. In like manner, a pleasurable sight or a suggestive thought will quicken the pulse of an intelligent man, whereas his stupid brother may be the spectator of festal or solemn scenes and the auditor of noble eloquence with scarcely a change.

The highly sensitive organism is one in which the reactions of sensibility on the circulation, and of the circulation on the sensibility, are most direct and rapid. This is often the source of weakness and inefficiency—as we see in certain feminine natures of both sexes, wherein the excessive sensitiveness does not lie in an unusual development of the nervous centres, but in an unusual development of the direct connection between brain and heart. There are men and women of powerful brains in whom this rapid transmission of sensation to the heart is not observable; the nervous force discharges itself through other channels. There are men and women of small brains in whom "the irritability" is so great that almost every sensation transmits its agitating influence to the heart.

And now we are in a condition to appreciate the truth which was confusedly expressed in the ancient doctrine respecting the heart as the great emotional organ. It still lives in our ordinary speech, but has long been banished from the text-books of physiology, though it is not, in my opinion, a whit more unscientific than the modern doctrine respecting the brain (meaning the cerebral hemispheres) as the exclusive organ of sensation. That the heart, as a muscle, is not endowed with the property of Sensibility—a property exclusively possessed by ganglionic tissue—we all admit. But the heart, as the central organ of the circulation, is so indissolubly connected with every manifestation of Sensibility, and is so delicately susceptible to all emotional agitations, that we may not improperly regard it as the ancients regarded it, in the light of the chief centre of feeling; for the ancients had no conception of the heart as an organ specially endowed with sensibility—they only thought of it as the chief agent of the sensitive soul. And is not this the conception we moderns form of the brain? We do not imagine the cerebral mass, as a mere mass, and unrelated to the rest of the organism, to have in itself sensibility; but we conceive it as the centre of a great system, dependent for its activity on a thousand influences, sensitive because sensibility is the form of life peculiar to it, but living only in virtue of the vital activities of the whole organism. Thus the heart, because its action is momently involved in every emotion, and because every emotion reacts upon it, may, as truly as the brain, be called the great emotional centre. Neither brain nor heart can claim that title exclusively. They may claim it together. EDITOR.

ATALANTA IN CALYDON.[1]

ANOTHER drama of Periclean Athens in the dialect of the Thames. Mr. Swinburne will again sing for us in these latter days the old-world story of how the whole country side of Ætolia turned out, after due libations and much martial oratory, to conquer one overgrown wood-pig, and how severely the press of heroes suffered in the engagement. A strange state of things, surely, it sounds to us in these days of Whitworth. Even below the mediæval civilisation pitch: for the knight made it a point of honour to slay his dragon single-handed, and in a sportsmanlike manner. Strange, too, how permanently rooted this legend of the boar-hunt became among the Ætolians, for as we put St. George and his Dragon on our guineas, so they had this boar and the spear that killed him on their coinage.

Mr. Swinburne has in the main told his story very well, and there is a freshness and a remarkable promise about his book which entitles him to be counted henceforward among our contemporaneous minor poets.

When it is said that Mr. Swinburne can write most delicate and harmonious blank verse—and his blank verse is more evenly unexceptionable than his lyrics—all is not said. His English is pure and extremely fluent; his rhythm is graceful and dignified; his lyrics are often melodiously flexible. But, more than this, he possesses an intense and incisive observation of the external aspects of things; his words chisel them out as clearly as in marble. But, with all this decision of surface and outline, Mr. Swinburne never seems to go much deeper than externals: he never seems to reach the marrow and pith of any object, mental or physical. Perhaps this very shallowness, with all its nicety of finish and ignorance of anything beyond its own reach, is more purely characteristic of the average pagan and of classical times, than if Mr. Swinburne had attempted to engraft our northern self-analysis upon the light, beautiful cadences of his Calydonian fatalism. But here comes in the jar and difficulty of all modern-antiques. Goethe cut the knot in *Iphigeneia* by making his characters simply noble-minded Germans in classical dresses, with the scenic back-ground of an ideal Scythia. And yet Goethe, when he chose, could reproduce the pure Greek spirit, and wed thereto all the intensity of northern feeling; as in his Ganymede and the Prometheus fragment. Which last, though merely a fragment, stands out as unrivalled as the mutilated Theseus of the Elgin marbles.

But, to return to our author, it is in some of Mr. Swinburne's most

[1] ATALANTA IN CALYDON: A Tragedy. By ALGERNON CHARLES SWINBURNE. Moxon & Co., London. 1865.

successful passages, where the harmony and expression are nearly unexceptionable, that this very want of depth will strike the reader most forcibly, and will make him feel like a person who has tasted a very sweet ice-biscuit which crumbles into nothing in his mouth. Mr. Swinburne is thus the very antipodes to Mr. Browning, whose over-concentration of meaning is for the concrete, if not for the ideal, reader, a serious hindrance to the pleasure derived from that author's perusal. The Laureate alone of living, and in company with a few dead men, can give us good tough meaning clothed in the melody of the nicest ear.

It is in our truly national measure, blank verse, that Mr. Swinburne has achieved his most undoubted success. Our blank verse of the nineteenth century, as at present elaborated by its greatest masters, Keats and Mr. Tennyson, seems, at any rate in mere verbal rhythm and movement, superior to that of all preceding English poetry. The typical Tennysonian pauses and disruptions, the improved flow of one line upon the next, the craftily managed discords and surplus syllables thrown in here and there to give edge and variety to the subsequent melody, the nice choice of words in which vowels and liquids predominate—these are a few of the most salient features which cannot fail to stamp the blank verse of the present era as a thing *per se* and of special note in all subsequent poetic annals. Shakspeare, for instance, did not think it worth his while to smooth and modulate his periods into the rhythms of our modern *Hyperion*. Where in rare and detached passages Shakspeare does so, it is quite unconsciously done, and not the result of artistic arrangement. But strangely enough we do get lines of his with quite a nineteenth century ring about them; as in *King John*—

"Large lengths of seas and shores."

or again, in *Henry VI.*, Part iii.—

"And this word 'love,' which greybeards call divine,
Be resident in men like one another,
And not in me. I am myself alone."

Neither did the surpassing excellencies of Milton lead him in precisely this direction, though he verged so nearly thereupon, that it remained for Keats, his direct and manifest imitator, to make known and to develop to their utmost all the capabilities of blank verse; instance the opening lines of *Hyperion*, and further on, at the Titan's entrance to his palace, and soliloquy on his approaching fall. Shelley's blank verse, again, is quite different; but at times he too gravitates into the typical rhythm, as in those lovely lines of the *Prometheus*, which might have been written by Keats—

"Peace is in the grave.
The grave hides all things beautiful and good:
I am a god and cannot find it there."

Since, therefore, Keats and Tennyson, working upon the materials of their predecessors, have consolidated a noble vehicle of blank verse, it would be apparent folly in present and future poets to refuse to adopt and assimilate into their style the peculiar excellencies of those who have preceded them. And yet, though the man of science manifestly is allowed to take up his researches at the point where his forerunners have left them, it is still the fashion in much current criticism to decry and condemn every new verse-writer as a mere copyist of Tennyson, because he cannot help falling into the rhythms and cadences of his contemporaries. If Macaulay's New Zealander ever turns his attention to poetical criticism he must discover from internal evidence, though both authors' names be lost, that *Œnone* and *Hyperion* are the product of the same century; yet who at the present day would dream of reproaching the Laureate because he has assimilated something of the spirit of Keats? Why should poetry be the only trade in which the apprentice is not allowed to show any traces of his master's workshop? Raphael, greatest of painters, copied Perugino servilely enough at one time; shall what is allowed to the man rich in genius be denied to his poorer brethren?

Mr. Swinburne is perfectly free from any beyond legitimate influence of Keats or Tennyson, yet would not the movement of the following beautiful and simple lines have been very different if he had written them fifty years ago? Althæa has just thrown the brand into the fire which is to destroy her son—

> "Girls, one thing will I say and hold my peace.
> I that did this will weep not nor cry out,
> Cry ye and weep: I will not call on gods,
> Call ye on them; I will not pity man,
> Show me your pity. I know not if I live;
> Save that I feel the fire upon my face
> And on my cheek the burning of a brand.
> Yea the smoke bites me, yea I drink the steam
> With nostril and with eyelid and with lip
> Insatiate and intolerant; and mine hands
> Burn, and fire feeds upon my eyes.
>
> * * * * *
>
> Yet, O child,
> Son, first-born, fairest—O sweet mouth, sweet eyes,
> That drew my life out through my sucking breast,
> That shone and clove my heart through—O soft knees
> Clinging, O tender treadings of soft feet,
> Cheeks warm with little kissings—O child, child,
> What have we made each other? Lo, I felt
> Thy weight cleave to me, a burden of beauty, O son,
> Thy cradled brows and loveliest loving lips,
> The floral hair, the little lightening eyes,
> And all thy goodly glory."

Thus also Meleager, just at his death, addresses his mother. The old philosophy of acquiescence is touchingly rendered :—

> "Since extreme love and sorrowing over much
> Vex the great gods, and over-loving men
> Slay and are slain for love's sake; and this house
> Shall bear much better children; why should these
> Weep? but in patience let them live their lives
> And mine pass by forgotten: thou alone,
> Mother, thou sole and only, thou not these,
> Keep me in mind a little when I die
> Because I was thy first-born."

Mr. Swinburne follows his Greek prototypes in keeping as much as possible the whole action and incidents of the drama off the stage. Thus the heroes who arrive for the hunt are described from a distance as they come into sight, something after the manner of the chieftain catalogue in the "Seven against Thebes." The account of the boar-hunt itself comes through the mouth of a herald; and successively, the quarrel about the skin, with the slaughter of his uncles by Meleager, and finally the manner of his own mysterious seizure by disease, when the brand begins to burn—each and all, are narrated, not acted. The description of the hunt itself is very spirited, and reads like a well-known picture of Snyders', done into blank verse. The whole is worth perusal, although too long for quotation here. Take, however, a fragment where Meleager waits for the boar's final rush :—

> "But Meleager, but thy son,
> Right in the wild way of the coming curse
> Rock-rooted, fair with fierce and fastened lips,
> Clear eyes, and springing muscle and shortening limb—
> With chin aslant indrawn to a tightening throat,
> Grave, and with gathered sinews, like a god."

Here is a somewhat similar passage, wherein Althæa contrasts the infant with the full-grown Meleager :—

> "Wherefore I kissed and hid him with my hands,
> And covered under arms and hair, and wept,
> And feared to touch him with my tears, and laughed;
> So light a thing was this man, grown so great
> Men cast their heads back, seeing against the sun
> Blaze the armed man carven on his shield, and hear
> The laughter of little bells along the brace
> Ring, as birds singing or flutes blown, and watch,
> High up, the cloven shadow of either plume
> Divide the bright light of the brass, and make
> His helmet as a windy and wintering moon
> Seen through blown cloud and plume-like drift, when ships
> Drive, and men strive with all the seas and oars
> Break and the beaks dip under, drinking death." .

Here is Atalanta herself at the hunting, chiseled out in words like a marble Artemis.

> "Arcadian Atalanta, with twain hounds
> Lengthening the leash, and under nose and brow
> Glittering with lipless tooth and fire-swift eye;
> But from her white-braced shoulder the plumed shafts
> Rang, and the bow shone from her side."

Our space forbids indulgence in any more lengthy extracts; but the tragedy is nowise exhausted by those already given. Many short isolated passages and expressions of much beauty occur, as—

> "And the mad people of windy mountain ways
> Laid spears against us like a sea."

Or—

> "Seeing thy head glitter and thine hand burn its way
> Through a heavy and iron furrow of sundering spears."

Or take such detached expressions as "These fatal from the vintage of men's veins;" and "Clothed round with the blush of the battle." By the way, Mr. Swinburne has evidently read his Hebrew Prophets with much care; in fact, his diction is often intensely Biblical. His Arcadians "shoot out lips" like the enemies of the Psalmist (Ps. xxii.); or what can be more Scriptural than such lines as these?—

> "And in the night shall no man gather fruit."
> "Sweet were they towards me living."

Little stray bits of Ezekiel and Jeremiah are continually cropping out of Mr. Swinburne's lines. But it is rather respectable than otherwise to be indebted to such time-honoured authorities.

Now for a little verbal criticism. Not serious blemishes truly; but it is worth while for so promising a writer as Mr. Swinburne to have an eye to the smallest details.

> "Narcissus, and the low-lying melilote
> And all of goodliest blade and bloom that springs," &c.

Now melilot is not specially low-lying; indeed, it will even grow sometimes to the height of four feet. Anyhow, it would be difficult to find narcissus and melilot in bloom together; and when we come in another place upon "darkest ivy-buds," apparently gathered somewhere in the ideal Ætolian landscape, one may say that ivy-buds are *not* dark, and that we have here three flowers, one of early spring, another of middle summer, and the last of latest autumn, all out together in characteristic floral anachronism. Surely, too, the epithet "green-haired waters" is rather violent, though it gives no bad idea of a pool with submerged grasses and pond-weeds. Such words, too, as "irremeable," "snowy-souled," and "disfleshed" were better away, as also one line, a despair to Lindley Murray :—

> "Not without God are visions born and die."

Note also such a line as—

"Alas thy beauty! alas thy body! alas thy head!"

where the classicism is too crudely rendered to be palatable to the English reader. It sounds strange, too, to mention a lady's son to her as "a sect of thee." Mr. Swinburne will do well, also, to beware of alliteration, that quicksand of modern verse, *e.g.*,

"And foam in reddening flakes and flying flowers."

We have also "mutual mouth of marriages," and "flowers in fields of fight," &c.

The construction, too, in a pretty simile between Atalanta laughing and the daybreak, at p. 70, is hopelessly misty. Then it is worth comparing Mr. Swinburne's "golden-girdled bees" with the Laureate's "yellow-banded" ones, and noting how the younger poet lays on gold-leaf, while the elder is content with yellow ochre. Perhaps Mr. Swinburne will consider such criticism about flowering months and bee-bands as utterly trivial. But Mr. Tennyson (no bad example) is most careful never to have a flower out at the wrong time. We all know the story of how he added to the "purple-winged cicala" in the *Œnone* of his first edition, a conscientious note that the insect might not occur in the Troad, and how he omitted the passage itself in subsequent editions. Surely the old parallel of poet and painter holds good here, and if the latter introduces a spider in a sixteen-foot canvas, he is bound to paint him the right colour or not at all.

Mr. Swinburne is too much given to comparing everything with "flames" and "flowers;" and again, "flames" with "hair." Which last metaphor Mr. Tennyson has already used in *Guinevere*. Shelley has appropriated the "mother of months" in the *Revolt of Islam* (canto iv. 1). But these are mere coincidences which every writer must fall into. But it is more difficult to understand on what principle Mr. Swinburne has written his prose argument to a quasi-Greek play in old English. We have heard of people speaking broken English to foreigners, with some vague idea that this will be more intelligible than the pure and undiluted vernacular; but surely old English is no whit nearer to Ætolia than old Welsh. It is only just, however, to Mr. Swinburne, to say that he has mimicked admirably the diction of such prose romances as Malory's version of the *Mort d'Arthure*.

In conclusion, *Atalanta* deserves to be read by every one who takes an interest in contemporaneous poetry. The blemishes are few, and the beauties are many. No critic ever was able to predict from a first attempt the capabilities of any author; but few works of greater promise have appeared of late years. Even from this early effort Mr. Swinburne may claim a place among contemporaneous minor poets, and very possibly may hereafter work his way to a still further eminence.

J. LEICESTER WARREN.

ON ATOMS.

"I sing of atoms."—*Rejected Addresses.*

DIALOGUE.—Hermogenes et Hermione interloquuntur.

Hermione.—What strange people those Greeks were! I was reading this morning about Democritus, "who first taught the doctrine of atoms and a vacuum." I suppose he must have meant that there is such a thing as utterly empty space, and that here and there, scattered through it, are things called atoms, like dust in the air. But then I thought, "What *are* these atoms?" for if this be true, then, these are all the world, and the rest is—nothing!

Hermogenes.—Yes. That is the natural conclusion: unless there be something that does not need space to exist in; or unless there be *things* that are not material substances; or unless space itself be *a thing*: all which is deep metaphysic, such as I am just now rather inclined to eschew. But, dear Hermione, how am I to answer such a host of questions as you seem to have raised—all in a breath? The Greeks! Yes; they were a strange people—so ingenious, so excursive, yet so self-fettered; so vague in their notions of things, yet so rigidly definite in their forms of expressing them. Extremes met in them. In their philosophy they grovelled in the dust of words and phrases, till, suddenly, out of their utter confusion, a bound launched them into a new sphere. There is a creature, a very humble and a very troublesome one, which reminds me of the Greek mind. You might know it for a good while as only a fidgety, restless, and rather aggressive companion, when, behold, hop! and it is away far off, having realised at one spring a new arena and a new experience.

Hermione.—Don't! But a truce to the Greek mind, with its narrow pedantry and its boundless excursiveness. The excursiveness was innate, the pedantry superinduced—the result of their perpetual rhetorical conflicts and literary competitions. I have read the fifth book of Euclid and something of Aristotle; so you need not talk to me on that theme. Do tell me something about these atoms. I declare it has quite excited me; 'specially because it seems to have something to do with the atomic theory of Dalton.

Hermogenes.—Higgins, if you please. But the thing, as you say, is as old as Democritus, or perhaps older: for Leucippus, Democritus's master, is said to have taught it to him. Nay, there is an older authority still, in the personage (as near to an abstraction as a traditional human being can be) Moschus (not he of the Idyls). But the fact is that the notion of THE ATOM—the *indivisible*, the *thing* that has *place, being*, and *power*—is an absolute necessity of the human thinking mind, and is of all ages and nations. It underlies all our notions of being, and starts up, *per se*, whenever we come to look closely at the intimate objective nature of things, as much as space and time do in the subjective. You have dabbled in German metaphysics, and know the distinction I refer to.

Hermione.—You don't mean to say that we are nothing but ATOMS! —Place! being! power! Why, that is I, it is you, it is all of us. Nay, nay. This is going too fast.

Hermogenes.—Perhaps it is.—(You have forgot thought, by-the-bye, and will.)—But I am not going to make a single hop quite so far. We shall divide that into two or three jumps, and loiter a little in the intermediate resting-places. But, to go back to your atoms and a vacuum. What does a vacuum mean?

Hermione.—Vacuum? Why, emptiness, to be sure! I mean empty space. Space where *no thing* is. I am not so very sure that I can realise that notion. It is like the abstract idea of a lord mayor that Pope and Atterbury talk about: and in getting rid of the *man*, the gold chain and the custard are apt to start up and vindicate their claim to a place in the world of ideas. And yet I do mean something by empty space. I mean *distance*—I mean *direction*: that steeple is a mile off, and not *here* where we sit; and it lies south-east of us, and not north or west. And if the steeple were away, I should have just as clear a notion of its *place* as if I saw it there. There now! But then distance and direction imply two *places*. So there are three things anyhow that belong to a vacuum; and let me tell you, it is not everything that three things positively intelligible can be "predicated" of (to speak your jargon).

Hermogenes.—Dear me, Hermione! how can you twit me so? Jargon! Every speciality has its "jargon." Even the Law, that system of dreams, has its "jargon"—the more so, to be sure, because it *is* a system of dreams, or rather of nightmares (God forgive me for saying so!). Well, then, you seem to have tolerably clear notions about a vacuum—at least I cannot make them clearer. Much clearer, anyhow, than Des Cartes had, who maintained that if it were not for the foot-rule between them, the two ends of it would be in the same place. Still there is much to be said about that same *Vacuum*, especially when contrasted with a *Plenum*, which means (if it mean anything) the *exact opposite of a vacuum*. In other words, a "jam," a "block," a "fix." But, on the whole, I lean to a vacuum. The other idea is oppressive. It does not allow one to breathe. There is no elbow-room. It seems to realise the notion of that great human squeeze in which we should be landed after a hundred generations of unrestrained propagation.[1] One does not understand how anything could get out of the way of anything else.

Hermione.—Do come back to our dear atoms. I love these atoms: the delicate little creatures! There is something so fanciful, so fairy-like about them.

Hermogenes.—Well; they have their idiosyncrasies. I mean, they obey the laws of their being. They comport themselves according to their primary constitution. They conform to the fixed rule implanted in them in the instant of their creation. They act and react on each other according to the rigorously exact, mathematically determinate relations laid down for them *ab initio*. They work out the preconceived scheme of the universe by their—their——

Hermione.—Their? Stop, stop! my dear Hermogenes. Where will you land us? Obey laws! Do they know them? Can they remember them? How else can they obey them? Comport themselves according to their primary constitution! Well, that is so far intelligible: they are as they are, and not as they are not. Conform to a fixed rule! But then they must be able to apply the rule as the case arises. Act and react according to determinate relations? I suppose you mean relations with each other. But how are they to know those relations? Here is your atom A, there is your atom B (I speak as you have taught me to speak), and a long interval between them, and no link of connection. How is A to know where B is; or in what relation it stands to B? Poor dear atoms! I pity them.

Hermogenes.—You may spare your sympathy.] They are absolutely blind and passive.

Hermione.—Blind and passive! The more the wonder how they come to perceive those same relations you talk about, and how they "comport themselves," as you call it (*act*, as I should say), on that perception. I have a better theory of the universe.

Hermogenes.—Tell it me.

Hermione.—In the beginning was the nebulous matter, or *Akasch*. Its boundless and tumultuous waves heaved in chaotic wildness, and

---

(1) For the benefit of those who discuss the subjects of Population, War, Pestilence, Famine, &c., it may be as well to mention that the number of human beings living at the end of the hundredth generation, commencing from a single pair, doubling at each generation (say in thirty years), and allowing for each man, woman, and child an average space of four feet in height, and one foot square, would form a vertical column, having for its base the whole surface of the earth and sea spread out into a plane, and for its height 3,674 times the sun's distance from the earth! The number of human *strata* thus piled one on the other would amount to 460,790,000,000,000.

all was oxygen, and hydrogen, and electricity. Such a state of things could not possibly continue; and as it could not possibly be worse, alteration was here synonymous with improvement. Then came——

Hermogenes.—Now it is my turn to say, Stop, stop! *Solvuntur risu tabulæ.* Do let us be serious. Remember, it was you who began the conversation. *Je me suis seulement laissé entraîner.* The fact is, I have only so far been trying you, and I see you are apt. There lies the real difficulty about these atoms. These same "relations" in which they stand to one another are anything but simple ones. They involve all the "ologies" and all the "ometries," and in these days we know something of what that implies. Their movements, their interchanges, their "hates and loves," their "attractions and repulsions," their "correlations," their what not, are all determined on the very instant. There is no hesitation, no blundering, no trial and error. A problem of dynamics which would drive Lagrange mad, is solved *instanter*, "*Solvitur ambulando.*" A differential equation which, algebraically written out, would belt the earth, is integrated in an eye-twinkle; and all the numerical calculation worked out in a way to frighten Zerah Colborn, George Bidder, or Jedediah Buxton. In short, these atoms are most wonderful little creatures.

Hermione.—Wonderful indeed! Any how, they must have not only good memories, but astonishing presence of mind, to be always ready to act, and always *to* act without mistake, according to "the primary laws of their being," in every complication that occurs.

Hermogenes.—Thou hast said it! That is just the point I knew you must come to. The *presence of* MIND is what solves the whole difficulty; so far, at least, as it brings it within the sphere of our own consciousness, and into conformity with our own experience of *what action is.* We know nothing but as it is conceivable to us from our own mental and bodily experience and consciousness. When we know we act, we are also conscious of will and effort: and action without will and effort is to us, constituted as we are, unrealisable, unknowable, inconceivable.

Hermione.—That will do. My head begins to turn round. But I hardly fancied we had got on such an interesting train. We will talk of this again. More to-morrow. Now to the feast of flowers the children are preparing.

J. F. W. HERSCHEL.

THE PRINCIPLES OF SUCCESS IN LITERATURE.

In the development of the great series of animal organisms, the Nervous System assumes more and more of an imperial character. The rank held by any animal is determined by this character, and not at all by its bulk, its strength, or even its utility In like manner, in the development of the social organism, as the life of nations becomes more complex, Thought assumes a more imperial character; and Literature, in its widest sense, becomes a delicate index of social evolution. Barbarous societies show only the germs of literary life. But advancing civilisation, bringing with it increased conquest over material agencies, disengages the mind from the pressure of immediate wants, and the loosened energy finds in leisure both the demand and the means of a new activity: the demand, because long unoccupied hours have to be rescued from the weariness of inaction; the means, because this call upon the energies nourishes a greater ambition and furnishes a wider arena.

Literature is at once the cause and the effect of social progress. It deepens our natural sensibilities, and strengthens by exercise our intellectual capacities. It stores up the accumulated experience of the race, connecting Past and Present into a conscious unity; and with this store it feeds successive generations, to be fed in turn by them. As its importance emerges into more general recognition, it necessarily draws after it a larger crowd of servitors, filling noble minds with a noble ambition.

There is no need in our day to be dithyrambic on the glory of Literature. Books have become our dearest companions, yielding exquisite delights and inspiring lofty aims. They are our silent instructors, our solace in sorrow, our relief in weariness. With what enjoyment we linger over the pages of some well-loved author! With what gratitude we regard every honest book! Friendships, profound and generous, are formed with men long dead, and with men whom we may never see. The lives of these men have a quite personal interest for us. Their homes become as consecrated shrines. Their little ways and familiar phrases becomed endeared to us, like the little ways and phrases of our wives and children.

It is natural that numbers who have once been thrilled with this delight should in turn aspire to the privilege of exciting it. Success in Literature has thus become not only the ambition of the highest minds, it has also become the ambition of minds intensely occupied with other means of influencing their fellows—with statesmen, warriors, and rulers. Prime ministers and emperors have striven for distinction as poets, scholars, critics, and historians. Unsatisfied with the powers and privileges of rank, wealth, and their conspicuous position in the eyes of men, they have longed also for the nobler privilege of exercising a generous sway over the minds and hearts of readers. To gain this they have stolen hours from the pressure of affairs, and disregarded the allurements of luxurious ease, labouring steadfastly, hoping eagerly. Nor have they mistaken the value of the reward. Success in Literature is, in truth, the blue ribbon of nobility.

There is another aspect presented by Literature. It has become a profession : to many a serious and elevating profession ; to many more a mere trade, having miserable trade-aims and trade-tricks. As in every other profession, the ranks are thronged with incompetent aspirants, without seriousness of aim, without the faculties demanded by their work. They are led to waste powers which in other directions might have done honest service, because they have failed to discriminate between aspiration and inspiration, between the desire for greatness and the consciousness of power. Still lower in the ranks are those who follow Literature simply because they see no other opening for their incompetence ; just as forlorn widows and ignorant old maids thrown suddenly on their own resources open a school—no other means of livelihood seeming to be within their reach. Lowest of all are those whose esurient vanity, acting on a frivolous levity of mind, urges them to make Literature a plaything for display. To write for a livelihood, even on a complete misapprehension of our powers, is at least a respectable impulse. To play at Literature is altogether inexcusable : the motive is vanity, the object notoriety, the end contempt.

I propose to treat of the Principles of Success in Literature, in the belief that if a clear recognition of the principles which underlie *all* successful writing could once be gained, it would be no inconsiderable help to many a young and thoughtful mind. Is it necessary to guard against a misconception of my object, and to explain that I hope to furnish nothing more than help and encouragement ? There is help to be gained from a clear understanding of the conditions of success ; and encouragement to be gained from a reliance on the ultimate victory of true principles. More than this can hardly be expected from me, even on the supposition that I have ascertained the real conditions. No one, it is to be presumed, will imagine that I can have any pretension of giving recipes for Literature, or of furnishing power and talent where nature has withheld them. I must assume the presence of the talent, and then assign the conditions under which that talent can alone achieve real success. No man is made a discoverer by learning the principles of scientific Method; but only by those principles can discoveries be made; and if he has consciously mastered them, he will find them directing his researches and saving him from an immensity of fruitless labour. It is something in the nature of the Method of Literature that I propose to expound. Success is not an accident. All Literature is founded upon psychological laws, and involves principles which are true for all peoples and for all times. These principles we are to consider here.

II.

The rarity of good books in every department, and the enormous quantity of imperfect, insincere books, has been the lament of all times. The complaint being as old as Literature itself, we may dismiss without notice all the accusations which throw the burden on systems of education, conditions of society, cheap books, levity and superficiality of readers, and analogous causes. None of these can be a *vera causa*; though each may have had its special influence in determining the production of some imperfect works. The main cause I take to be that indicated in Goethe's aphorism: "In this world there are so few voices and so many echoes." Books are generally more deficient in sincerity than in cleverness. Talent, as will become apparent in the course of our inquiry, holds a very subordinate position in Literature to that usually assigned to it. Indeed, a cursory inspection of the Literature of our day will detect an abundance of remarkable talent—that is, of intellectual agility, apprehensiveness, wit, fancy, and power of expression—which is nevertheless impotent to rescue "clever writing" from neglect or contempt. It is unreal splendour; for the most part mere intellectual fireworks. In Life, as in Literature, our admiration for mere cleverness has a touch of contempt in it, and is very unlike the respect paid to character. And justly so. No talent can be supremely effective unless it act in close alliance with certain moral qualities. (What these qualities are will be specified hereafter.)

Another cause, intimately allied with the absence of moral guidance just alluded to, is *misdirection* of talent. Valuable energy is wasted by being misdirected. Men are constantly attempting, without special aptitude, work for which special aptitude is indispensable.

"On peut être honnête homme et faire mal des vers."

A man may be variously accomplished, and yet be a feeble poet. He may be a real poet, yet a feeble dramatist. He may have dramatic faculty, yet be a feeble novelist. He may be a good story-teller, yet a shallow thinker and a slip-shod writer. For success in any special kind of work it is obvious that a special talent is requisite; but obvious as this seems, when stated as a general proposition, it rarely serves to check a mistaken presumption. There are many writers endowed with a certain susceptibility to the graces and refinements of Literature which has been fostered by culture till they have mistaken it for native power; and these men, being really destitute of native power, are forced to imitate what others have created. They can understand how a man may have musical sensibility and yet not be a good singer; but they fail to understand, at least in their own case, how a man may have literary sensibility, yet not be a good story-teller or an effective dramatist. They imagine that if they are cultivated and clever, can write what is delusively called a "brilliant style," and are familiar with the masterpieces of Literature, they must be more competent to succeed in fiction or the drama than a duller man, with a plainer style and slenderer acquaintance with the "best models." Had they distinctly conceived the real aims of Literature this mistake would often have been avoided. A recognition of the aims would have pressed on their attention a more distinct appreciation of the requirements.

No one ever doubted that special aptitudes were required for music, mathematics, drawing, or for wit; but other aptitudes not less special are seldom recognised. It is with authors as with actors: mere delight in the art deludes them into the belief that they could be artists. There are born actors, as there are born authors. To an observant eye such men reveal their native endowments. Even in conversation they spontaneously throw themselves into the characters they speak of. They mimic, often quite unconsciously the speech and gesture of the person. They dramatise when they narrate. Other men with little of this faculty, but with only so much of it as will enable them to imitate the tones and gestures of some admired actor, are misled by their vanity into the belief that they also are actors, that they also could move an audience as their original moves it.

In Literature we see a few original writers, and a crowd of imitators: men of special aptitudes, and men who mistake their power of repeating with slight variation what others have done, for a power of creating anew. The imitator sees that it is easy to do that which has already been done. He intends to improve on it; to add from his own stores something which the originator could not give; to lend it the lustre of a richer mind; to make this situation more impressive, and that character more natural. He is vividly impressed with the imperfections of the original. And it is a perpetual puzzle to him why the public, which applauds his imperfect predecessor, stupidly fails to recognise his own obvious improvements.

It is from such men that the cry goes forth about neglected genius and public caprice. In secret they despise many a distinguished writer, and privately, if not publicly, assert themselves as immeasurably superior. The success of a Dumas is to them a puzzle and an irritation. They do not understand that a man becomes distinguished in virtue of some special talent properly directed; and that their obscurity is due either to the absence of a special talent, or to its misdirection. They may probably be superior to Dumas in general culture, or various ability; it is in particular ability that they are his inferiors. They may be conscious of wider knowledge, a more exquisite sensibility, and a finer taste more finely cultivated; yet they have failed to produce any impression on the public in a direction where the despised favourite has produced a strong impression. They are thus thrown upon the alternative of supposing that he has had "the luck" denied to them, or that the public taste is degraded and prefers trash. Both opinions are serious mistakes. Both injure the mind that harbours them.

In how far is success a test of merit? Rigorously considered it is an absolute test. Nor is such a conclusion shaken by the undeniable fact that temporary applause is often secured by works which have no lasting value. For we must always ask, What is the nature of the applause, and from what circles does it rise? A work which appears at a particular juncture, and suits the fleeting wants of the hour, flattering the passions of the hour, may make a loud noise, and bring its author into strong relief. This is not luck, but a certain fitness between the author's mind and the public needs. He who first seizes the occasion, may be for general purposes intrinsically a feebler man than many who stand listless or hesitating till the moment be passed; but in Literature, as in Life, a sudden promptitude outrivals vacillating power.

Generally speaking, however, this promptitude has but rare occasions for achieving success. We may lay it down as a rule that no work ever succeeded, even for a day, but it deserved that success; no work ever failed but under conditions which made failure inevitable. This will seem hard to men who feel that in their case neglect arises from prejudice or stupidity. Yet it is true even in extreme cases; true even when the work once neglected has since been acknowleged superior to the works which for a time eclipsed it. Success, temporary or enduring, is the measure of the relation, temporary or enduring, which exists between a work and the public mind. The millet seed may be intrinsically less valuable than a pearl; but the hungry cock wisely neglected the pearl, because pearls could not, and millet seeds could, appease his hunger. Who shall say how much of the subsequent success of a once neglected work is due to the preparation of the public mind through the works which for a time eclipsed it?

Let us look candidly at this matter. It interests us all; for we have all more or less to contend against public misconception, no less than against our own defects. The object of Literature is to instruct, to animate, or to amuse. Any book which does one of these things succeeds; any book which does none of these things fails. Failure is the indication of an inability to perform what was attempted: the aim was misdirected, or the arm was too weak: in either case the mark has not been hit.

"The public taste is degraded." Perhaps so; and perhaps not. But in granting a want of due preparation in the public, we only grant that the author has missed his aim. A reader cannot be expected to be interested in ideas which are not presented intelligibly to him, nor delighted by art which does not touch him; and for the writer to imply that he furnishes arguments, but does not pretend to furnish brains to understand the arguments, is arrogance. What Goethe says about the most legible handwriting being illegible in the twilight, is doubtless true; and should be oftener borne in mind by frivolous objectors, who declare they do not understand this or do not admire that, as if their want of taste and understanding were rather creditable than otherwise, and were decisive proofs of an author's insignificance. But this reproof, which is telling against individuals, has no justice as against the public. For—and this is generally lost sight of—the public is composed of the class or classes directly addressed by any work, and not of the heterogeneous mass of readers. Mathematicians do not write for the circulating library. Science is not addressed to poets. Philosophy is meant for students, not for idle readers. If the members of a class do not understand,— if those directly addressed fail to listen, or listening, fail to recognise a power in the voice,—surely the fault lies with the speaker, who, having attempted to secure their attention and enlighten their understandings, has failed in the attempt? The mathematician who is without value to mathematicians, the thinker who is obscure or meaningless to thinkers, the dramatist who fails to move the pit, may be wise, may be eminent, but as an author he has failed. He attempted to make his wisdom and his power operate on the minds of others. He has missed his mark. *Margaritas ante porcos!* is the soothing maxim of a disappointed self-love. But we, who look on, may sometimes doubt whether they *were* pearls thus ineffectually thrown; and always doubt the judiciousness of strewing pearls before swine.

The prosperity of a book lies in the minds of readers. Public knowledge and public taste fluctuate; and there come times when works which were once capable of instructing and delighting thousands lose their power, and works, before neglected, emerge into renown. A small minority to whom these works appealed has gradually become a large minority, and in the evolution of opinion will perhaps become the majority. No man can pretend to say that the work neglected to-day will not be a household word to-morrow; or that the pride and glory of our age will not be covered with cobwebs on the bookshelves of our children. Those works alone can have enduring success which successfully appeal to what is permanent in human nature—which, while suiting the taste of the day, contain truths and beauty deeper than the opinions and tastes of the day; but even temporary success implies a certain temporary fitness. In Homer, Sophocles, Dante, Shakspeare, Cervantes, we are made aware of much that no longer accords with the wisdom or the taste of our day—temporary and immature expressions of fluctuating opinions—but we are also aware of much that is both true and noble now, and will be so for ever.

It is only posterity that can decide whether the success or failure shall be enduring; for it is only posterity that can reveal whether the relation now existing between the work and the public mind is or is not liable to fluctuation. Yet no man really writes for posterity; no man ought to do so.

"Wer machte denn der Mitwelt Spass?"

("Who is to amuse the present?") asks the wise Merry Andrew in *Faust*. We must leave posterity to choose its own idols. There is, however, this chance in favour of any work which has once achieved success, that what has pleased one generation may please another, because it may be based upon a truth or beauty which cannot die; and there is this chance against any work which has once failed, that its unfitness may be owing to some falsehood or imperfection which cannot live.

III.

In urging all writers to be steadfast in reliance on the ultimate victory of excellence, we should no less strenuously urge upon them to beware of the intemperate arrogance which attributes failure to a degraded condition of the public mind. The instinct which leads the world to worship success is not dangerous. The book which succeeds accomplishes its aim. The book which fails may have many excellencies, but they must have been misdirected. Let us, however, understand what is meant by failure. From want of a clear recognition of this meaning, many a serious writer has been made bitter by the reflection that shallow, feeble works have found large audiences, whereas his own work has not paid the printing expenses. He forgets that the readers who found instruction and amusement in the shallow books could have found none in his book, because he had not the art of making his ideas intelligible and attractive to them, or·had not duly considered what food was assimilable by their minds. It is idle to write in hieroglyphics for the mass when only priests can read the sacred symbols.

No one, it is hoped, will suppose that by what is here said I countenance the notion which is held by some authors—a notion implying either arrogant self-sufficiency or mercenary servility—that to succeed, a man should write down to the public. Quite the reverse. To succeed, a man should write up to his ideal. He should do his very best; certain that the very best will still fall short of what the public can appreciate. He will only degrade his own mind by putting forth works avowedly of inferior quality; and will find himself greatly surpassed by writers whose inferior workmanship has nevertheless the indefinable aspect of being the best they can produce. The man of common mind is more directly in sympathy with the vulgar public, and can speak to it more intelligibly, than any one who is condescending to it. If you feel yourself to be above the mass, speak so as to raise the mass to the height of your argument. It may be that the interval is too great. It may be that the nature of your arguments is such as to demand from the audience an intellectual preparation, and a habit of concentrated continuity of thought, which cannot be expected from a miscellaneous assembly. The scholarship of a Scaliger or the philosophy of a Kant will obviously require an audience of scholars and philosophers. And in cases where the nature of the work limits the class of readers, no man should complain if the readers he does not address pass him by to follow another. He will not allure these by writing down to them; or if he allure them, he will lose those who properly constitute his real audience.

A writer misdirects his talent if he lowers his standard of excellence. Whatever he can do best let him do that, certain of reward in proportion to his excellence. The reward is not always measurable by the number of copies sold; that simply measures the extent of his public. It may prove that he has stirred the hearts and enlightened the minds of many. It may also prove, as Johnson says, "that his nonsense suits their nonsense." The real reward of Literature is in the sympathy of congenial minds, and is precious in proportion to the elevation of those minds, and the gravity with which such sympathy moves: the admiration of a mathematician for the *Mécanique Celeste*, for example, is altogether higher in kind than the admiration of a novel reader for the last "delightful story." And what should we think of Laplace if he were made bitter by the wider popularity of

Dumas? Would he forfeit the admiration of one philosopher for that of a thousand novel readers?

To ask this question is to answer it; yet daily experience tells us that not only in lowering his standard, but in running after a popularity incompatible with the nature of his talent, does many a writer forfeit his chance of success. The novel and the drama, by reason of their commanding influence over a large audience, often seduce writers to forsake the path on which they could labour with some success, but on which they know that only a very small audience can be found; as if it were quantity more than quality, noise rather than appreciation, which their mistaken desires sought. Unhappily for them, they lose the substance, and only snap at the shadow. The audience may be large, but it will not listen to them. The novel may be more popular and more lucrative, when successful, than the history or the essay; but to make it popular and lucrative the writer needs a special talent, and this, as was before hinted, seems frequently forgotten by those who take to novel writing. Nay, it is often forgotten by the critics; they being, in general, men without the special talent themselves, set no great value on it. They imagine that Invention may be replaced by culture, and that clever "writing" will do duty for dramatic power. They applaud the "drawing" of a character, which drawing turns out on inspection to be little more than an epigrammatic enumeration of particularities, the character thus "drawn" losing all individuality as soon as speech and action are called upon. Indeed, there are two mistakes very common among reviewers: one is the overvaluation of what is usually considered as literary ability ("brilliant writing" it is called; "literary tinsel" would be more descriptive) to the prejudice of Invention and Individuality; the other is the overvaluation of what they call "solid acquirements," which really mean no more than an acquaintance with the classics. As a fact, literary ability and solid acquirements are to be had in abundance; invention, humour, and originality are excessively rare. It may be a painful reflection to those who, having had a great deal of money spent on their education, and having given a great deal of time to their solid aquirements, now see genius and original power of all kinds more esteemed than their learning; but they should reflect that what is learning now is only the diffused form of what was once invention. "Solid acquirement" is the genius of wits become the wisdom of reviewers.

IV.

Authors are styled an irritable race, and justly, if the epithet be understood in its physiological rather than its moral sense. This irritability, which responds to the slightest stimulus, leads to much of the misdirection of talent we have been considering. The greatness of an author consists in having a mind extremely irritable, and at the same time steadfastly imperial :—irritable that no stimulus may be inoperative, even in its most evanescent solicitations; imperial, that no solicitation may divert him from his deliberately chosen aims. A magisterial subjection of all dispersive influences, a concentration of the mind upon the thing that has to be done, and a proud renunciation of all means of effect which do not spontaneously connect themselves with it— these are the rare qualities which mark out the man of genius. In men of lesser calibre the mind is more constantly open to determination from extrinsic influences. Their movement is not self-determined, self-sustained. In men of still smaller calibre the mind is entirely determined by extrinsic influences. They are prompted to write poems by no musical instinct, but simply because great poems have enchanted the world. They resolve to write novels upon the vulgarest provocations: they see novels bringing money and fame; they think there is no difficulty in the art. The novel will afford them an opportunity of bringing in a variety of scattered details; scraps of knowledge too scanty for an essay, and scraps of experience too meagre for independent publication. Others, again, attempt histories, or works of popular philosophy and science; not because they have any special stores of knowledge, or because any striking novelty of conception urges them to use up old material in a new shape, but simply because they have just been reading with interest some work of history or science, and are impatient to impart to others the knowledge they have just acquired for themselves. Generally it may be remarked that the pride which follows the sudden emancipation of the mind from ignorance of any subject, is accompanied by a feeling that all the world must be in the state of darkness from which we have ourselves emerged. It is the knowledge learned yesterday which is most freely imparted to-day.

We need not insist on the obvious fact of there being more irritability than mastery, more imitation than creation, more echoes than voices in the world of Literature. Good writers are of necessity rare. But the ranks would be less crowded with incompetent writers if men of real ability were not so often misdirected in their aims. My object is to define, if possible, the Principles of Success—not to supply recipes for absent power, but to expound the laws through which power is efficient, and to explain the causes which determine success in exact proportion to the native power on the one hand, and to the state of public opinion on the other.

The laws of Literature may be grouped under three heads. Perhaps we might say they are three forms of one principle.

They are founded on our threefold nature—intellectual, moral, and æsthetic.

The intellectual form is the *Principle of Vision*.
The moral form is the *Principle of Sincerity*.
The æsthetic form is the *Principle of Beauty*.

It will be my endeavour to give definite significance, in succeeding chapters, to these expressions, which, standing unexplained and un-illustrated, probably convey very little meaning. We shall then see that every work, no matter what its subject-matter, necessarily involves these three principles in varying degrees; and that its success is always strictly in accordance with its conformity to the guidance of those principles.

Unless a writer has what, for the sake of brevity, I have called Vision, enabling him to see clearly the facts or ideas, the objects or relations, which he places before us for our own instruction, his work must obviously be defective. He must see clearly if we are to see clearly. Unless a writer has Sincerity, urging him to place before us what he sees and believes *as* he sees and believes it, the defective earnestness of his presentation will cause an imperfect sympathy in us. He must believe what he says, or we shall not believe it. Insincerity is always weakness; sincerity even in error is strength. This is not so obvious a principle as the first; at any rate it is one more profoundly disregarded by writers.

Finally, unless the writer has grace—the principle of Beauty I have named it—enabling him to give some æsthetic charm to his presentation, were it only the charm of well-arranged material, and well-constructed sentences, a charm sensible through all the intricacies of *composition* and of *style*, he will not do justice to his powers, and will either fail to make his work acceptable, or will very seriously limit its success. The amount of influence issuing from this principle of Beauty will, of course, be greatly determined by the more or less æsthetic nature of the work.

Books minister to our knowledge, to our guidance, and to our delight, by their truth, their uprightness, and their art. Truth is the aim of Literature. Sincerity is moral truth. Beauty is æsthetic truth. How rigorously these three principles determine the success of all works whatever, and how rigorously every departure from them, no matter how slight, determines proportional failure, with the inexorable sequence of a physical law, it will be my endeavour to prove in the chapters which are to follow.

EDITOR.

THE IRON-MASTERS' TRADE-UNION.

"Masters are always and everywhere in a sort of tacit but constant and uniform combination not to raise the wages of labour above their actual rate. Masters, too, sometimes enter into particular combinations to sink wages even below this rate."

ADAM SMITH.

ALL who watch our social progress have long been aware of periodical convulsions of Industry, which of late have been growing more frequent and more ominous. And now the public has learnt with bewilderment that a local dispute about wages between six firms and their men can suddenly swell to the scale of a national event. They have seen whole counties smitten as by the stroke of a famine, a great trade (the second in the kingdom), paralysed, vast combinations of capitalists and workmen ranging over half England, and 200,000 souls brought to the verge of abject want, before the rest of their countrymen understood the dispute. These struggles, from their scale, results, and obstinacy, from the marvellous organisation they imply, from the prospect of a boundless reserve of power behind one side and the other, open to the thoughtful politician visions of industrial battles and convulsions to come, of which these are but the symptoms and prelude. As these disputes grow less lawless, they grow more disciplined; what they forego in direct violence, they acquire in indirect destructiveness. They are gaining the system and energy of true political struggles; they threaten the public peace, at least as much as the markets; they are becoming wars of classes for rights, institutions, and power. In the stagnation of actual politics these things are, to those who can discern the times, the true public questions of the day. Nor can the nation see without interest and anxiety a great branch of its industry struck down, as it were, by another Lancashire famine, self-imposed and self-maintained.

It may be useful whilst the embers of the latest of these great civil wars are smouldering in the Black Country, to scrutinise the doctrines on which the dispute has been popularly judged. Economic science has been loudly invoked, and a body of maxims have been announced as obvious and irrefragable truth. It is true that political economy, with all its rational exponents, professes to teach us tendencies rather than results, general laws, not special rules. It is true that the application of its laws to practice, being simply a branch of the general philosophy of society, is amongst the most difficult problems of thought. But, notwithstanding this, we have heard a very difficult dispute summarily judged on a few misunderstood and general maxims.

What has happened is something of this kind. The manufacturers of iron reduce the wages of their men ten per cent. on the ground of a fall in the price of their wares. In a certain district the men refuse the new terms. A strike takes place. Forthwith a chorus of denunciation begins. Strikes are painted by a thousand pens as a sort of public crime, if not an insurrection against lawful authority. The consequences of resistance are cast on the men, as if the act was solely theirs, and the masters were passive victims. Selfishness, infatuation, ruin are the only terms which can describe it. Then trip glibly forth an array of economic dogmas which, though never found in economic writers of repute, are somehow invested with authority. It is an axiom of science, they assure us, that a strike can never avert a fall of wages. It is an ultimate fact that a fall of wages flows from natural causes beyond the control of employer or employed. It is a recognised law, we are told, that wages *must* fall in a falling market; if prices fall, profits must fall, and if profits fall, wages must fall. The rate of wages depends by eternal necessity on the state of the "wages-fund," and fluctuates as this is diminished or increased. All this, by immutable laws of nature, and artificial attempts to resist a reduction of wages, are as hopeless as artificial attempts to withstand the tides. It is notorious, they tell us, that the price of iron has fallen; and it follows by logical necessity that the strike of the iron-workers is suicidal, ignorant, and criminal.

A new element is introduced. The strike of the particular workmen is maintained by the contributions of about one-fifth of the workmen of the entire trade. An unnatural attempt, they cry, to interfere with the freedom of the market. Combinations to check the regular working of competition, the simple bargain of one individual with another, are as irrational as they are unjust. Combination is opposed to the spirit of Free Trade. Next the masters combine. They close their works to all the workmen alike. A general lock-out over a great part of England is announced to continue until the workmen on strike shall accept the reduced terms. This, we are told, is the exact counterpart of the act of the men. The men combine to strike; the masters combine to lock-out. The lock-out is forced on the masters by the strike. They are driven to resort to it to preserve the existence of capital at all. It is a simple measure of defence, inevitable in itself, and very effectual in its results. The lock-out is the perfect equivalent of the strike, or differs from it only as an involuntary act of self-preservation differs from a voluntary act of aggression.

Such are some of the current doctrines we have heard respecting the dispute in the iron trade. It is the attempt of the following pages to show that these propositions are one and all totally false. They are vicious in theory and untrue in fact. Far from it being true that the onus of a strike can be imputed to the men who refuse, rather than to the masters who impose, new terms, the onus really lies on those who insist on the change. A strike in itself is criminal and infatuated, just as much as other refusals to deal are criminal and infatuated, and not a whit more. The rate of wages is as much beyond human control as other contracts, and not the least more. So far from the rate of wages "necessarily" falling when prices fall in the same trade, it frequently, and indeed usually, rises whilst prices fall. So far from the rate of profits "necessarily" falling when prices fall, it usually rises whilst prices fall. So far from the rate of wages invariably falling or rising with the "wages-fund," or any other fund, or, indeed, anything at all, it is often in particular occupations, over long courses of years, absolutely fixed, and that in the largest, most highly-paid, and most highly-skilled trades. So far from fluctuations in the rate of wages being the rule, the rule is rather that it is stationary. So far from attempts to affect the rate of wages artificially being hopeless, it hardly ever varies in the principal trades from any other cause. So far from combinations of workmen interfering with the freedom of the labour-market, it is almost impossible without them to test it fairly. So far from combinations being unjust, the absence of them is practical slavery. A lock-out such as that we have seen, far from being the exact counterpart of a strike, is its exact opposite. Instead of being simply defensive, it is essentially aggressive. Far from attaining its end of reducing wages, it almost necessarily raises them, by forcing the labourers to emigrate. A lock-out, far from succeeding in crushing combination, almost invariably promotes it. Instead of suppressing unions, it strengthens, and sometimes originates, them. Far from being a public necessity, it is usually a gratuitous public disaster. Far from being justified by economic principles, it is the most complete denial of every rational principle of economy at once. In short, if these positions are made good, we may see grounds for believing that a number of doctrines have been solemnly imposed on the public as irrefragable axioms of economic science, which are fallacies in logic, and untrue in fact. And on this tissue of sophism and misconception great bodies of our countrymen have been loudly and severely condemned.

The facts, after careful personal inquiry by the writer, appear to be these:— A branch of the makers of iron known as the puddlers, who knead the metal in the furnace, have recently been associated in a trade-union which embraced about one-fourth of the workmen in the trade. The iron-masters have also been associated for many years in regular district societies, at the quarterly meetings of which the prices of iron have been usually fixed. By a somewhat undefined and irregular custom, which can scarcely be called an agreement, wages have for some years loosely followed the prices of bar-iron in the ratio of one shilling in the pound. At the opening of last year, both stood nearly at the rate at which, for a long period, they had been more than ten years ago. In July last, the price of iron was reduced £1 at the regular quarterly meeting, but no reduction in wages followed. In January of this year, by agreement between the whole body of iron-masters, a fortnightly notice was given of a reduction of wages of 10 per cent. After long discussion in the union and trade, the bulk of the workmen accepted these terms. The unionist puddlers, however, in North Staffordshire, who number some 1,000 men, and are employed at different works by six firms, refused to accept the reduction, and ceased their work, *but offered officially to meet the masters half way by accepting a reduction of five per cent.* This they did at their own spontaneous desire, with the sanction, though not at the instigation, of the union, from which they received promise of support. They alleged, as a ground of difference in wages, certain peculiarities in their case, relating to the profits of the employer and their own earnings, which, perhaps, nothing but immense local knowledge can enable any one to estimate correctly. They asserted that the metal they worked was of a quality to increase their labour in working to the extent of one or two hours per diem; that the cost of living was higher, and the cost of production was lower. They insisted generally that the fall in price was an incident of the product-market, and that no variation in the demand and supply of their labour existed. Upon this strike taking place, the associated iron-masters, mustering nearly all those of the midland and northern districts, gave notice of a general lock-out—of their intention to close their works absolutely and generally on a given day, and to keep them closed until the North Staffordshire puddlers returned to their work. Upon this the union reconsidered their decision to support their brethren on strike. The executive of both northern and southern divisions gave formal directions to them to withdraw, and publicly refused to continue contributions. It is certain that this was acted on, and that from that day to the present time (May 1), no union funds were applied to the support of the men on strike. They still, however, refused to yield. Divisions in the union followed: the northern section separated from the southern, and both were at issue with the men in North Staffordshire. Before the lock-out commenced, the union authorities offered to give any guarantee that should be required, that the men on strike should not be supported by their funds. This was not accepted, and on the day named the lock-out was actually enforced by all the iron-masters in the districts mentioned. By this act an immense body of men, directly or indirectly connected with the trade, were thrown out of work, Large towns were suddenly brought to a stand; various trades were convulsed, and 200,000 persons were said to be threatened with destitution. Violent indignation was produced, and a perceptible agitation ran through the whole body of working men in England. The strike still continued. Negotiations ensued with the union without any definite result, except to prove that it actually abandoned the men on strike, and had no longer any control over them. The masters of the northern district at length separated from the southern, and withdrew the lock-out after a suspension of some weeks. The masters of the southern division continued it some weeks longer, but at last agreed to withdraw it. The men on strike remained unaffected during the lock-out; the works were still without men. At last, after a contest of sixteen weeks, it is believed the masters will accept the terms originally proposed by their men, of a reduction of 5 per cent.; and on this the strike would be brought to a close.

Let us now consider the true character of these proceedings. The strike and lock-out are totally distinct, and rest on different principles. What is a strike in the abstract? The master of a workshop gives notice that he will reduce wages on a certain day ten per cent. His men refuse. What is it that each asserts? The employer asserts that the relation of supply and demand of labour has varied; that he less needs workmen, or that there are more of them. They assert that there are not more, or that they are not less needed. It is a simple question of fact. No bargain can be made, and what is called a strike occurs. The question is then put to the test. If the master is right, unemployed workmen gradually come in, or he finds himself in little need of workmen at all. If the men are right, he fails to find them, or he has such pressing need of them that he sends for his old workmen, and accepts their terms. Reduced to its simplest proportions, a strike is nothing more than this. It is a right which is absolutely inseparable from the commonest intercourse between men. Precisely similar transactions occur hourly in every relation of life. Wherever men are free to deal with each other, each party to the bargain must be free to offer or to decline a proposal. If the owner of a house, or a horse, or a coat, find that the public declines to give the price he asks, the equivalent of a "strike" has occurred. If two servants in a house ask at once for a rise of wages, and "give notice" on refusal, they have caused a real, though certainly a small, "strike." Every time a houseful of lodgers refuse to pay increased rent, every time well-known customers refuse to deal with a tradesman, every time the Bank of England raises its rate of discount, "strikes" occur. Unless there were this ultimate power in reserve, an absolute condition of slavery would result; and much of the absurd horror with which "strikes" are denounced is due to the fact that the labourer is still systematically regarded, not as an equal party to a bargain, but as the dependant and instrument of the employer. When two people who meet to deal are unable to arrange a bargain, it is generally impossible to say which party refuses, and which makes an offer. Both usually do both. Each makes his own offer and declines that of the other. It is impossible to throw the onus of the refusal on one side more than on the other absolutely. A strike respecting wages occurs just as often from the employer enforcing new rates as from his refusing them; and whether the men make a demand, or the capitalist. Yet it is very common to have all the misery caused by "a strike" imputed to the men, as if it was their act more than that of the employers; whereas of course without other knowledge it is just as unreasonable to blame the men for refusing the masters' terms as it would be to blame the master for refusing the men's.

It is plain indeed that this dispute as to facts must occasionally be put to the practical test. Of moral and social considerations (on which hereafter something will be said) no question is raised here. The question will now be discussed on purely economic grounds, and on the recognised maxim of economists, that the wages or remuneration of the labourers depend on a comparison of their numbers with the actual demand for their labour. It is plain that this is a question of fact which no argument can prevent being occasionally put to the proof. Let us introduce into our example a new element—combination. The men who refuse the employers' terms seek during the proof for that which the employer has to support him in the interval—a reserve fund. The capitalist can live on his capital, and wait till the issue is decided. The men without a fund cannot wait, for they cannot live; they are unable to reach another market, or to test the state of their own. They combine and form such a fund. The union is the capital of the labourer. But by this the fairness of the test is not affected; or rather it is not fair without it. If there are available workmen they will be found, whatever may be the support given to the displaced. If there are not available workmen, the support only enables the men on strike to live long enough to prove it. To deny them this is practically to deny them the power of ever bringing the state of the market to experiment. Intimidation, moral or physical, ought to be and is restrained by the full power of the law. But speaking broadly, a body of men refusing the offer of their employer are perfectly entitled, whilst bringing that offer to the test of facts, to exist by the assistance of their fellow-workmen. If that assistance is given generally, it is the best possible proof that their fellow-workmen are not anxious to take their places, *i.e.*, that there is no superabundant supply of labour. The highest possible degree of concert and organisation amongst the workmen, so long as it is confined to testing by direct and lawful means the true state of demand and supply of labour, and attempts no threat or coercion towards their fellow-workmen or their employers, in no degree affects the fairness of the experiment. The supply of labour, of course, implies not the actual number of legs and arms unemployed, but the number of competent men who are seeking particular employment. If that number is limited by mutual agreement, by combination to remove a certain portion, or to support a certain portion without employment, by any legitimate form of persuasion short of injury, actual or threatened, by them or any one else, the case is not affected. So long as men are simply and heartily unwilling to engage in any employment, or are able to dispense with it, it is ridiculous to inquire how it is they are unwilling to accept the offers that are made to them. It is not uncommon to see in newspaper articles that the combinations of workmen are a violation of the "immortal principles of free trade;" as if free trade prevented any body of dealers from agreeing to put any price they please upon their own commodities. Some theorists have gone so far as almost to persuade themselves that economic transactions are purely physical facts, and that any act of volition is a hopeless attempt to interfere with immutable laws of nature. Of course every act of trade whatever is an act of the human will; and whether that will is determined by motives derived from each individual's reflection, or from consultation with others, from mere self-interest, from benevolence, from pride, or from honour, does not affect the question, provided no semblance of coercion is used. Combinations to affect wages, it may plausibly be said, can rarely obtain their object, as they will be defeated by competition; but it is childish to pretend that they do not form a perfectly natural element in the supply of labour. If every workman is free to refuse terms which are offered him (and if he were not free to do this he would be a slave), he must be equally free to consult with his fellow-workman, and to accept or refuse the terms offered in concert with him. He must be also free to borrow money from his fellow-workman to enable him to live during his refusal, or to reach another market, and of course he is free to lay by a sum out of his own earnings to do this. And no less certainly a body of workmen, each of whom individually is quite free to do this, must be collectively free to make this provision. Indeed, unless they do so they are practically at the mercy of their employer, and must accept any terms he likes to give them, as Adam Smith conclusively shows. Any amount of organisation to effect this object is perfectly legitimate, and the completeness of the machinery by which the test is applied cannot in the least alter the efficacy of the test. The querulous commonplaces about combination interfering with the legitimate action of supply and demand can arise only out of two suppositions: either that bargains are absolutely determined by an external fate, or that men are bound to act as if they were not social beings.

In truth, the real masters of Political Economy have over and over again pointed out not so much the abstract right but the positive necessity for combinations amongst the men. Adam Smith and Mr. Mill emphatically show that it is the first condition of fair bargaining respecting labour. Without combination, without a reserve fund, without the means of existence, the labourer is practically at the mercy of a capitalist, just as a starving man in a prison is at the mercy of a man who offers him a loaf. Capital, indeed, itself is a combination. It is the combined product of a number of labourers. The capitalist represents a great association of workmen himself. He deals with the whole of their united power at his back. And that he should meet any body of labourers on terms even approximately equal, it is essential that they should be combined with a somewhat equivalent power.

There is, however, another very sufficient reason for combination amongst workmen. Besides the fact that every capitalist himself represents an association of labour, capitalists as a body are always in a state of open or secret combination themselves; and this in a way that no power can control and no skill can detect. It is a combination very indefinite, very variable, but perfectly real and immensely powerful. As Adam Smith tells us, "Masters are always and everywhere in a sort of tacit but constant and uniform combination, not to raise the wages of labour above their actual rate." Since very powerful combinations exist, and must exist, among employers, it is monstrously unjust to prevent the fullest liberty of combination to the men. And, indeed, such combinations should be strongly promoted as essential to counteract a power so vast, and capable of abuse, in the hand of their employers. Those who complain of trades unions of workmen have never suggested a remedy for trades unions of masters—unions far more dangerous and far less responsible.

Now what is the true limit and legitimate scope of such a combination? Until some equitable or moral basis is acknowledged as the true grounds of dealing between man and man, until it is anti-social to appeal to the haggling of the market, no simpler measure for the profits of classes has yet been proposed than the comparison of the demand with the supply of labour. Under any possible state of things the bargain of capital and labour must occasionally be left to be decided by experiment. To deny either party entire freedom to do this on their own responsibility and at their own risk would be to subject one to slavery to the other. But society has a right to say, This issue of fact must be tried fairly and simply. The side which attempts to succeed by forcing the other to surrender by violence, or by intimidation,—by using accidental and external means of injury,—by crushing those who assist the opponent,—by harming those who depend on him, or on whom he depends—ceases to be making a bargain at all, but is settling a question of the market by the use of personal oppression.

If the captain of a ship in a populous port seeking seamen for a voyage offers such wages as he thinks fit, which the seamen decline to accept, each waits for another offer, and the question is put to the test—what is the ordinary rate which seamen will take and captains will give? We may take a second case. The same captain, having his crew in mid ocean, insists on reducing their wages by one-half, and unless they yield, threatens to refuse them food and water. He is resolute and armed. The men must accept his terms; unless they are obstinate enough to die or strong enough to kill him. These two cases differ—

differ in kind rather than degree. Both may be legal. Both are appeals in a sense to force. In both, their necessities determine the bargain. But in the one case the market rate of wages has been determined; in the other nothing but the adroitness of the captain.

Now, in the view here taken, the strike of the men was a transaction similar to the first, and therefore, though possibly unreasonable in its circumstances, legitimate in principle; whilst the lock-out of the masters was of the nature of the second, and utterly unjustifiable in principle and method. The one was a transaction which economy and society must always regard as possible; the other, one which both have the fullest right to repudiate. If I go to a baker who asks me tenpence for his loaf and insist on having it for eightpence, I can finally prove that my demand is right only by buying as good and as large a loaf for eightpence from his neighbour. But if I go to the baker and say, "Sell me the tenpenny loaf for eightpence, or I will deprive your son of his post, or terminate the lease of your house, or call in the money you owe," I do nothing to settle the point in dispute. I may possibly gain my end; but it is the interest of the public that my conduct be denounced.

Now the strike of the puddlers may have been economically unsound; it may have been utterly irrational; but it cannot, like the lock-out, be so decided on independent grounds. This is a question of figures, with which few men in England are able to deal completely. The public and the newspapers appear to decide it in a summary way; but the present writer assuredly will totally abstain from so doing. The men who struck may be hopelessly wrong, or they may be distinctly right. Their labour may possibly, in the balance of the market, be worth much more, or it may be worth much less, than they demand. Certainly no attempt will be made to decide that here; but a few words of criticism may not be out of place on some of the arguments which have been used to judge it. So far from the strike being obviously a blunder, economically speaking there are several *primâ facie* reasons for believing the strike to be not altogether without warrant from the state of the market. In the first place, there is the signal fact that for more than three months the North Staffordshire works have remained without any workmen ready to go in, in spite of incessant efforts to obtain them —in spite of the lock-out; and although no single infraction of law has been reported, and at last the masters have accepted the compromise originally offered by the men, it certainly does seem that whilst workmen are urgently needed, they cannot be obtained at the price of the masters, though they can at the price of the men. If the right and wrong of a strike is only to be tested by facts, it does seem that facts answer not altogether against the men. It has been argued that the strike has been condemned and discountenanced by the whole body of workmen, and even denounced by the northern division of the union. But this was obviously due to public and prudential grounds, not to economic. The only practical proof that the strike is discountenanced by the body of workmen would be that they were ready to take their places; and that proof, in spite of every inducement, has not been given. We come next to the supposed axiom that wages must naturally fall because prices in that market have fallen, and we are assured that it is an eternal law of political economy that wages must fall in a falling market. This is one of the glib fallacies with which these questions are so easily disposed of. If wages are measured by the proportion which the demand bears to the supply of labour, there is no necessity at all that wages should fall in any given trade because the prices that are obtained in it fall. Prices and wages, *in a particular trade*, may vary in every conceivable ratio. In some cases a fall of price leads to a vast increase of consumption, and therefore of demand for labour; and therefore wages may rise, and that permanently. This was the case of the growing cotton manufacture, and, indeed, of every quickly increasing trade, where prices rapidly sank, whilst wages rapidly rose. In some cases a rise of prices leads to a vast decrease of consumption, and therefore of demand for labour, and therefore wages may fall. This is the case of the late Lancashire distress, when prices rapidly rose and wages rapidly sank. In some cases a fall of prices is caused by a decrease of consumption which involves a decrease of demand for labour; whilst labour, by emigration or other causes, may decrease still more rapidly, and in this case prices may fall whilst wages actually rise; a case of which there are frequent instances in the American war. Sometimes consumption remaining the same and labour remaining the same, an influx of capital may, by competition, at once reduce prices and raise wages. In fact, there is no absolute connection whatever between the rise of price in a particular manufacture and the rise of wages of those engaged in it. And this is but another instance of the hollowness of the economic maxims which public writers seek to impose on a commercial people. The truth is, that the attempt to make wages depend on prices, instead of making prices depend on wages, is thoroughly unsound and unnatural, and cannot possibly issue in anything but discord. The real and natural relation is rather between profits and wages, and not between prices and wages, and the attempt to substitute the latter for the former in the iron trade is something very like an ingenious artifice. A rise of 10 per cent. in price might possibly increase profits 100 or even 200 per cent., whilst wages were increased only 10 per cent. We may suppose the bar of iron to sell for ten guineas per ton, the profit on it to be ten shillings; then an increase in price of one pound per ton, supposing (what is possible, but unlikely) the cost of production to remain the same, would amount to 200 per cent. Supposing (what is probable) half the cost of production, viz., for coal, premises, plant, superintendence, taxes, &c., to remain in the gross unaltered, and the other half of the cost to be increased 10 per cent., the increase of profit would still be 100 per cent., and so on for every 10 per cent. These figures are merely hypothetical, but far from impossible; still they seem to show that an increase of wages in proportion to price bears no definite relation whatever to the increase of profits. The rule is that an increase of price diminishes instead of increasing profits, and a fall of price increases them, as every shopkeeper knows. The attempt to establish a regular dependence of wages on prices is so utterly unnatural and unjust, that it must lead to continual confusion until it is abandoned. In the gradual improvement and development of production, a vast number of articles of consumption—and iron is no exception—steadily decrease in price, whilst the wages of the artificers who produce them steadily and naturally rise. The price of a knife, of a nail, of a coat, of a piece of cotton goods, of a mirror, of a steam-engine, have certainly declined, whilst the wages of the makers of them have certainly risen. The great and general fall of the price of corn unquestionably did not cause a similar reduction in the wages of the labourers who produced it. On the contrary, in many parts of England, the very causes which reduced prices in corn, raised the wages of the cultivators. In every growing and improving trade, the natural tendency is for prices to fall and wages to rise; profits, of course, often increasing 10, 50, or 100 per cent. The attempt to persuade the workmen to make their earnings dependent on the price of the goods produced is so preposterous, that it is difficult to believe that men of business ever made it in good faith.

A great deal has been made of the supposed understanding that wages should vary as prices. In the first place, such an understanding has not really been acted on, if ever made. In the next place, there is no recognised body with whom, on the part of the men, such an understanding could be made. But whether it ever existed or not, it is far too unnatural to be maintained. Prices might very easily be sinking whilst the demand for labour was excessive, and the supply of it small, and in such a case it is preposterous to suppose that the workmen would accept a reduction, whilst every fact of the market was in their favour, and their employers were possibly doubling their profits. There is nothing to prevent profits from rising whilst prices are sinking, for they usually do, as in the development of the cotton trade. Or again, in a very unfavourable market, whilst gross returns are greatly diminished, the loss might be so skilfully thrown on the cost of production that no diminution of net profits should ensue. It is hence impossible to show that wages must infallibly fall either through a fall in price or even a very diminished rate of gross returns. There is indeed but one natural ratio with which, if it is to fluctuate at all, the rate of wages should correspond, and that is the rate of *net* profit. If wages fluctuate in some fixed ratio with this, they may continue to bear something like the same proportion to the fund from which they are derived—the fund out of which both wages and profits issue. But the state of this fund is precisely the fact which is most religiously kept secret from the men as well as the public. It therefore comes round, on every point of view, to this—that it is impossible to judge *à priori* what is the natural rate of the wages of the labourers in any trade, and, therefore, whether any particular demand they make is warranted by the state of the market, *until the rate of the accumulation of capital in the trade and of the profits of the capitalist be authentically put in proof*.

Not only is price no measure of the natural rate of wages, not only are gross returns no measure of it; but it is quite possible that *net* profits may be no infallible standard. The net profits of an employer may be decreasing greatly, yet still if he needs labourers and cannot get them at his own price, he must pay the wages they ask. Of course he will not do so if their demands prevent him from receiving the lowest return for his capital he will accept; but until that point is reached he will pay the wages they ask. The fact that business and profits are diminished is a far from conclusive reason that the wages of the workmen must necessarily fall. The wages of workmen may fall when the supply of their labour is in excess of the demand. But this relation is the point in question, and this alone.

It may sound almost a paradox to some persons, but no position is capable of more overwhelming proof—that there is no economic necessity at all that the rate of wages should fluctuate in any particular trade. In all the more highly skilled trades the rate of wages remains absolutely stationary for periods of ten and twenty years together, and only varies to rise at distant intervals. The wages of the engineers, one of the most powerful and highly paid of all the trades, have never varied for more than ten years. Masons, carpenters, bricklayers, painters, cotton-spinners, and countless other trades, in every district of England, under conditions the most various, those highly skilled as well as the least skilled, have been over still longer periods paid at the same rates. Of course when less business is done a smaller gross sum is paid in wages. But it is obvious that there are at least three ways in which this can be done, any one of which satisfies economic necessity. The same number of labourers may be employed for a shorter time, or a smaller number of labourers may be employed for the same time, or a lower rate of wages may be paid. All or any of these may be combined; but there is no greater *necessity* for the last of these methods being adopted than for any other. To assure us, as self-styled economists assure us, that the rate of wages *must* fluctuate on this or that ingeniously framed ratio, is a proposition as rational as that the population of London must fluctuate in the ratio of the population of England.

No doubt there is a certain truth at the bottom of even so transparent a fallacy as this. The real teachers of the science certainly have established certain conditions—capital, population, profits, and so forth—on which the rate of wages in the long run depends. But of course they mean that these form the *limits* within which the rate of wages is confined. If the gross returns of the iron trade are £30,000,000, *and cannot be increased*, of course wages and profits in the gross can never exceed that amount; but *within this limit* every variation of rate and proportion is possible, and there is not a growing trade in the kingdom in which this proportion might not be immensely varied.

If there is one doctrine which political economy has more than any other assiduously set itself to impress on the public, it is that the wages or remuneration of labour depend on the proportion between capital in search of labour and labour in search of capital. Yet, in spite of this axiom, we see public writers, and the public generally, deciding disputes about wages *whilst both these data are totally unknown*. Nay, we usually, as in this case, hear strikes of the workmen condemned in the name of this very doctrine by people who profess total ignorance of both the indispensable sides of the equation. It is repeated to us, *ad nauseam*, that wages depend on the demand for and the supply of labour; yet after all that has been written, not a word has been uttered respecting the two real questions in issue—What have been the relative profits of the iron-masters, and what are the relative numbers of the iron-workers? Science assures us that a certain conclusion will follow from the comparison of one set of figures with another. And there are persons who seem to suppose that these figures may be seen written in the sky, or may be assumed at will.

The real history of the state of the iron trade appears to be this. Under the effect of the American war, of the development of railways, of iron-clad ships, and engineering in many parts of the world, an unparalleled demand for iron in recent years has set in. That demand was met by a rise of price amounting to 10, 20, and then 30 per cent. This rise of price, far from checking demand, enormously increased profits, which rose in some cases 50, 100, in others 200, in others 300 per cent. Gains so sudden and prodigious attracted fresh capital; foreign capitalists came into the field, and competition and over-stocking necessarily reduced prices. The wages of labour, however, in the meantime had advanced 10, 20, and at most 30 per cent., a rate which did not act as such a stimulus to the supply of labour as the enormous rate of profit did to the supply of capital. And it is notorious that capital can rush into a demand far quicker than skilled labour. On the contrary, the causes of the rise of price—American war, colonial enterprises, &c.—drained off great numbers of the very workmen whom capital most required at home. At that moment, perhaps, of unusual demand for labour, without greatly increased supply of it, an organised effort of the workmen might possibly have raised wages prodigiously above even 30 per cent. It was not made, and the influx of foreign capital into the trade greatly lowered prices, and gradually diminished colonial and foreign demand. Trade became comparatively slack, profits comparatively small. There still, however, remained sufficient demand and sufficient profit to give fair employment to the labourers, and as their numbers had not been increased there was no superabundance of labour. On the contrary, the tendency of the capital which came in and reduced prices by competition would be to bid for the labourers and raise their wages. This is a simple explanation of the phenomenon that profits largely decrease, whilst wages rather tend to rise than to fall. A fact somewhat singular it appears to employers! But the singularity of it resides in this—that the vast increase of wages which the labourers might have obtained during the high prices, had they used their power, *all went to swell the profits of the employer*.

The illustration of this would occupy more space than can here be given to it, but a careful study of the statistics of the trade[1] will show the following results

(1) See Hunt's Mineral Statistics, Ryland's Iron-Trade Circular, &c., &c.

—(1) A vast increase in production, *i.e.* of demand for labour; (2) No corresponding increase in the supply of labour; (3) An enormous increase of profits; (4) No corresponding increase of wages.

The growth of the iron manufacture is a matter of national history. It is well known that within the last forty years it has doubled itself ten times, with an annual rate of increase of 20 or 30 per cent. Of course this gigantic growth represents a corresponding rate of profit, and justifies M'Culloch's remark, that "larger fortunes have been made in this than in any department of industry." Recent events have in the last few years raised these profits into still more fabulous proportions, and it is well known that the increase of the iron trade mainly sustained the national revenue on the collapse of the cotton trade. The trade reports during last year teem with accounts of new companies forming, new works opening, and vast business doing in the entire trade. No doubt desperate competition naturally reduced the high prices during the latter part of 1864, but this was but one of the ordinary and temporary fluctuations to which this trade is peculiarly liable. The year 1865, however, began with a state of trade not so bad but what the iron-masters' organ can write that it opens "not without promise of fair results and tolerably remunerative prices." And this before the reduction of wages. We learn also that thirty-three new furnaces were building, which may reassure persons who fear the iron trade of England is in a state of collapse. The latest trade reports are still more satisfactory, and one goes so far as to represent its condition as actually "buoyant." Altogether we will trust that, in spite of some occasional mysteries of the market, the demand for English iron has not yet died out of the human race.

Remembering Adam Smith's maxim, that wages depend on the increase, not the extent, of business, it is a little singular to find that the wages of puddlers are still just what they were previously to 1854. In the Blue Book published by the Children's Employment Commission, they are estimated at twenty-eight shillings per week. A careful inquiry (putting aside some extravagant statements in newspapers) will make them now about thirty to thirty-five shillings, on an average all the year round—about on a level with the wages of the highest scale of skilled labour. The same blue book gives us the statement of an iron-master of the extreme want of labourers in these words:—
"The supply of hands is not actually insufficient to do the work which is needed, but there is no further available supply." The facts of the strike indeed prove this to be as true now as it was then. In spite of every effort for sixteen weeks the North Staffordshire works have been empty, and if anything were needed to prove that the labour market was not overstocked, it might be found in the threats of the newspapers, that "six hundred puddlers from Russia," or "five hundred puddlers from Prussia, were expected next week,"—doubtless in new suits of buckram.

Let us now proceed to consider the lock-out of the employers. And first, in the abstract, what is the kind of combination legitimate in their case? Of course it is perfectly open to them to act in combination to test the question of fact. In reality, capitalists—as we have seen—are in a permanent state of combination to raise prices and to reduce wages. Whether the masters of any trade are legally incorporated and have paid secretaries or not, is of little consequence, so long as they really act in combination. As a matter of fact the association of masters has actually existed in Staffordshire for more than twenty years, whilst that of the men is only in its infancy. It is perfectly notorious that quarterly meetings of iron-masters have for a long period fixed the price of iron and the rate of wages. The natural answer to the combination of the workmen to limit the supply of labour, was a combination of capitalists to obtain it freely. It is perfectly open to them to support a brother capitalist during the test of the labour market by aiding him to obtain workmen, by supplying him with funds or credit, by undertaking or guaranteeing his contracts, or by any reasonable method by which he can dispense with his refusing workmen. They can use their vast command of the channels of publicity, their experience of the markets, and their wide relations with capitalists of every kind, to maintain themselves. There never was a strike in which all this was not done more or less effectually; often it is done with extraordinary energy and even without any strike or threat of one; it is being invisibly accomplished by silent associations of capitalists to promote their own interest. This is the reasonable counterpart of the combination of the men. It embraces almost any amount of active co-operation, and evidently leaves room for influence more powerful and far-reaching than that of the men. In the recent strike, indeed, as in all great contests, the full resources of this machinery have been called into play. The principal iron-masters of the centre and north of England have been organised into a single body. The moral pressure which has been so often denounced in the union, has been exercised with full vigour amongst them. They have had funds for common purposes; they have concerted a variety of expedients to supply each other with material, with labourers. They have taken such joint measures in the iron market, in the money market, and entered into such mutual agreements as they thought fit. It was of course open to them to have subscribed by a per-centage out of their profits a sum to sustain the full profits of their threatened brethren, precisely as the men subscribed funds out of their earnings for theirs.

But having availed themselves of the full force of this combination, the iron-masters proceeded to a very different step. They combined to close the whole of their workshops on a given day, and announced that they would remain closed until the North Staffordshire men were again at work. Directly or indirectly, it is said, 200,000 persons throughout the kingdom were suddenly thrown into destitution. How does this act answer to the test which has just been laid down ? It does nothing to show whether there was a superabundant supply of labour in the market. It throws no light on the question—what is for the moment the natural level of wages ? It simply suspends the decision. The real issue is whether the demand for labour exceeds or falls short of the supply. And the answer of the lock-out is to punish and disable all the labourers. The measure, in fact, is simply penal. It is avowedly intended only to terrify, coerce, or harass the whole body of labourers so as to paralyse their combination, and prevent the state of the market from being tried. It is in reality a mere industrial *coup-d'état*. If it were intended as a means of testing the market, if it were a trade necessity, if there were financial or other motives for such a proceeding, if the state of the iron trade made a general suspension of manufacture requisite, it might be otherwise. But nothing of the kind was ever alleged in this case. The lock-out was devised and justified as a simple means of conquering the whole body of workmen, and of preventing them from supporting each other during the experiment. It could have no other end. It possibly acted as a very powerful engine to obtain a certain end—so would physical force—but neither could prove anything as to the simple matter of fact which was in issue. It is, in fact, this character of terrorism and aggression which is the salient feature of the lock-out. It was indeed denied that the object of the lock-out was the suppression of the union, but it is obvious that its avowed motive was to suppress the purpose for which the union existed, viz. mutual support. It aimed at punishing or pauperising every member of a combination. If, as has been said above, combination amongst the men is legitimate and even necessary to enable them to bargain on equal terms, penal inflictions on the right of combination are attempts to reduce the men to unequal terms. The combinations of masters are as legitimate as those of the men, provided they are directed to legitimate objects; but combinations of masters to crush combinations of men are abuses of power, and intended directly to reduce the men to the helplessness of isolation. We have often heard of late the question—If men may fairly combine to strike, why may not masters combine to lock-out?—the logic of which is a verbal antithesis that would justify combinations to rob.

The obvious answer is that they cannot fairly combine to punish their men for combining. When workmen combine for a rise of wages, masters can combine (and they invariably do) to reduce them; but neither side can in reason punish the other for exercising this natural right. The moment we draw the true parallel on the side of the men to this lock-out on the part of the masters, we see the truth of this position in a striking light. The true parallel to the lock-out would be this. Let us suppose that a committee of the Union of Iron-workers gave a fortnight's notice to every employer that they required a rise of 10 per cent. in their wages; that every firm reluctantly agreed to it except the iron-masters of North Staffordshire, who, with promises of assistance from the other capitalists, refused. We have next to suppose that the committee of the men's union gave orders to every iron-worker in the kingdom suddenly to cease to work, whether employed by a master who had assisted the North Staffordshire masters or not. Suppose the orders of the committee were that no man should work for any employer for any wages under any conditions or in consideration of any promise until the North Staffordshire masters had agreed to the terms of the union; that the whole body of employers were ordered to force their North Staffordshire brethren to adopt the men's terms, to take into their immediate employment the whole of the workmen on strike at the advanced rates, to force them to surrender their contracts, and to reduce them to bankruptcy if they still resisted.

This is the true parallel of the lock-out, and it can safely be said not only that nothing approaching to this can be seen in the Staffordshire strike, but that no body of workmen in the kingdom ever ventured upon or thought of so wanton an exercise of power. We have only to trace this case to its full parallel to imagine the amount of just indignation which such a proceeding would call out. The public feeling would at once stigmatise such an act as systematic oppression and terrorism,' and would see that it aimed at settling a question of the market by coercion and intimidation. The mere exercise of public opinion in such cases shows us in fact that there is some other limit to action in these matters beside that of law. When we say that these questions must be left to be decided by strength we certainly do not mean that *any* exercise of strength is reasonable. If both parties may do their best to gain their terms, it is yet clear there are a great many things they may not do. Industrial wars, like national wars, have their own recognised code. In the first place, they may do nothing illegal. The masters are certainly not free to win by sending for a regiment of dragoons, or the men by setting fire to their employers' works. Neither are all things not illegal justifiable. We hear in much loose talk that the masters "may do what they will with their own;" that they "must" protect themselves, and should answer force by force. Scarcely in all things. There are a great many things strictly legal which would greatly promote the objects of either side, which opinion would certainly condemn most vigorously. The master of a factory situated in a very open country might very easily adopt effectual means of coercing his refractory hands if he chanced to own every baker's and butcher's shop in the entire district, or every spring of water and every house within reach. Since a stroke of his pen could deprive an entire population of water, food, and shelter in a moment, by strict process of law, he could bring a trade question to a very speedy end. Yet opinion would condemn in the loudest manner so monstrous an abuse of accidental power. Again, on the other side, the men on strike might chance to acquire the very unsatisfactory balance-sheet of their employer, or to possess some secret which could ruin him in character or fortune, and might possibly in ways strictly legal induce him quickly to assent to their terms, or they might with very strict legality refuse to work the pumps if his property were on fire, or they might ruin the banker who lent him money, or the butcher who supplied him with meat, or in fifty ways harass, injure, or ruin him. It is nothing to say that these devices would not be successful, or would not be successful long. It is quite conceivable that they could be practised under very possible conditions. The point which concerns us is this— would they not one and all be condemned by public opinion on one side and on the other as attempts to attain a momentary profit by mere extraneous pressure? There is again another class of expedient which would raise still louder indignation. It is quite possible that one party to a dispute might have in its power a device which might be perfectly legitimate as against the other, but entail immense and disproportionate injury on the rest of the community. The contractors and workmen who were building a fortress in a great national crisis, or the constructors of a new class of guns indispensable in the turning point of a great war, or the masters and sailors of a fleet laden with corn at a moment of general famine, might, it is quite conceivable, engage in a dispute, quite legitimate by itself, which would inflict utter ruin on their country. Opinion would not be slow to visit those severely who were the direct authors of so desperate an act.

The public good sense therefore seems to have struck out two rough practical rules on which to base its judgment respecting these trade struggles. The one is, that it will condemn all attempts in either party to win by simply injuring or terrifying the other; the second is, that it will condemn every act the immediate consequence of which is to injure large masses of persons totally disinterested in the contest. There is, perhaps, a small class of very logical economists who, true to the sacred law of supply and demand, are content to sanction every act within the limits of the law of the land by which either side can force the other to submit. They trust to the grand compensating principle of "competition," and assure us that under its providential dispensation the wildest excesses of human passions work together to the common good. To such theorists the wholesale eviction of a starving population or the deportation of a county are but links in the chain of human happiness. Such men would see the battle of labour fought out with every weapon which ingenuity and exasperation can suggest (provided no Act of Parliament be infringed). It seems the less necessary to consider this view because it more and more is felt repugnant to public morality. We have passed the stage of serene acquiescence in public oppression. If in a trade dispute the master gains his end by suddenly casting the wives and children of his men on to a barren moor, or the men gain their end by forcing his creditors to call in their debts, the public conscience does, and more and more will continue to, step in and pronounce that party in the wrong. Economists of a certain school may vow that it is strictly according to their science. But men of the least political instinct must see that this is not political economy at all, but a degraded system of politics. Reasonable men will see that there are some means to an end which are legitimate, and some which are not; and that there are certain means of forcing an opponent to terms, which society has the right to condemn.

Now, when the men of North Staffordshire struck, that is, refused the new terms of the masters, they may have mistaken egregiously the state of the market; they may have demanded more than their labour was worth; they may have been acting in a wrong-headed, selfish, and ignorant spirit, but their action was limited to bringing that question to the test, and supporting themselves whilst they did so. It is not alleged that the law was infringed. There is no proof that they tried to beat the masters by resorting to extraneous means of coercion. They did not seek, though they possibly had some means, to ruin or injure every brother capitalist who supported them, nor did they refuse to enter the yard of every member of the masters' association. Their action was confined to refusing (rightly or wrongly) the wages that were offered by their employer; it did not seek to ruin every one on whom he depended. Nor, on the other hand, did they strike against a single disinterested person. It would have been thought a wild injustice, indeed, if the men had struck against every master in North Staffordshire, whether he accepted their terms or did not; whether he aided their opponents or not; whether they had any difference with him or not, merely as a warning to him to give no countenance to his brethren. Lastly, the strike was, at least, a narrowing of the contest. It minimised the evils to all parties, and especially to the dependent but unconcerned parties. This, in itself, is of immense value to society. If a trade struggle must unhappily be fought out, it is of the last consequence to the public that the area of the campaign as far as possible be localised, and society has a perfect right to complain that either party wantonly extend the evil.

The lock-out, however, was a totally different proceeding. Men were locked out by their masters, not for refusing the terms that were offered, but for helping others who did. It was avowedly penal in its object. Its sole aim was to crush combination. The second feature of it was still worse. It struck indiscriminately the innocent and the guilty alike. It struck, too, where the innocent were a large majority of the whole. The Ironworkers' Union at most includes a quarter of the whole body. Three-fourths of the whole have therefore no influence over it, nor it over them. The great bulk of the men locked out had never refused the masters' terms, nor abetted those who had, however much they sympathised with them, nor could they compel them to accept the terms. It is easy for newspapers to repeat phrases about the necessity of the innocent suffering with the guilty; but it is peculiarly repugnant to English feeling to know that three innocent men are intentionally struck in order that a fourth may be mastered. There is a third feature in the lock-out which, from the social and national point of view, is even yet more unjust. The lock-out was an avowed attempt to extend the struggle and the suffering to the widest possible area. A grand and overpowering blow was to be struck, at which the whole labouring body of England should quail. It was to be a *coup-d'état* of imperial scale and force. It is precisely this feature of it which the public and the political reasoner has the best right to condemn. The original act of some 1,000 workmen to resist an alteration in wages, supported by some ten times that number of their associated brethren, is to be met by a grand stroke of policy by which 200,000 persons, more or less, in various parts of England, are plunged into want, by which the trade of prosperous towns is paralysed, the operations of industry in every district are dislocated, whole districts stricken as by a famine or plague, and a national disorder inflicted deep enough to tell strongly on the annual revenue of the nation. It may be that all this suffering and ruin were absolutely unavoidable, but the English public in its calmer moments will seek a reckoning and answer from the direct rather than the indirect authors of this suffering, and will require strict proof of the " necessity " for creating a national calamity.

It is barren logic to repeat that the act of the masters was just as legitimate as that of the men. As against the men, we can suppose that it was; but as against society, it was not. This is no question of abstract rights. It is one of the exercise of rights. It is not a metaphysical or scientific question. It is essentially a political and social one. And in politics there are a great many abstract rights, the exercise of which society will authoritatively condemn. A man roughly attacked by a footpad in the street may have a perfect right to disable his opponent, but not by discharging in the midst of a crowd a six-barrelled pistol at random. And when a man finds that he cannot get the best of a bargain, except by a step which will ruin fifty of his neighbours, society (whatever economists may say) will simply require him to forego it.

Tried by this test there is very rarely a strike which is not on purely social grounds unjustifiable. A time must come when the sense of self-preservation in a class calls on them to act even at the cost of much injury to society about them. But it is a serious and stern responsibility; and the men who struck in North Staffordshire have much to answer for, even supposing that their claim is reasonable in itself. It should, however, be remembered that in this case, as in most others of the kind, the other workmen who suffer are more or less assenting or sympathising parties. Were it not so, a strike would rarely be possible, as the "under hands" would take the place of the "puddlers," the smiths of the engineers, the labourers of the bricklayers, and so on, for which work they are more or less prepared. But if the strike of North Staffordshire is worthy of condemnation on social and moral grounds, as a selfish injury by a body of men to others ten times their number, what is to be said of the lock-out which affected the population of counties and the trade of a kingdom, and which was planned altogether on a scale of reckless indifference, before which the evils of the largest strike sink into insignificance?

So much for the general policy of the lock-out. But there are features in its mode of execution which are very significant. It was even in its form penal. It offered no alternative. No terms of submission were suggested. It was totally different from a simple refusal to deal. The men were locked out until something else occurred in another part of the kingdom, over which the bulk of them had as little control as over the action of the tides. The northern division of the men's union, before the lock-out commenced, formally separated themselves from the men on strike, offered any guarantee of good faith, and actually refused to contribute a penny. The balance-sheets of a union are far from secret, and any infraction of this guarantee could have been instantly detected. The two divisions of the men indeed actually engaged in a quarrel of their own whilst the masters locked both out on the ground of their union. Supposing every unionist in the trade had been (as they were not) in strict concert, and under perfect discipline, they formed scarcely a quarter of the whole; and to coerce the executive (supposed to be so despotic) by putting the screw on a large body of men with whom they had nothing to do, is a little like taking a besieged city by driving into it the women and children of the surrounding country. This dealing, however, with the union, as a legal and authoritative body, is in itself a little singular. The lock-out proceeded entirely on the ground that it was to compel the union to take a certain course. The masters said that the union had originated the strike and therefore must withdraw it. The executive replied, that they had tried but could not; and the lock-out was an expedient which aimed at compelling them to do so. But if in these trade disputes the masters are to deal directly with the officers of the union, these bodies must be made as authoritative as possible, not systematically opposed and denounced; at least the laws which make such associations incapable of being incorporated should be revised. If they still are so irregular in their action, if their officers are still so irresponsible, so indefinite, and have an authority so uncertain, the cause is that in the state of the law these unions are the best form of irregular association which the men can obtain, that their form and action is the best that poor men disowned by the law can invent, because the public and the statute-book forbid them to become permanent and recognised institutions. If the union is now to be held responsible for the action of the entire body of workmen in a trade, and the whole body of workmen are to be responsible for it, the least that justice requires is that they should be properly legalised and publicly strengthened. It would no doubt be better for all sides if the unions were more powerful and had more definite authority; but the claim comes with a bad grace from those who have laboured for years to crush, discredit, and repudiate them. With a singularly bad grace indeed does this come from the iron-masters of the North of England, who were engaged some months of last summer in extinguishing the union of these very puddlers in the Bradford and Leeds district—who locked out the whole of their men to enforce the "declaration," that they were not, and would not become, members of any society which regulated wages or employment—and whose men at this very moment are obliged to work, with their signatures to this actual "declaration." The Associated Ironmasters of Yorkshire lock out the men to make a union impossible. The Associated Masters of Northumberland and Stafford lock out their men to compel the union to exhibit more energy. Conduct so capricious and unreasonable as this is as certain to provoke resistance as it is certain to prove ineffectual.

Very ineffectual it has proved. There is a certain order of economists to whom the issue in any commercial question is the sole test that can be applied. If a strike succeeds, it is right and just. If it fails, it is wrong. In every matter of bargain we are told the true view is the one which succeeds. Brought to this test the lock-out was utterly wrong because it utterly failed. It was undertaken to put an end to the North Staffordshire "strike," and it was announced that it should last until that "strike" was closed. As a matter of fact it was withdrawn without having done anything but greatly aggravate the local dispute. The Association of Masters could not last; but in sections they made their peace as best they could with their men. They certainly did not exhibit themselves that perfect union and discipline which they exacted from the men. They covered their divisions and retreat by such pleas as they could. But it is just as preposterous to pretend that the lock-out was withdrawn because it had answered its end, as they said in the north, as to say that it was withdrawn from motives of humanity, as they did in the south. The lock-out was withdrawn because it became impossible to persevere in it, and because it was found to be doing more harm than good, as every impartial observer could perfectly see. Whatever was the value of the guarantee by the union not to support the strike, that guarantee was given before the lock-out commenced, and nothing was easier than to know whether that guarantee was being maintained. If it be said that the object of the lock-out was simply to make it quite certain that no support would be given to the "strike," it certainly puts the policy of such a measure in a very odious light. Before proceeding to convulse the trade of the kingdom, and to desolate a province, it was surely the duty of the masters to ascertain as a fact beyond dispute that the acts and assurances made by the authorities of the union were essentially insincere and evasive. Everything shows that it was impossible for the northern half of the union to do more than they did, or to show more entire good faith than they have shown. So that it comes to this, that an engine of such ruinous force as a lock-out was to be suddenly put in use to prevent a possible act of the men, because a certain Association of Masters chose to be very suspicious or very impatient.

We have heard very much of the absolute necessity of this measure, that it was an act of self-preservation which the masters were compelled to adopt.

Public opinion will certainly require very close investigation of the real "necessity" of a measure which is to threaten the peace and prosperity of the kingdom so seriously. How comes it then that this lock-out was the one course possible? It was a question of the superabundance of labour. Now if the men on strike had been all the time supported in luxury by external aid, or their own accumulated savings, if they had remained out for years together, and had been kept in permanent idleness by any means whatever, that would not in the least have prevented the unemployed labourers who were said to be waiting to take their places from accepting the terms of the employers. Of course, if force, physical or moral, were put upon the unemployed labourers to prevent them from filling up the vacant places, there are laws stringent enough to reach both. And very sharply these laws are worked. If the unemployed surplus of labourers decline on other grounds of their own to take the places of the men on strike—from sympathy, from persuasion, from scruple, or any other similar motive—they are not seeking that employment, and of course are not *in the market* at all. Those motives may be supplied or sustained by their brethren, refreshed by exhortation, or stimulated by information; but what is there in all this to make "necessary," and "unavoidable," and "indispensable," the reduction of the whole body of labourers to starvation? If there are labourers willing to take the offered terms, they will be found in time if the laws are honestly enforced. If such labourers are not found, and are still wanted, offers must be raised till they are attracted. That is to say, if the places of men on "strike" cannot be filled up, the men must be taken back on their own terms, as we have seen. Such is the plain explanation on the ordinary theories of economists of an ordinary strike for wages, and judged by this test the strike in North Staffordshire was a simple appeal to the facts of the market, which events have justified; the lock-out is an attempt to remove the question from that issue, and to decide it by personal oppression.

The argument by which this supposed "necessity" has been usually explained is, that unless the masters had resorted to the sweeping measure of prevention they would have been all conquered "in detail," that the lock-out was made "indispensable" by the "usual tactics" of the men. That is to say, that the men would have struck seriatim against each master in turn, and they, one after another, would have been forced to yield. Certainly they would, if the state of the labour market justified the demands of their men; but certainly not if it did otherwise. If there took place a strike against A, and he so failed to find labourers, and so much needed them, that he had to raise his terms, and then B had to do the same, and so on all through the list of employers, it would be the most convincing possible proof that there was *not* a superabundance of labourers, and that wherever it was tried, under whatever state of the market, men could not be found to accept the terms of the employer. The fact, in any dispute as to wages, that the masters are certain to be beaten one by one in every case, is perfectly conclusive proof that the labour market is against them, and that wages are sure to be raised. The case might not be fairly tried where a single capitalist is in special conditions, and it may be quite right that the body of capitalists take care that none of their number be overcome from want of time or assistance, or reasonable freedom of action. Such help is the reasonable combination of the capitalists, and is the exact counterpart of the unions of the men. There may of course be possibly a real *numerical* surplus of unemployed labourers, but if they have their own reasons to refuse employment, they cease to form a portion of the effective supply of labour, just as unemployed funds cease to form a part of effective capital. And so long as the effective capital in a trade holds the same relation to the effective supply of labour there is no reason that wages should vary. No amount of combination between capital on the one side and labour on the other can prejudice the experiment, provided that combination on both sides confines itself to the legitimate end of *strengthening its own side, not of crippling or injuring or threatening the other.*

It is no doubt quite possible that a close combination of workmen, possessed by exceptional circumstances of a virtual monopoly, might force up wages to that point that they threatened to absorb all profits. There may have been rare and small cases in which this has been done. In that case, no doubt, capital will cease to employ labourers at all, and will pass into other channels. It is quite unnecessary to assume, as has sometimes been done, that wherever capital has passed into other channels, it has done so under the pressure of exorbitant demands for wages. It has only followed the largest profits. But the case is conceivable. Wherever such an event occurs, or is imminent, it may be very reasonable and just that the capitalists should combine to suspend their operations simultaneously, and cease to employ the labourers at all. It is far from being the object of this paper to argue that in no conceivable case is it reasonable that capitalists should cease to be employers altogether. Our present purpose is only concerned to see that such a case is totally different from the present case of the lock-out. It never was suggested that it was caused by commercial necessity, by the state of orders, by reasons of prudence. Its sudden withdrawal and the immediate resumption of active work shows that it was nothing of the kind. Indeed, to make an act of the kind reasonable, full explanation of its cause, ample notice to all concerned, and willingness to modify its consequences, would at any rate be expected by the public, and of course would be actually shown by the capitalists. The sympathy and help of the public has been frequently asked, not indeed by, but for the iron-masters, on the ground that the demands of their men were tending to expel capital by absorbing profits.

If this were really the case, the best, and indeed the only means of effectually checking this tendency would be the public demonstration of the fact. There is but one satisfactory demonstration possible, short of the actual migration of capital, which is the actual scrutiny of the profits of capital. If some of the leading firms could succeed in satisfying the public, their own men, or confidential referees, that their profits were actually being exhausted by wages, the men are quite shrewd enough to withdraw from the suicidal course of draining their own well dry. But so long as this is refused, and the case is suggested only in the columns of morning newspapers, the men will scarcely be induced to believe it. As applied to the iron trade, indeed, outcries about the imminent annihilation of profits are probably worth about as much as the perennial wail of the British farmer over the extinction of agriculture. If the real justification of the lock-out is said to be this, that the profits of the capitalists were vanishing under the high rate of wages, and that the masters were "forced," to preserve capital in the trade at all, to warn the labourers of their blunder, it cannot be too sharply insisted that the direct and simple way of meeting the danger was to state it, and after stating it to prove it by proper reference to the books of account. As nothing of the kind has ever been attempted (and it could easily have been accomplished by the agency of confidential arbitrators, without any prejudicial publicity), there is very good reason to suppose it could not be done, and the final yielding of the masters would show that the plea is untrue. Indeed, whilst employers systematically refuse to disclose the necessary conditions for estimating the market (even to confidential and independent judges), it is out of the question that their men should acknowledge their demands to be untenable. It is perfectly ridiculous to suppose that one party to a bargain can expect the other to close it on the faith of figures to which he himself alone has access. There is something quite *naïf* in the idea, not seldom propounded, that workmen are bound, in common sense, to permit a reduction of wages every time that their employer assures them that he cannot afford to give more. Yet this is the simple meaning of those who complain that workmen do not instantly recognise the relative diminutions of the "wages-fund"—the actual state of that wages-fund being kept a profound secret from them. It is repeated day by day, in every possible form, that strikes for wages are suicidal and unreasonable, because there is only a certain fund applicable to the payment of wages, *but what that fund may be the employers alone are permitted to know.*

The truth is, that the complaint of capitalists that a strike for increase of wages is unreasonable, as depriving them of the fair profits of capital, is of all possible pleas that which is most fatal to their own maxims. It points out in strong light the necessity for complete publicity of the facts *on both sides,* before the true state of the market can be judged of. It points also to the relation of natural justice, now too often forgotten, between wages and *profits.* Thirdly, it practically abandons the ground that the natural measure of wages is the proportion of capital to labour, and points to considerations of equitable distribution.

The lock-out, indeed, as the means of terminating a strike, is the completest denial of the rule that wages naturally follow supply and demand. If, when the labour market is overstocked, wages will naturally fall, there is no necessity to use violence to decide a question which facts can prove by themselves. In reality, no lock-out was ever attempted except when the employers were tolerably certain that no labourers can be found on the offered terms. The more certain they are that labourers are in the market and ready to come in, the less likely are they to resort to the expense and risk of a lock-out, in the attempt to compel them. They do so because they believe that violent pressure alone will force the labourers to terms. That is to say, they only lock out to enforce terms which the state of the market by itself will not justify.

These lock-outs are, in fact, becoming now a regular feature of our industrial system. They are now, from time to time, tried on the part of the employers, in one trade after another, and it may be said that there is no known instance of any real counterpart on the part of the men. The workmen never yet in any trade combined to strike work against every employer in the trade, with the avowed object of forcing them to withhold all connection with a certain set of employers, who were in dispute with a certain section of their workmen. The master engineers throughout England, the coal masters of Yorkshire, the master builders of London, and those of the midland districts, the Yorkshire iron-masters, as well as some others, have at different times attempted by a lock-out to extinguish a strike. In every instance the real object of the movement was to crush combination, the first and most natural right of the workman. In every case the lock-out has been a complete failure, disguised occasionally by an apparent triumph,[1] but virtually a damaging defeat. The effect of the lock-out in every case has been to produce great irritation, not only in the particular body of workmen affected, but in the whole mass of the artisan population. It has been defeated invariably by the support which it has created for the objects of it amongst the rest of the community. In every case the union has been greatly increased and strengthened, and in some cases almost created by it. It is pretty clear also that a systematic lock-out, unless it succeed by the first violence of the blow, must very speedily be withdrawn. The feeling it awakens calls out,

---

(1) In the case of the Amalgamated Engineers, and in that of the Yorkshire iron-workers, the signature of the "Declaration" of non-membership of a union was nominally enforced, but, it is well known to both parties, was practically an unmeaning form. The union of both flourishes.

in fact, the very spirit of combination which it is its object to suppress. The prosperity of the great engineers' union dates from the close of the great lock-out in 1851, that of the Yorkshire colliers from the lock-out of 1858. The triumphant reply to the policy of the lock-out is the rapid development of the union in every trade in which it has been tried. There is this peculiarity about the lock-out which makes it a resource of only momentary power: the longer it continues, the more overpowering is the temptation it holds out to some of the manufacturers to make their own fortunes by deserting their class,—a temptation which it has been proved to satiety the capitalists are much less able to resist than the workmen. On the other hand, its inevitable consequence, if protracted, is to force the labourers into other fields, and thus to reduce the very supply of labour which it was intended to promote. Labourers do not flow over the earth quite as freely as some economists imagine, but still they migrate rather more easily than capital invested in fixed establishments, and the effect of an obstinate lock-out is invariably to produce so great a scarcity of labourers, that wages rise immediately it is withdrawn. A lock-out, as a rule, is the cradle of emigration, of unions, of co-operation, of association of every kind. It evokes a spirit of resistance and organisation, by which the trades are united amongst themselves, and one with another, by which every resource of the whole operative order is strengthened and stimulated, by which every latent class feeling is fanned into desperation.

On every ground, therefore, economical, political, and moral, a lock-out such as that which we have seen is utterly indefensible. Economically, it abandons the principles on which capital professes to rest. It substitutes for the measure of supply and demand the test of the power to injure, and prevents a simple question of fact from being decided by the issue of events. It imitates and exaggerates the worst blunders and injustices of the workmen. It promotes the very result it is aimed at preventing. Politically, it inflicts without economic justification vast evils on the public, produces an extraordinary amount of class animosity and social agitation, and elevates a local dispute into a national disturbance. Morally, it is nothing but avarice working, through cruelty, on a scale and with a system which throws into the shade the worst excesses of the workmen at the worst times of trade selfishness. It exhibits, in its most stupendous form, in the natural heads of society, a wanton contempt of every true social duty, which threatens the existence of society itself. On moral grounds, it is true, the recent strike of the men (as are all strikes) is open to similar blame, though in a far lower degree, and with far more excuse. But no such pitiful retort, no barren logic of economic sophistry, can long blind thoughtful men to the belief that the lock-out itself is no less than a great crime against the nation.

FREDERIC HARRISON.

PUBLIC AFFAIRS.

WITHIN the scope of our first fortnightly record there comes, unhappily, one of those great crimes in high places which are at once recognised by the common instinct of mankind as landmarks in history. The murder of President Lincoln, which yet agitates the civilised world, must rank high in the category of those cardinal events which influence the destinies of the human race. The man was so well known—photography, and steam, and electricity have so far lessened the effect of time and distance, that we are moved by sentiments of horror, pity, and indignation, as though we all saw the deed committed before our very eyes. It is impossible to speculate with any profit on the result of an act perpetrated under circumstances of peculiar tragic interest, by one who must have been politically insane; but we can at once aver that no possible combination of circumstances could have created such a feeling in favour of the Federal government as the violent death, by the hands of a Southern sympathiser, of Mr. Lincoln in the Washington theatre. Let it be at once understood that we do not believe any Southern statesman, politician, or general — we had almost said gentleman — planned, suggested, or was cognisant of the foul design, or was privy to its execution; but let us at the same time, in the interests of truth, declare our conviction that Mr. Lincoln was assassinated in pursuance of a conspiracy to take the lives of the prominent leaders of the Federal government, which was planned and executed by partisans of the South, or of States Rights and Slavery. The murder of the President might, if isolated, be taken as the act of a madman; but the simultaneous assault on Mr. Seward forces us to think there was a plot for a political assassination, concocted by at least two sane men, as we do not believe madmen can conspire. There will be no very decided manifestation of feeling on the part of the Southern leaders respecting the crime, or we are much mistaken; and if the murderers have been discovered, it has not been by Southern aid. Let it be remembered how absolutely personal the animosity of the people of the Slave States is in all its characteristics. They hated such men as Lincoln and Seward with an intensity not to be credited by those ignorant of the passion which animated the hand that struck Sumner to the ground in the Senate, and that sought, in many a debate before secession, to adjust political differences on the field of honour. Mr. Lincoln was, to the Southern mind, the type of a despot, a tyrant, a plunderer, and a felon. He was to the South an "Illinois baboon, influenced by whisky and fanaticism," who, by some inscrutable decree of Providence, was armed with satanic power to afflict and scourge them, and to trample on their rights. The Federal troops were styled "Lincoln's mercenaries" or "assassins;" the Federal navy was called "Lincoln's piratical flotilla;" the Federal judges were termed "Lincoln's myrmidons;" and the people of the Northern States were designated "Lincoln's slaves." The Federal prisons were "Lincoln's dungeons." Those who used these phrases never intended to produce any such effect on the minds of their followers as that which led bold and desperate men to plot against the life of the President and his cabinet, as though they were the sole depositories of Federal power, but they did intend to fire the Southern heart. If we did not know that revenge is blind and hate unreasonable, we might feel some wonder that the President was not murdered before the fall of Richmond and the flight of Mr. Davis. It is when a cause is triumphant that its champions are most hated and feared. Mr. Lincoln, through the whole of his political life, expressed his opinions with singular moderation, and had never been engaged in any violent controversy with a political opponent. The men of the pistol sought other antagonists. His selection for the candidature was due to the mildness of character which raised him above or depressed him beneath personal antipathies; and it was Mr. Seward, we believe, who suggested his name at the time, when the Republicans were deliberating on the best mode of securing success, as that of a man who had no violent foes. It would not be fair to say Mr. Lincoln was determined to eradicate slavery when he came into office, but he certainly belonged to a party which was resolved to prevent the extension of slavery. On his election as President he enunciated the doctrine "that no State can lawfully get out of the Union," and "that acts of violence within any State against the authority of the United States, are insurrectionary or revolutionary, according to circumstances." In his inaugural address he declared, "I have no purpose, directly or indirectly, to interfere with the institution of slavery in the States where it exists; I believe I have no lawful right to do so, and I have no inclination to do so." But at the same time he saw and feared the coming of the contest by which slavery under his administration was doomed.

Believing that no government ever provided an organic law for its own termination, he announced that "he would take care that the laws of the Union shall be executed in all the States, unless his rightful masters, the American people, should withhold the requisite means, or direct the contrary;" and at the same time he expressed his conviction, "that all the controversies then distracting the United States arose from constitutional questions relating to slavery." "One section of our country," said he, "believes slavery is right, and ought to be extended; while the other believes it is wrong, and ought not to be extended." And in his view the constitution did not decide the question one way or the other. The constitution did not expressly say whether fugitive slaves should be surrendered; the constitution did not expressly say whether Congress might prohibit slavery in the territories; the constitution did not expressly say that Congress must protect slavery in the territories. These questions then were to be decided by the majority of the people; but Mr. Lincoln added, "that he had no objection that an amendment of the constitution, which should provide that the Federal government should never interfere with the domestic institutions of the States including that of persons held to service, should be made express and irrevocable." Such propositions the South rejected with scorn; though they were warned by Mr. Lincoln that he would maintain the Union. "In your hands, my dissatisfied fellow-countrymen, and not in mine, is the momentous issue of civil war. You can have no conflict without being yourselves the aggressors; this government will not assail you." But at the time when Mr. Lincoln uttered these words the Southern leaders had already prepared for the arbitrament of war, and within little more than a month the guns of Charleston gave forth the response of the South to Mr. Lincoln's promises and professions. "In this act, discarding all else, they have forced upon the country the distinct issue—immediate dissolution, or blood." Such was Mr. Lincoln's language in his first message to Congress on the 4th July, 1861. It has been the fashion with the Southern leaders and sympathisers to accuse Mr. Lincoln of being personally responsible for the bloodshed and misery of the war which for four years has desolated the South; but it can scarcely be maintained, with any show of reason, that the chief magistrate of the United States was bound to surrender all the rights of government, and the public property of the whole Union to violence which success alone could scarcely have legalised. Such an act of treason to the Union would have been speedily punished by the North, and the Federal government would thenceforth have been directed by men less humane and moderate than Abraham Lincoln. It is quite true, that if Mr. Lincoln's opinions had been the same as those of Mr. Buchanan, no attempt would have been made to coerce the Southern States into submission; but Mr. Lincoln was elected because he held opinions different from those of Mr. Buchanan; and in the contest which arose when the South appealed from the ballot to the bullet, the march of events compelled Mr. Lincoln to make a direct war on the institution of slavery. In his third annual message in 1863, he alluded to the organisation of "coloured persons" into the war service. A preliminary proclamation announced the coming of emancipation, not, however, as the accomplishment of a principle, but as a military necessity. "According to our political system," he said, "as a matter of civil administration the general government had no lawful power to effect emancipation in any State." The necessity of resorting to it came as a military measure; once adopted, however, Mr. Lincoln resolved that emancipation should be permanent. "While I remain in my present position I shall not attempt to retract or modify the emancipation proclamation, nor shall I return to slavery any person who is free by the terms of that proclamation or by any of the acts of Congress." The proclamation of amnesty was contingent upon taking an oath of fidelity to the constitution and Union, and to the recent slave legislation of Congress, and by degrees, as the struggle proceeded, the policy of Mr. Lincoln's administration became definite and precise, and the war which was waged against the Confederates in the field was also directed against the domestic institution which was one of the State Rights for which they contended. By his acts Abraham Lincoln became a great man; because greatness is an attribute of all men who are the agents by which any immense social or political changes are effected. By his steadfastness and honesty of purpose he gradually gained the respect of the large mass of people in the Northern States who were at first inclined to resent the choice of one of uncouth manners, strange aspect, and quaint speech, as their chief magistrate. As director of the vast armies and navies placed at his disposal, Mr. Lincoln displayed the best quality which a man in his position could possess. He never hesitated to reject incompetent commanders, no matter how important their support, how influential their following might be. Personal favour, intimate relations, or close political connection might secure the nomination of an officer, but never preserved him for a moment in a place which he was unfit to fill; and when at length men of capacity and genius came to the front, Mr. Lincoln gave them his whole confidence, armed them with the fullest powers, and never for an instant was distracted by an unworthy fear for his own popularity, or by any jealousy of the reputations he so generously extended and magnified. With the capitulation of General Lee and the fall of Richmond, the first phase of the great conflict inaugurated on, if not by, his election, was brought to a close, for we do not believe in the possibility of any further military resistance being offered by the South to the Federal armies. So far Mr. Lincoln may be considered as having conducted the contest to a successful termination. The second phase, involving the adjustment of even greater difficulties, might have presented questions beyond his grasp; but whatever he was called upon to do in the first, he did well. As his accession to power was clouded by the menace of civil war, and by the dread of the assassin's dagger, so its close was brightened by victory and by a death which enthusiasm may be pardoned for considering as a martyrdom. Not that Mr. Lincoln courted such an end, but that he would not have deviated from his course right or left to have avoided it. Speaking of the disguise he assumed on his way to Washington, he declared he was bound to protect his life as it had become the property of the nation, and it was his duty to take his oath of office; but there is nothing in his career to authorise the belief that he did not possess physical as well as moral courage. He was the first to cross the Potomac, and to appear among the demoralised troops after the first battle of Bull Run, and although the duties of his position forbade his accompanying the Federal armies on the field, he on more than one occasion witnessed their operations against the enemy, and actually suggested the movement which led to the fall of Norfolk. Men now recall the sombre tone of his last address, but like many humourists, Mr. Lincoln was of a grave and rather melancholy temperament. His jesting and his love of anecdote bore traces of his early life in the Far West; and his religion, which was not demonstrative, save so far as it was exhibited in a blameless life and in the purest domestic relations, was tinged with a strong fatalism. It is stated with every show of authority that a presentiment of some evil, or a deterring influence of some sort or other, rendered the President unwilling to go to the theatre on the fatal night of the 14th of April; but it is little likely that men so determined as the assassins who set their lives on the hazard of the dreadful enterprise, would have been baulked in their purpose. His intention to be present was known; and the knowledge possessed by the assassin of the stage enabled him to accomplish his purposes and effect his retreat with wonderful celerity and impunity. All the mechanism of murder was completed—the doors and passages secured—the desperate leap upon the stage meditated—perhaps the very instant calculated beforehand.

History, although it abounds with instances of political assassination, presents nothing at all parallel to this crime. Wilkes Booth, a ranting actor, of extreme violence in his political views, a man of irregular life and of stormy passions, whose brain was no doubt affected by the heated atmosphere and alcoholic life of political bar-rooms, evinced in the commission of the deed an extraordinary amount of dexterity, courage, cruelty, and calmness. One may imagine the President, who had a childish simplicity in his moments of relaxation, indulging in the contented chuckling laughter peculiar to him, as, with his great gaunt body leaning forward, his brawny hands thrust through his thick black locks, his full dark eyes fixed on the stage, he listened to the exaggerated eccentricities of "Our American Cousin," whilst the murderer was hovering in the passage behind the box, or peeping through the crevice he had contrived, at every movement of his intended victim. The theatre was crowded to excess, and no doubt hundreds of people were criticising the President and Mrs. Lincoln when the assassin entered. He broke away from Mr. Lincoln's sole male companion so rapidly that the President had not even time to turn ere Booth, with the surest aim, had discharged the deadly weapon, and it is said that for a moment Mrs. Lincoln, who sat close to her husband, was ignorant of the calamity that had befallen her. The audience, waiting for the appearance of a favourite actress on the stage, were suddenly startled by the report of a pistol, and by the fall or leap of a man from the President's box upon the stage, who, brandishing a dagger, and exclaiming "*Sic semper tyrannis*," vanished at the side. Whether he added "the South is avenged," or not, matters but little, if it be true that the man who attacked Mr. Seward so resolutely also uttered words which are the motto of Virginia as he escaped, because the two men were evidently animated by the notion that they were avenging the wrongs of the South, and that they were ridding the world of tyrants.

The successful attempt to murder the President took place before thousands of spectators; the unsuccessful assault on Mr. Seward was perpetrated under more extraordinary if not desperate circumstances. Through the streets of Washington, filled with soldiers, surrounded by fortifications and patrols, there rode, whilst the citizens were still awake and stirring, a solitary man to the house of the Secretary of State, then lying on his sick-bed from the effects of an accident which rendered him as helpless as a child, but which at the same time, as the assassin well knew, rendered it necessary for him to have the aid of others. Two of Mr. Seward's sons and two male attendants were actually about his bed, or in the adjoining room, when the desperado, under a plea which at once provoked suspicion and resistance, forced his way up the hall, and with incredible strength, fury, and rapidity, struck down every obstacle between him and his victim, and plunged his dagger again and again in Mr. Seward's body; then stepping over the bleeding bodies of Mr. Seward's two sons and of his two attendants, the man rushed into the street, exclaiming, "*Sic semper tyrannis*," leaped upon his horse, and galloping along the side of the square in which the Secretary's house is situated, was lost to sight.

Ere the body of the murdered President was laid in the grave Wilkes Booth and one of his accomplices had been hunted down, and like wild beasts had turned to bay. The wretch, who died with curses on his lips, and who for three hours of mortal agony tested the mercy of his captors by his blasphemies, can scarcely receive an apotheosis except from the men who planned the murders of St. Alban's and the burning of New York. We are not aware of any modern sect who worship ferocious felony. His accomplice awaits justice. We can only hope Mr. Stanton's assertions will prove to be utterly unfounded, and that only two wretches like Wilkes Booth and Harrold vexed humanity at one and the same time. The American people at least seem to think so, and in all this terrible tragedy nothing has been so touching and so grand as the calm dignity of the Northern people.

An attempt to make political capital out of deeds like these would be inexpressibly vile, but it would be equally discreditable to be deterred from the expression of all the abhorrence excited by such atrocities by any fear that our motives should be misconstrued. When from all quarters of the civilised world, in every variety of language, the sad wail of horror and of sympathetic emotion rolls over the Atlantic, it would be strange indeed if Englishmen did not, in their common speech, proclaim to the American people the feelings with which so foul a murder and so great a crime have filled them. Stranger would it be, indeed, if the American people misunderstood or misrepresented the motives and the causes of such utterances of our sorrow. Probably, however, the letter of the Queen, the words of sympathy uttered by one widowed mother to another in her hour of grief, will produce a greater effect on the minds of the American people than the addresses in both Houses of Parliament, the meetings of corporations, and the public assemblages of citizens, in every town throughout the kingdom. Even the singular want of judgment—no, on reflection, not singular—manifested by Lord Derby cannot detract from the value of the great popular exhibition to which Mr. Lincoln's death has given rise, and the effect of which may be traced in the language of Mr. Adams and of other Americans of less political and social weight.

Those who are curious in anniversaries may remark that Mr. Lincoln was assassinated on the very day four years of the surrender of Fort Sumter, and on the very day when the guns of Charleston had saluted the reappearance of the United States flag over the historic ruin once more commanded by Robert Anderson. Mobile, the last port, or indeed town, of any consequence possessed by the Confederates, was carried by storm five days previously. It is difficult to believe that the work of the new President will need much of either fleets or armies, although it may not be so much a matter of police as some sanguine Northerners are inclined to think. Whether Johnston has been captured or not, whether General Kirby Smith commands 20,000 or 40,000 men, whether Magruder is at the head of 15,000 or 50,000 men, is of comparative insignificance now that the Southern leaders have lost their armies, their capital, their generals, and, in fact, all the outward and visible signs of established government on which they claimed the act of recognition at the hands of the great powers of Europe. Mr. Davis is now a fugitive, and the most sanguine of Southern partisans can scarcely maintain that he can find in Texas or Arkansas a base of operations against the Federal power more substantial than he found in Virginia or Georgia. But there are still enormous difficulties to be overcome in the work of reconstruction; and indeed, in our judgment, these are so far insuperable, as to place the restoration of the Union, as it was before the war, beyond the limit of possibility. But the old Union was aggressive and menacing; the old Union protected and guaranteed slavery; the old Union was arrogant, offensive, uncompromising, and dangerous. For most of these characteristics it was indebted to Southern politicians and statesmen; and we have yet to see whether the American people, chastened by many sufferings, and loaded with great debt, will be as minacious and troublesome as the representatives of the *quasi* sovereign states who so long directed the foreign policy of the United States of America. If the Federal government be obliged to maintain an army in every State, and a governor in every city of the South, we think the task will be found unsuited to the genius of American institutions, and beyond the elasticity of even American resources. The confiscation advocated by the extreme abolitionists, accompanied by projects of colonisation, is still less likely to be successful, for we must then suppose that the people who require armies and fleets to coerce them into submission to the Union, will quietly allow bands of civilians to dispossess them of their own, or that the State will maintain armies and fleets to keep the colonists in possession, and thus perpetuate a frightful anarchy. The only hope of a successful solution lies in the fact that a considerable amount of what is called Union sentiment appears to crop out under the shadow of the American eagle as it wings its way through the South. In most large towns the Federal rule has been accepted without enthusiasm, indeed, but without such violent repugnance as renders the hope of establishing civil administration utterly impossible.

In the trans-Mississippi region it is averred that the nucleus of a new confederacy has been already formed; and speculators talk of slave states to be formed in Sonora, and in the dependencies of King Gwin; but for all governmental purposes the North has won Missouri, Kentucky, Virginia, Louisiana, South Carolina, and the seabords of the Gulf and Atlantic States, and a guerilla war does not offer much prospect of success in Georgia, North Carolina, Florida, Mississippi, or Alabama. The evil counsellors who have suggested a foreign war as a means of escape from domestic troubles, and as a bond of re-union, are not likely to have weight with Mr. Johnson, whose interview with Sir Frederick Bruce has created a very favourable impression in this country with respect to the moderation and ability of the new President.

England and France will be more at ease about Canada and Mexico when they hear professions of peace and good will from the chief of their powerful neighbour; although there is a suspicious stream of emigration spoken of in the direction of the Emperor Maximilian's dominions, and the presence of delegates from Canada in this country shows that the provinces are not quite satisfied or at rest on that ground. It is a favourite argument with the Canadians against the national purse, that in case of a war with Great Britain, their country would become the scene of hostile operations; but at the same time they should recollect that their connection with Great Britain would furnish one of the strongest inducements to the United States to go to war with us,—in other words, that the risk of war between the two countries would be diminished almost to a vanishing point if Canada did not belong to Great Britain. Wolfe's great conquest stands very much in the same relation to us that Algeria does to France—each is the *damnosa hæreditas* of a former age which cannot well be got rid of. The army maintained by the French in Algeria is very nearly as large as that which we are obliged to keep on foot in Hindostan. The military governor of the province is often tempted to override the Arab bureaux, and to come into conflict with the civil administration, and Marshal Macmahon has, it is said, carried matters to such a pitch that the Emperor's presence is required to adjust the quarrels between civil and military officers of government. M. Emile Girardin, indeed, has gone so far as to advise that Algiers should be given up to the Algerines, but the utterances of *La Presse* are not regarded always with the respect to which the writer considers them entitled. It is not likely that a ruler so shrewd, even though he be so visionary, as the Emperor of the French, would excite discontent in France by conferring the supreme power in Algeria on Abdel Kader, or any other Mussulman. But it is by no means unlikely that he may introduce important if not startling changes in the present system of administering the affairs of a country which, as yet, has given little return to France for great sacrifices in blood and treasure, except fitting her army for war. Many people regard the Emperor's departure as a proof that he thinks European affairs are of no very pressing moment, and the Duke of Persigny may indeed have communicated some pleasing intelligence from Rome. One is at a loss to understand how the Pope could have brought himself to communicate with the principle of evil incarnate in Victor Emmanuel, unless novel ideas and strange counsels were slowly filtering into the Vatican. It is at least curious that a scarcity of bishops in the Peninsula should have produced a result which a plethora of soldiers and arguments failed to accomplish. *Terque quaterque beati!* Happy people of Italy, who have ten times as many apostolic hands to bless you as the children of Catholic Ireland or even ultra Catholic Bavaria. The only reason given by those who ought to know, for the Pope's letter to Victor Emmanuel, is his anxiety to get the vacant dioceses filled again; but the mission of M. Vegezzi may give an opportunity for establishing an understanding, which the Duke of Persigny can at least facilitate, in reference to more important matters. It is hinted that some wicked people in France are almost as tired of Napoleon *dieu et Empereur*, as the Romans are of the troops of his nephew. There are some persons, indeed, who are very ready to take offence. Even the erection of a statue or two offends them, and these may be found in England as well as in France.

It is not for a journalist, if it be for any man, to justify the ways of God to princes, and to point divine morals or adorn providential tales; but the death of the Cesarewitch at Nice might tempt indiscreet politicians and bad logicians of Sarmatian proclivities, to expatiate on the woes of Poland as a pendant to the sorrows of the amiable Empress, and of the well-meaning and kindly disposed Emperor, who are weeping by the side of that early bier. Whom the gods love die young, and although a great portion of the human race may lose something in the grave which has opened for the new Marcellus, it may be, too, that he has been spared an ordeal too terrible and a trial too great for his strength in the future of his country.

The Prussians are about to commemorate their valorous deeds at Düppel by a great memorial, but they do not seem quite so willing to fight for their share of the prey with the Austrian bird, though they are flapping their wings over Kiel. It is just at the moment when a great referendary and umpire in many European questions is likely to be needed, that the Belgian Ulysses sickens, and is nigh to death's door, with the weight of his unaccepted arbitrament in the Brazilian quarrel still weighing heavily on Lord Russell. Not a glance is cast northwards by the people of France at the prosperous little kingdom which is said to be the object of their ambition, and it is probable that if Leopold dies now, his son will reign in his stead.

In home affairs the most important event has been the introduction and discussion of Mr. Gladstone's budget, because we cannot regard a two nights' debate and a doctored division as any settlement of the Reform question. It is to be hoped that the reduction on tea will go into the pockets of the consumers instead of those of the wholesale dealers; but the twopence in the pound to be remitted on the income is a hard practical fact which no official agency can disrefute.

On the Edmunds case, the public has pronounced an opinion, which is not in reality much stronger than the censure conveyed in the studied phraseology of the Lords' Committee interpreted by Lord Derby; and as out of evil comes good, we may expect that the government will take steps to prevent official "irregularities" which would not do discredit to a bureau of the old style in Moscow or St. Petersburg. Lord Granville will no doubt deprive Mr. Edmunds of his pension, but he cannot remove the stain which has fallen on the ermine of Lords, and which has covered the white with little black tails. Sir George Grey, who is the most sore vexed of ministers, is threatened with a great difficulty in the Road murder case, in which Miss Constance Kent steps forward to prove to all the world how little use our modern police system is in detecting the authors of crime. The suicide of Admiral Fitzroy gives a melancholy notoriety to the fortnight.

NOTICES OF NEW BOOKS.

THE GRAMMAR OF ORNAMENT. By OWEN JONES, Architect. Illustrated by Examples from various Styles of Ornament. 112 Plates. Day and Son, London.

THE inventor of movable types, says the venerable Teufelsdröckh, was disbanding hired armies, cashiering most kings and senates, and creating a whole new democratic world. Has any one yet said what great things are being done by the men who are trying to banish ugliness from our streets and our homes, and to make both the outside and inside of our dwellings worthy of a world where there are forests, and flower-tressed meadows, and the plumage of birds; where the insects carry lessons of colour on their wings, and even the surface of a stagnant pool will show us the wonders of iridescence and the most delicate forms of leafage? They, too, are modifying opinions, for they are modifying men's moods and habits, which are the mothers of opinions, having quite as much to do with their formation as the responsible father—Reason. Think of certain hideous manufacturing towns where the piety is chiefly a belief in copious perdition, and the pleasure is chiefly gin. The dingy surface of wall pierced by the ugliest windows, the staring shop-fronts, paper-hangings, carpets, brass and gilt mouldings, and advertising placards, have an effect akin to that of malaria; it is easy to understand that with such surroundings there is more belief in cruelty than in beneficence, and that the best earthly bliss attainable is the dulling of the external senses. For it is a fatal mistake to suppose that ugliness which is taken for beauty will answer all the purposes of beauty; the subtle relation between all kinds of truth and fitness in our life forbids that bad taste should ever be harmless to our moral sensibility or our intellectual discernment; and—more than that—as it is probable that fine musical harmonies have a sanative influence over our bodily organisation, it is also probable that just colouring and lovely combinations of lines may be necessary to the complete well-being of our systems apart from any conscious delight in them. A savage may indulge in discordant chuckles and shrieks and gutturals, and think that they please the gods, but it does not follow that his frame would not be favourably wrought upon by the vibrations of a grand church organ. One sees a person capable of choosing the worst style of wall-paper become suddenly afflicted by its ugliness under an attack of illness. And if an evil state of blood and lymph usually goes along with an evil state of mind, who shall say that the ugliness of our streets, the falsity of our ornamentation, the vulgarity of our upholstery, have not something to do with those bad tempers which breed false conclusions?

On several grounds it is possible to make a more speedy and extensive application of artistic reform to our interior decoration than to our external architecture. One of these grounds is that most of our ugly buildings must stand; we cannot afford to pull them down. But every year we are decorating interiors afresh, and people of modest means may benefit by the introduction of beautiful designs into stucco ornaments, paper-hangings, draperies, and carpets. Fine taste in the decoration of interiors is a benefit that spreads from the palace to the clerk's house with one parlour.

All honour, then, to the architect who has zealously vindicated the claim of internal ornamentation to be a part of the architect's function, and has laboured to rescue that form of art which is most closely connected with the sanctities and pleasures of our hearths from the hands of uncultured tradesmen. All the nation ought at present to know that this effort is peculiarly associated with the name of Mr. Owen Jones; and those who are most disposed to dispute with the architect about his colouring, must at least recognise the high artistic principle which has directed his attention to coloured ornamentation as a proper branch of architecture. One monument of his effort in this way is his "Grammar of Ornament," of which a new and cheaper edition has just been issued. The one point in which it differs from the original and more expensive edition, viz., the reduction in the size of the pages (the amount of matter and number of plates are unaltered), is really an advantage; it is now a very manageable folio, and when the reader is in a lounging mood may be held easily on the knees. It is a magnificent book; and those who know no more of it than the title, should be told that they will find in it a pictorial history of ornamental design, from its rudimentary condition as seen in the productions of savage tribes, through all the other great types of art—the Egyptian, Assyrian, ancient Persian, Greek, Roman, Byzantine, Arabian, Moresque, Mahommedan-Persian, Indian, Celtic, Mediœval, Renaissance, Elizabethan, and Italian. The letter-press consists, first, of an introductory statement of fundamental principles of ornamentation—principles, says the author, which will be found to have been obeyed more or less instinctively by all nations in proportion as their art has been a genuine product of the national genius; and, secondly, of brief historical essays, some of them contributed by other eminent artists, presenting a commentary on each characteristic series of illustrations, with the useful appendage of bibliographical lists.

The title "Grammar of Ornament" is so far appropriate that it indicates what Mr. Owen Jones is most anxious to be understood concerning the object of his work, namely, that it is intended to illustrate historically the application of principles, and not to present a collection of models for mere copyists. The plates correspond to examples in syntax, not to be repeated parrot-like, but to be studied as embodiments of syntactical principles. There is a logic of form which cannot be departed from in ornamental design without a corresponding remoteness from perfection; unmeaning, irrelevant lines are as bad as irrelevant words or clauses, that tend no whither. And as a suggestion towards the origination of fresh ornamental design, the work concludes with some beautiful drawings of leaves and flowers from nature, that the student, tracing in them the simple laws of form which underlie an immense variety in beauty, may the better discern the method by which the same laws were applied in the finest decorative work of the past, and may have all the clearer prospect of the unexhausted possibilities of freshness which lie before him, if, refraining from mere imitation, he will seek only such likeness to existing forms of ornamental art as arises from following like principles of combination.

GEORGE ELIOT.

SOME ACCOUNT OF GOTHIC ARCHITECTURE IN SPAIN. By G. E. STREET. With Woodcuts. John Murray, London. 1865.

THIS very handsome volume is, it may be hoped, only an instalment of what architectural Spain will yield if Mr. Street and other similarly qualified explorers are encouraged to draw and measure in the great Peninsula. The *raison d'être* for such a publication, and the spirit in which Mr. Street has undertaken it, may be judged from a few words in his preface. After summing up the labours of his predecessors, he says:—

"Seeing how complete is the ignorance which up to the present time we have laboured under, as to the true history and nature of Gothic architecture in Spain, I commit this volume to the reader with a fair trust that what has been the occupation of all my leisure moments for the last two or three years—a work not only of much labour at home, but of considerable labour also in long journeys taken year after year for this object alone—will not be found an unwelcome addition to the literature of Christian art."

This programme has been carried out by Mr. Street with the taste and conscientious labour which are naturally to be looked for at the hands of one of our leading architects, who, like Mr. Butterfield, Mr. Burgess, or Mr. Waterhouse, is not more distinguished above some of his contemporaries for the creative power with which he handles his art, than for the pains which he takes to complete every portion to the best of his own ability. The field which the book covers includes the Cathedrals of Burgos, Salamanca, Zamora, Leon, Santiago, Avila, Siguenza, Toledo, Valencia, Tarragona, Barcelona, Gerona, Lerida, Tudela, and Pamplona, with about as many other churches of importance. For almost all Mr. Street has supplied us with excellent plans, which in the majority of instances are either the first ever properly laid down, or the first accessible in England; and he has filled his book with careful illustrative woodcuts. Engraved on the scale adopted, they have perhaps a little too much the effect of diagrams—a style into which the author's wish to avoid false picturesqueness and to tell the essential truth has probably led him. Is it too much to hope that some wealthy Englishman may be found to do for Spain what Mr. Gally Knight honourably attempted for Italy, and to entrust Mr. Street with the preparation of a volume of full-sized engravings?

It will be seen that several of the most popularly known buildings of Spain, as those of Seville and Granada, are not included in the series. Mr. Street has omitted them because they have been often described (he might have added, and greatly overrated as pieces of architecture), and because he wished to investigate "how the Christians and not how the Moors built in Spain in the middle ages." And, so far as the book goes, the result of the investigation would seem to be that the Christians built as the French taught them. Mr. Fergusson's view, that "Gothic" in the common use of the term was exclusively due to the genius of Northern and Upper-Central France appears to be amply confirmed by Mr. Street's experience. As we turn over his beautiful book the scales fall from our eyes. Beneath the elaborate excrescences of ornamental work which have hitherto been described or drawn as the essential features of a Spanish church, appears the severe but lovely outline of a French thirteenth century building. One noble cathedral after another is traced to French architects or to French ecclesiastics. In Spain, as elsewhere, the great thirteenth century shines forth in its strange creative fertility. This may be called the first lesson of the book. The second would be, that beyond what was thus planted in the country by foreign hands the true Gothic took no root in Spain. So soon as the French impulse died away, the genuine spirit of the Iberian race, which appears to be more thoroughly incapable of art than any other (at least) of Western Europe, asserts itself. We find now a few not very valuable Moresco suggestions, and a considerable infusion of a bad style of decoration from Flemish and German sources; but, wanting any native sympathy, Gothic architecture rapidly declined in Spain; and we can hardly, judging from the specimens given, rate the cathedrals of the fifteenth century higher than those later works which Mr. Street summarily dismisses as Pagan—an epithet, by the way, which (in his estimation) seems to connote something extremely wrong. As models of convenient, though not of graceful, arrangement, there is, however, much to be learned from the enormous structures which the wealth of the wealthiest nation of the fifteenth and sixteenth centuries lavished over the land; and everything which Mr. Street tells of them is almost as new to English readers as if he were describing the architecture of the Argentine Republic. He has done us a great service, which is the more estimable as the work of a man engaged in an engrossing business; but one is often tempted to believe that it is only those who seem to have no leisure for anything who somehow find time for everything. Let us hope that he will write us more books, and build us, not only more churches, but (what is a much greater need) more houses in a style fit for civilised men to look at.

F. T. PALGRAVE.

HAUNTED LONDON. By WALTER THORNBURY. Illustrated by F. W. FAIRHOLT, F.S.A. Hurst and Blackett, London.

THE author of "Haunted London" is a book-maker by profession, and as a manufacturer of literary ware we suppose his chief aim is to turn out an article which will please the public and satisfy his publishers. These motives are no doubt legitimate, and if Mr. Thornbury is more anxious to produce what will attract his readers than to gain respect and approval in the world of letters, his critics, although they may believe him to be capable of better things, have no reason to complain. That he is careless, inartistic, inaccurate, Mr. Thornbury has been often told, and appears willing to acknowledge; but he knows at the same time how to be lively, readable, and often extremely entertaining, and such virtues will hide a multitude of literary defects.

"Haunted London," although a loosely-written compilation, may be commended for these qualities. It is an agreeable book, and one to which we can recur again and again. The whole composition is, indeed, a medley drawn from various but obvious sources. The very words employed by his authorities are frequently used again by Mr. Thornbury without special acknowledgment; he makes statements twice over, and statements which are not always correct; he sometimes draws over several paragraphs what might be better told in a few lines; and of the original remarks scattered through the volume, some offend against good taste and others against good grammar. Mr. Thornbury is as free with his offensive appellations as a Billingsgate woman with her tongue; it must be owned, however, that he praises with an almost equal prodigality, and every man or woman introduced into his pages is dubbed with some epithet to signify the writer's approval or contempt.

Thus we have "that sluggish, muddy-minded, and certainly out-witted man Sir Thomas Fairfax," "that fussy time-server Bishop Burnet," "that pompous impostor and contemptible dauber Kent," "that eccentric heretic Whiston," "that learned and amiable gentleman Mr. Evelyn," "that dangerous Mrs. Knipp," "handsome Jack Bannister," "thrifty Garrick," "choleric and Quixotic Lord Herbert," and so on *ad nauseam*. This might be regarded as a trifling fault if it did not occur so frequently; there are other faults in the volume which are more important and equally offensive. Nevertheless, in spite of these drawbacks Mr. Thornbury's gossip is not without its charm. He does rightly indeed in calling the volume "patchwork," but, regarded as patchwork, we see in it more to praise than to condemn.

It will be remembered that in "The Town," a volume of which we are never weary, Mr. Leigh Hunt describes in his charming manner the remarkable characters and events associated with that portion of the metropolis which lies between St. Paul's and St. James's. Mr. Thornbury starts from Temple Bar, walks westward, till he turns up St. Martin's Lane, and passes from thence through Long Acre and Drury Lane to Lincoln's Inn Fields. A portion of the same ground is therefore covered by both writers. It would be invidious to compare them. Let it suffice to say that Mr. Thornbury does fealty to the essayist by following carefully in his steps. "Haunted London" will not supersede "The Town;" it will not, we venture to say, affect in the slightest degree the circulation of Mr. Cunningham's "Hand-book." To the one volume we shall always refer for racy anecdote and suggestive criticism, to the other for useful statistics and trustworthy information. Mr. Thornbury's work will also claim attention in leisure moments, for, although never brilliant, it is seldom dull, and bears the marks of having been compiled by a writer who has an honest liking for his subject. If "Haunted London" deserved even less praise than we have awarded it, Mr. Fairholt's delightful illustrations would suffice to preserve it from corruption.

JOHN DENNIS.

TITI LUCRETI CARI DE RERUM NATURA LIBRI SEX. With a Translation and Notes. By H. A. J. MUNRO, M.A., Fellow of Trinity College, Cambridge. 2 Vols. Bell and Daldy, London.

Mr. MUNRO is one of the most eminent of our scholars, and has chosen the most difficult of editorial tasks, in the restoration of a text which must, to the end of time, remain greatly conjectural. He has followed closely, yet critically, the lead of Lachmann, who, with all his boldness, was so sagacious and so learned that Hermann properly cautioned those who dissented from his views to consider whether the fault did not lie with them. It is certain that Lachmann's acuteness has enabled him to reconstruct a lost archetype, as palæontologists have reconstructed vertebrate types, now no longer in existence; but scholars are not ready to accept all the details; and Mr. Munro, with a profound veneration for what Lachmann has done, does not hesitate occasionally to correct him. On the success with which he has performed his delicate and laborious task we must leave more competent critics to decide; our notice is intended only for the wider public that may desire to know what are the claims of this edition on attention.

First, we remark that it is an eminently useful edition. In the distribution of its matter, no less than in the succinct elaborateness of its contents, it is quite a model. The first volume contains the text in clear and elegant type, settled after minute and exhaustive collation, and *illustrated* by a prose translation at the foot of each page—very remarkable among translations of the classics for the extraordinary vigour and felicity with which it renders the meaning and beauty as well as ruggedness of the original. Lucretius is undoubtedly a splendid writer. He has passages unsurpassed in Latin poetry. But he is also at times a rugged and prosaic writer, and very much of his poem is as fatiguing to the æsthetic as it is to the philosophic sense. With Mr. Munro's admirable version at the bottom of the page many a reader, we suspect, will at times gratefully quit the original, to move more rapidly and pleasantly through the duller passages in prose, recurring to the verse when the poet rises again into eloquence.

The second volume contains a minute account of the formation of the text, the critical apparatus, and a long commentary, which might easily have been longer, but which Mr. Munro, with a wise fortitude controlling editorial impulses, has kept within very moderate compass. This commentary ought to be in the hands of all who are studying Lucretius. It is very suggestive and instructive reading. It implies even more than it displays—a wide and various erudition at the service of a candid and thoughtful mind. Indeed, throughout these volumes we are impressed with a sense of the reticence of power.

EDITOR.

DR. DE JONGH'S

(Knight of the Order of Leopold of Belgium)

LIGHT-BROWN

COD LIVER OIL

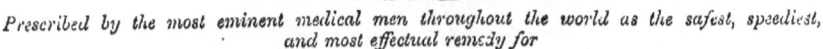

Prescribed by the most eminent medical men throughout the world as the safest, speediest, and most effectual remedy for

Consumption, Asthma, Chronic Bronchitis, Coughs, General Debility, Rheumatism, Gout, Diseases of the Skin, Rickets, Infantile Wasting, and all Scrofulous Affections.

The distinctive characteristics which have gained for Dr. DE JONGH'S Oil so much celebrity, the entire confidence of the most eminent members of the Medical Profession, and an unprecedented amount of public patronage, may be thus concisely enumerated:—

I.—Its genuineness, purity, and uniform strength are ascertained and guaranteed.

II.—It contains all the active and essential principles that therapeutic experience has found to be the most effective in the operation of the remedy.

III.—It is palatable, easily taken, and creates no nausea.

IV.—It is borne with facility by the most delicate stomach, and improves the functions of digestion and assimilation.

V.—Its medicinal properties and remedial action have been found to be immeasurably greater than those of any other kind of Cod Liver Oil.

VI.—From the unequalled rapidity of its curative effects, it is infinitely more economical than any which is offered, even at the lowest price.

CONSUMPTION AND DISEASES OF THE CHEST.

The extraordinary virtues of Dr. DE JONGH'S LIGHT-BROWN COD LIVER OIL in Pulmonary Consumption may now be considered as fully established. No remedy so rapidly restores the exhausted strength, improves the nutritive functions, stops or diminishes emaciation, checks the perspiration, quiets the cough and expectoration, or produces a more marked and favourable influence on the local malady.

The following high testimony to the efficacy of Dr. DE JONGH'S Cod Liver Oil in Diseases of the Chest, is afforded by Dr. WAUDBY, late Physician to the Hereford Infirmary, from his own personal experience:—

"I can take DR. DE JONGH'S Oil without difficulty or dislike, and with as little inconvenience as water alone. Not only in my own case, but in many others I have seen, it has caused an improvement of chest symptoms, and an increase of weight, so soon and so lastingly, as to be quite remarkable. I believe DR. DE JONGH'S Oil to be the most valuable remedy we possess for chronic and constitutional disease."

GENERAL DEBILITY AND EMACIATION.

In cases of prostration and emaciation, where the vital forces are reduced, and where life appears to be even at its lowest ebb, the restorative powers of DR. DE JONGH'S LIGHT-BROWN COD LIVER OIL are remarkably manifested. By its administration the natural appetite is revived, and the functions of digestion and assimilation are improved, reanimated, and regulated; and, when its use has been steadily persevered in, its peculiar tonic and nutritive properties have entirely restored health and strength to the most feeble and deteriorated constitutions.

The actual benefit derived is thus described by BENJAMIN CLARKE, Esq., M.R.C.S., F.L.S., author of "Notes and Suggestions on Cod Liver Oil and its Uses:"—

"Having myself taken both the Pale and Light-Brown Cod Liver Oil for debility, I am able, from my own experience, to remark upon their effects and comparative usefulness as remedial agents. After the Pale Oil, and all other remedies that I could think of had failed, I tried, merely as a last resort, DR. DE JONGH'S Light-Brown Oil. I received immediate relief; and its use was the means of my restoration to health. In their sensible properties and chemical constituents the Pale Oil and DR. DE JONGH'S Light-Brown Oil are distinct medicines; and, from my observation of their mode of action and effects, I must believe that I have seen many patients die both in hospital and private practice, some of them of juvenile years, and others in the prime of life, who in all probability would have been cured if the medical properties of DR. DE JONGH'S Light-Brown Oil had been known as they are now, and its use prescribed."

[*For further Select Medical Opinions, see other side*

EFFICACY OF DR. DE JONGH'S OIL IN THE TREATMENT OF THE DISORDERS OF INFANCY AND CHILDHOOD.

In those severe disorders, *Infantile Wasting and Rickets*, from which children suffer so extensively, and which destroy so many infants, the good effects of this Oil are incontestably established, its operation being oftentimes so very remarkable as to cure the disease when every other remedy had failed, and all hope of saving life had been abandoned.

In cases of languid and imperfect nutrition often observed in children, where the appetite is capricious, and digestion slow and painful, and the body becomes weak and wasted, without any apparent disease, this Oil, after a few weeks, and sometimes in a few days, has produced the most extraordinary transition to a state of normal health. This effect is described by THOMAS HUNT, Esq., F.R.C.S., Medical Officer of Health to the populous district of Bloomsbury, in a communication to the *Medical Times and Gazette*:—

"In badly-nourished infants, DR. DE JONGH'S LIGHT-BROWN COD LIVER OIL is invaluable. The rapidity with which two or three tea-spoonfuls per diem will fatten a young child is astonishing. The weight gained is three times the weight of the Oil swallowed, or more; and, as children generally like the taste of the Oil, and when it is given them, often cry for more, it appears as though there were some prospect of deliverance for the appalling multitude of children who figure in the weekly bills of mortality issued from the office of the Registrar-General."

SELECT MEDICAL OPINIONS.

From innumerable medical and scientific opinions of the highest character in commendation of Dr. DE JONGH'S LIGHT-BROWN COD LIVER OIL, *the following are selected:—*

Sir HENRY MARSH, Bart., M.D.,
Physician in Ordinary to the Queen in Ireland.
"I consider DR. DE JONGH'S Light-Brown Cod Liver Oil to be a very pure oil, not likely to create disgust, and a therapeutic agent of great value."

Dr. LETHEBY,
Medical Officer of Health, and Chief Analyst to the City of London.
"The Oil corresponds in all its characters with that named 'Huile Brune,' and described as the best variety in the masterly treatise of DR. DE JONGH. It is, I believe, universally acknowledged that DR. DE JONGH'S Light-Brown Cod Liver Oil has great therapeutic power; and from my investigations, I have no doubt of its being a pure and unadulterated article."

Dr. LAWRANCE,
Physician to H.R.H. the Duke of Saxe-Coburg & Gotha.
"I invariably prescribe DR. DE JONGH'S Cod Liver Oil in preference to any other, feeling assured that I am recommending a genuine article, and not a manufactured compound in which the efficacy of this invaluable medicine is destroyed."

Dr. BARLOW,
Senior Physician to Guy's Hospital.
"I have frequently recommended persons consulting me to make use of DR. DE JONGH'S Cod Liver Oil. I have been well satisfied with its effects, and believe it to be a very pure oil, well fitted for those cases in which the use of that substance is indicated."

Sir JOSEPH OLLIFFE, M.D.,
Physician to the British Embassy at Paris.
"I have frequently prescribed DR. DE JONGH'S Light-Brown Cod Liver Oil, and I have every reason to be satisfied with its beneficial and salutary effects."

Dr. LANKESTER, F.R.S.,
Coroner for Central Middlesex.
"I consider that the purity of this Oil is secured in its preparation by the personal attention of so good a Chemist and intelligent a Physician as DR. DE JONGH, who has also written the best Medical Treatise on the Oil with which I am acquainted. Hence, I deem the Cod Liver Oil sold under his guarantee to be preferable to any other kind as regards genuineness and medicinal efficacy."

Dr. GRANVILLE, F.R.S.,
Author of the "Spas of Germany."
"Dr. Granville has found that DR. DE JONGH'S Light-Brown Cod Liver Oil produces the desired effect in a shorter time than other kinds, and that it does not cause the nausea and indigestion too often consequent on the administration of the pale oil."

EDWIN CANTON, Esq., F.R.C.S.,
President of the Medical Society of London.
"For several years past I have been in the habit of prescribing DR. DE JONGH'S Light-Brown Cod Liver Oil, and find it to be much more efficacious than other varieties of the same medicine which I have also employed with a view to test their relative superiority."

☞ Dr. de Jongh's Light-Brown Cod Liver Oil *is sold* ONLY *in bottles, each bottle being sealed with a stamped metallic capsule, and bearing beneath the pink outside wrapper a label with* DR. DE JONGH'S *stamp and signature, and to these capsules and marks purchasers are earnestly requested to pay particular attention.*

WITHOUT THESE NONE CAN POSSIBLY BE GENUINE.
FULL DIRECTIONS FOR USE ACCOMPANY EACH BOTTLE.

SOLE CONSIGNEES,
ANSAR, HARFORD & Co., 77, STRAND, LONDON, W.C.
And sold by all respectable Chemists and Druggists throughout the World.
IMPERIAL Half-pints, 2s. 6d.; Pints, 4s. 9d.; Quarts, 9s.

CAUTION.—*In consequence of the rapid effects produced by* DR. DE JONGH'S COD LIVER OIL, *and the small quantities required to be taken as compared with other kinds, some unscrupulous dealers, with a view to increased profit, endeavour, when* DR. DE JONGH'S OIL *is applied for, to recommend or substitute different varieties of so-called Cod Liver Oil, sold at a nominally low price. Purchasers are therefore solicitously cautioned against proposed substitutions.*

[TURN OVER.

MAPPIN, WEBB & CO.,
77 & 78, OXFORD-ST.; & 71 & 72, CORNHILL.

ELECTRO-SILVER PLATE.

Guaranteed Quality.	Plain Pattern.			Thread Pattern.			Ornamental Pattern.		
	£	s.	d.	£	s.	d.	£	s.	d.
Table spoons or forks, per doz.	1	7	0	2	14	0	2	16	0
Dessert spoons or forks ,,	1	1	0	2	0	0	2	0	0
Tea spoons, per doz.	0	10	6	1	4	0	1	4	0
Side dishes and covers, per set	8	10	0	10	0	0	16	0	0
Dish covers, per set of four ..	10	0	0	12	0	0	16	0	0
Fish carvers & forks, in cases	0	15	6	1	5	0	2	5	0
12 pairs dessert knives & forks	3	10	0	5	0	0	5	10	0
12 fish eating knives, in cases	1	18	0	2	16	0	3	0	0
Tea & Coffee services, per set.	4	10	0	7	0	0	9	10	0
Cruet frames, 4, 5 and 6 bottle	1	15	0	2	15	0	3	12	6
Bed-room candlesticks, each..	0	10	0	0	14	0	0	18	6
Toast racks, each	0	11	0	0	14	0	1	2	0
Salvers in all sizes, each	1	4	0	1	16	0	2	18	0
Butter coolers, every variety..	1	0	0	1	12	0	2	10	0

IVORY HANDLE TABLE KNIVES.
WARRANTED.

Blades secured to Handles. Best quality only.	Table Knives.		Cheese Knives.		Carvers.	
	s.	d.	s.	d.	s.	d.
3½ in. balance ivory, per doz.	11	0	9	0	3	6
3½ in. ,, better ivory....	13	0	10	0	4	6
3½ in. ,, white............	16	0	12	0	6	0
4 in. strong ,, ...	20	0	15	0	7	0
4 in. ,, ,, ...	25	0	18	0	9	0
4 in. full strength............	34	0	24	0	10	6
Round handles, silver ferrules	40	0	30	0	13	0
Electro-plated handles, any pattern..	26	0	22	0	8	6

Smaller quantities can be had at the above rate of prices which are the same as at the Manufactory, ROYAL CUTLERY WORKS, Sheffield.
Every Article exchanged if not approved.

CANTEENS AND PLATE CHESTS.

MAPPIN, WEBB & CO., Manufacturing Silversmiths, Cutlers, &c., have a large assortment of compact and convenient CANTEENS, from £5 5s., fitted with their unrivalled manufactures.

	£	s.	d.
12 Table forks..........................	1	16	0
12 Dessert ,, ...	1	7	0
6 Table spoons	0	18	0
12 Dessert ,, ...	1	7	0
12 Tea ,, ...	0	16	0
4 each, salt & egg ,, ...	0	13	4
1 Mustard ,, ...	0	1	8
1 Pair sugar tongs	0	3	6
1 Gravy spoon	0	7	0
1 Butter knife	0	3	6
1 Soup ladle	0	8	0
1 Gravy spoon	0	7	0
2 Sauce ladles	0	8	0
1 Fish carver and fork	0	12	6
12 Table knives	1	0	0
12 Cheese knives	0	15	0
2 Pair carvers	0	14	6
1 Steel	0	2	0
Oak chest	1	5	0
Complete	£13	4	6

FURNISHING IRONMONGERY.

The Show Rooms of Furnishing Ironmongery are replete with a large selection of
DRAWING & DINING-ROOM FENDERS & BEST STEEL FIRE IRONS.
Shower, Sponging, Hip and Open Baths.
ORNAMENTAL TOILET SETS.
AND EVERY REQUISITE FOR HOUSE FURNISHING.

Estimates, List of Prices, and costly Illustrated Catalogues forwarded on application, free.
Every Article warranted, and exchanged if not approved.

MAPPIN, WEBB AND CO.,
77 & 78, OXFORD STREET, WEST END; 71 & 72, CORNHILL, CITY.

THE LONDON WAREHOUSES ARE CELEBRATED FOR CONTAINING THE
Largest, most Modern and Elegant Stocks of Cutlery, Electro-Silver Plate, Furnishing Ironmongery, Dressing Bags, &c., in England.
Manufactory, THE ROYAL CUTLERY WORKS, SHEFFIELD.

MAPPIN, WEBB & CO.'S
TRAVELLING & DRESSING BAGS & CASES

Fitted with their unrivalled Cutlery and every Article of luxury and convenience of the first qua[lity]

CELEBRATED		THE WELL KNOW[N]
£2 2 0		£1 10 0
FOR GENTLEMEN.		FOR LADIES.
Waterproof Leather,		French Morocc[o]
Containing 14 most useful requisites.		Containing 13 most useful Toilet requisites.

Registered.
- Best Enamel Leather (Waterproof) "Oxford" Bag, fitted with most complete Writing and Dressing fittings of the first quality £11 0 0
- Ladies' Morocco Leather Ditto 11 0 0
- Ladies' Morocco Leather Dressing Bag with solid Silver fittings complete .. 7 0 0
- Ladies' Walnut Wood Dressing Case complete with solid Silver fittings 8 8 0
- Ladies' Coromandel Wood Brass Bound Dressing Case with solid Silver fittings complete 10 10 0
- Ladies' Hand Bags with outside pocket from 0 10 6

- Gentlemen's Leather Dressing Cases from £0 10
- Handsome Leather Despatch Box completely fitted with cutlery and writing materials 2 2
- Russia Leather Despatch Box complete with three porcelain slates, cutlery and writing materials 3 15
- Purses in great variety from 0 1
- Also the celebrated Seal skin Purse 0 13
- Ladies' Work Cases handsomely fitted 0 16
- Envelope Case, Blotter, Inkstand and Bookstand complete, in every variety, the set 4 10
- Students' Cases from 0 6

VOLUNTEER PRIZES, WEDDING, BIRTHDAY & CHRISTENING PRESENTS
Manufactured by MAPPIN, WEBB & CO.,
From 10s. to Fifty Guineas, always in Stock.

	1 Pint, 20s.	½ Pint, 27s.	3 Pints. £7 5s.	½ Pint, 40s.	½ Pints. 36s.
In Silver..	£5 5s.	£5	£21	£5 5s.	£4 15s.

Yachting, Rowing, Coursing and Rifle Shooting Prizes, in Silver and Electro-Silver,
A VAST SELECTION OF MOST ELEGANT DESIGN AND BEAUTIFUL FINISH. ALSO GALLERIES OF

GILT BRONZE AND MARBLE CLOCKS
of the Newest Design, the Movements of which are expressly manufactured for them.

Handsome Gilt Drawing Room Timepiece, complete with Shade and Stand	£1 17 6
Dining Room and Library Clocks in wood cases, commencing at	1 1 0
Lever Carriage Clocks	2 5 0

A large selection of Bronze Figures, Candelabras, Ormolu and Porcelain Candelabra, &c., &c.

MAPPIN, WEBB & CO.,
LONDON,
77 & 78, OXFORD STREET, WEST END; 71 & 72, CORNHILL, CITY.
Manufactory, THE ROYAL CUTLERY WORKS, SHEFFIELD.
AND AT PARIS, BRUSSELS, NAPLES AND FLORENCE.

[TURN OVER.

THE WHEELER AND WILSON
UNRIVALLED PRIZE MEDAL
LOCK-STITCH SEWING MACHINES,
FOR £9 AND UPWARDS.

These Machines have long stood pre-eminent for their elegance, durability, and simplicity; for the variety of work, the ease of management, the permanence of the sewing, the noiseless action, and the strength and beauty of the work performed.

It is a pleasant and healthy exercise, and an ornament in the drawing-room.
Fells or Hems any width, turning its own Hem as it stitches.
Gathers and sews on a band at the same time without basting.
Braids in beautiful designs with Cord or Braid.
Sews on Cord without basting.
Hems, enclosing a Cord at same time, without basting.
Binds any material without basting.
Marks any width of Tucks, and Stitches them without basting.
Trims Skirts with Braid, Velvet or Ribbon, without basting.
Quilts any material in any design with Silk or Cotton.

Illustrated and Descriptive Pamphlet, with Testimonials, Gratis and Post Free.
INSTRUCTIONS GRATIS TO EVERY PURCHASER.

OFFICES AND SALE ROOMS, 139, REGENT STREET, W.

NEW FOOD FOR INFANTS, specially prepared upon BARON LIEBIG'S principles by SAVORY and MOORE, surpasses all other substitutes for the Natural Food of Infants. Readily prepared for use without boiling or straining.

SAVORY and MOORE, New Bond Street; FORTNUM, MASON, & Co., Piccadilly; and all Retail Vendors; in tins, 1s., 1s. 6d., 2s., and 5s. each. Wholesale, CROSSE and BLACKWELL, and BARCLAY and SONS.

Health, Fresh Air & Pure Water.
CONDY'S PATENT DISINFECTING FLUID.

PURIFIES, deodorizes, and disinfects by the Agency of Nascent or Ozonic Oxygen—their active principle which, under all circumstances, is of an absolutely innoxious and wholesome nature. For this reason, these preparations can be employed for numerous domestic and personal purposes, besides those of ordinary disinfection, for which all other substances of the kind hitherto used, on account of their poisonous and otherwise objectionable character, are wholly unsuited and worthless. Among such useful employments may be specified the following:—

A simple and certain test for organic impurities in air or water.
Purifying drinking and other water.
Removing taint from meat, fish, poultry, and vegetables.
Washing butter, and removing rancidity and bad flavour.
Imparting mildness and flavour of age to new and coarse spirits.
Curing musty provender.
Cleansing wheat and other seeds from smut.
Developing the vitality of old seeds.
Maintaining the health of plants in pots and conservatories.
Preserving and restoring the freshness of cut flowers kept in water.
Destroying the blight of the potato, vine, hop, mulberry tree, &c.
A general remedy for the external diseases of animals.
Cleansing foul sores, poisoned wounds and bites, &c.
Allaying the irritation of flea-bites, mosquito bites, &c.
An antidote to all organic poisons.
Removing bad breath, and the odour of tobacco.
Washing the hair.
A purifying and refreshing addition to baths, bidets, and tubs.
A remedy for tender and perspiring feet.
Washing dogs and other domestic animals.
Purifying aquaria, bird-cages, &c.
Washing and purifying the bedding and clothes of infants.
Purifying the air of bed-rooms and close places.
Cleansing bottles, wine casks, beer barrels, dairy utensils, &c.
Purifying soapy and greasy sponges.
Cleaning pots, pans, dish-cloths, &c.
Cleansing and polishing plate and jewellery.
Refreshing the colours of old carpets, silks, and other stuffs.
Cleaning oil pictures.
Counteracting the smell of fresh oil paint.
Removing odours from fustian, flannels, new boots and shoes, &c.
Ordinary proportions for use—a teaspoonful to a pint of water.
In bottles, 1s., 2s., 4s.; or in gallon bottles, 5s. and 10s. each.

CONDY'S PATENT OZONIZED WATER.
Is perfectly pure, and specially adapted for toilet purposes and for the purification of water.
Price 2s., 3s. 6d., 6s., and 11s. Sold by all Chemists.

RESTORATIVE AND INVIGORATING DRAGÉES DÉ GELIS ET CONTÉ restores all natural secretions to healthful action, are a specific for debility, and invaluable to the nervous and dyspeptic. For Females and persons of weak constitutions they are superior to any other preparation of Iron, and are approved by the Paris Imperial Academy of Medicine. Paris—Rue Bourbon-Ville-Neuve. London—F. NEWBERY AND SON, 45, St. Paul's Churchyard. Price in Boxes, with Government Stamp, 2s. 6d. and 4s. 6d.; free by Post, 2s. 9d. and 4s. 10d. Write for Treatise, free by Post.

THE FURNISHING OF BED-ROOMS.

HEAL and SON have observed for some time that it would be advantageous to their customers to see a much larger selection of Bed-room Furniture than is usually displayed, and that to judge properly of the style and effect of the different descriptions of Furniture, it is necessary that each description should be placed in a separate room. They have therefore erected large and additional Show Rooms, by which they are enabled not only to extend their show of Iron, Brass, and Wood Bedsteads, and Bed-room Furniture, beyond what they believe has ever been attempted; but also to provide several small rooms for the purpose of keeping complete suites of Bed-room Furniture in the different styles.

Japanned Deal Goods may be seen in complete suites of five or six different colours, some of them light and ornamental, and others of a plainer description. Suites of Stained Deal Gothic Furniture, Polished Deal, Oak, and Walnut, are also set apart in separate rooms, so that customers are able to see the effect as it would appear in their own rooms. A Suite of very superior Gothic Oak Furniture will generally be kept in stock, and from time to time new and select Furniture in various woods will be added.

Bed Furnitures are fitted to the Bedsteads in large numbers, so that a complete assortment may be seen, and the effect of any particular pattern ascertained as it would appear on the Bedstead.

A very large stock of Bedding (HEAL and SON'S original trade) is placed on the BEDSTEADS.

The stock of Mahogany Goods for the better Bed-rooms, and Japanned Goods for plain and Servants' use, is very greatly increased. The entire stock is arranged in eight rooms, six galleries, each 120 feet long, and two large ground floors, the whole forming as complete an assortment of Bed-room Furniture as they think can possibly be desired.

Every attention is paid to the manufacture of the Cabinet work, and they have just erected large Workshops on the premises for this purpose, that the manufacture may be under their own immediate care.

Their Bedding trade receives their constant and personal attention, every article being made on the premises.

They particularly call attention to their Patent Spring Mattrass, the Sommier Élastique Portatif. It is portable, durable, and elastic, and lower in price than the old Spring Mattrass.

HEAL AND SON'S
ILLUSTRATED CATALOGUE OF
BEDSTEADS, BEDDING, AND BED-ROOM FURNITURE,
Sent free by Post.

196, 197, 198, TOTTENHAM COURT ROAD.

J. S. VIRTUE, PRINTER,] [CITY ROAD, LONDON.

www.ingramcontent.com/pod-product-compliance
Lightning Source LLC
Chambersburg PA
CBHW030318170426
43202CB00009B/1049